REMEMBRANCE
OF SWINGS PAST

Other Bantam books by Ron Luciano and David Fisher

THE FALL OF THE ROMAN UMPIRE
STRIKE TWO
THE UMPIRE STRIKES BACK

REMEMBRANCE OF SWINGS PAST

**Ron Luciano
and David Fisher**

BANTAM BOOKS
TORONTO · NEW YORK · LONDON · SYDNEY · AUCKLAND

REMEMBRANCE OF SWINGS PAST
A Bantam Book / May 1988

LIBRARY OF CONGRESS
Library of Congress Cataloging-in-Publication Data

Luciano, Ron.
    Remembrance of swings past/Ron Luciano and David Fisher.
    p.   cm.
    ISBN 0-553-05262-4
    1. Baseball—United States—Anecdotes, facetiae, satire, etc.
I. Fisher, David, 1946–   . II. Title.
GV873.L77 1988
796.357′ 0973—dc19   88-932
                                                       CIP

Published simultaneously in the United States and Canada

Bantam Books are published by Bantam Books, a division of
Bantam Doubleday Dell Publishing Group, Inc. Its trade-
mark, consisting of the words "Bantam Books" and the
portrayal of a rooster, is Registered in U.S. Patent and
Trademark Office and in other countries. Marca Registrada.
Bantam Books, 666 Fifth Avenue, New York, New York 10103.

PRINTED IN THE UNITED STATES OF AMERICA

BP   0 9 8 7 6 5 4 3 2 1

To my oldest and dearest friend,

_____

(fill in the blank)

ACKNOWLEDGMENTS

We greatly appreciated the assistance of the many people who helped revive the memories. These include Peter Guzzardi, Matt Shear, Kathy Jones, Lou Aronica, and the rest of the wonderful people at Bantam; John Boswell, Jonathan Boswell, and Patty Brown; Joanne Curtis; Bob DiNunzio, Sr. and Jr.; John Fox; Joe Gabarino; the Yankees' Harvey Greene; Bill Haller; Bob Huckbone; the Mets' Jay Horowitz and Arthur Richman; Randy Horshok; the Jesters; the people at the Luciano/I/O reunion; Mike McCarthy; Kevin McManus; the Yankees' Ann Mileo; Nina, Fonda, and Mary; the Nortons; Cecil Oldren; Cosmo Parisi; Buck Picciano; Dave Rossi; Joan Sinclair; Tony Termini; John Young; the Waltons; Steve Hirdt and the Elias Sports Bureau; Nell Rogers; Alfred Baman, Peter Miller, Charlie Lampach, and Catherine Smythe for their constant good humor under trying circumstances—my presence. Thank you all.

R.L.
D.F.

CONTENTS

1
A DAY AT THE PENNANT RACES

The Luciano Era," as it is proudly remembered in NBC Sports history, stretched from the halcyon days of 1981 all the way to the golden days of 1982. During that legendary period I served as color commentator on baseball's *Game of the Week*. At the end of that time Michael Weisman, who eventually became executive producer of NBC Sports, told me that television really wasn't quite ready for someone like me. I took that as a compliment; of course, I take anything as a compliment. But when I read recently that Weisman had telecast a portion of a National Football League game without using any broadcasters at all, I began to believe my time had finally arrived. So I called Weisman.

"NBC Sports," his secretary answered, "Michael Weisman's office."

"Hello," I said in my booming voice. "This is . . . Ron Luciano!"

"ABC Sports," she immediately replied, "Roone Arledge's office."

"You probably don't understand," I continued. "This is Ron . . . Luciano, former color commentator on the backup *Game of the Week*."

"Oh," she said. *"Buenos días, Televisión Español."*

Eventually that slight misunderstanding was cleared up

and Weisman picked up his phone. "Hey, Ron," he said, "it's good to hear your voice. But I'm a little busy right now. Can I ask you to call me back?"

"Sure, Mike," I said. "When would be a more convenient time?"

"Why don't you try next year?" he suggested. "June, maybe."

"Actually, I just need one minute, Mike. I have a few things I'd like to discuss with you and I was wondering if we could have lunch."

"Gee, that'd be great, Ron, honest. I'd really love to. Unfortunately, I've given up food."

The truth, I later discovered, was that Mike Weisman believed I was a jinx. The first thing that had happened after he'd hired me, he pointed out, was that major league baseball had gone on strike.

"That was a long time ago," I pointed out.

"I read your last book, Ronnie, which was published only two years ago. The one that included brief autobiographies of fifteen major leaguers?"

"So?"

"So ten of them are out of the majors, another one of them has been traded three times, Ray Miller was fired as Twins manager, and Charlie Hough broke his finger shaking hands!"

"That's not a jinx," I said with a laugh, "that's just bad luck."

Finally I managed to convince him that a belief in the existence of a jinx, an individual doomed to cast negative influence over a situation, was the hallmark of a primitive culture, and as a sophisticated human being, he certainly could not allow superstition to influence his decisions as head of the sports division of America's leading television network. At least not when they involved food. Weisman agreed to have lunch with me.

Two weeks later, the day before NBC was to televise the All-Star Game, the Directors' Union went on strike.

During lunch I told Mike that since my contract at NBC had expired I'd become an author, raconteur, and national spokesperson for the great Car-X Muffler company. Mike thought it was ironic that a company that installs mufflers, devices that decrease noise, had chosen me as a spokesperson. Finally I announced the real reason I had invited him to take me to lunch at an expensive New York City restaurant. "I've been watching NBC Sports faithfully for the past few years," I said. "I think I'm ready to go back to work!"

"That's great, Ronnie," Mike said. "What exactly is it you do again?"

"Mike, I'd like to go back to work for you as a color commentator."

I'll never forget his answer. "Waiter, check please."

I had anticipated a little resistance, but I have to admit his prolonged laughter surprised me. Eventually, he told me that there were three reasons he wouldn't rehire me: The people currently broadcasting *The Game of the Week* were superb. I had no talent. And that since I'd left baseball in 1981 the game had changed.

"Oh, sure," I agreed, "maybe I do have no talent. But that's been the secret of my success."

"What success?" he asked.

"That's the secret."

But I didn't agree with him that baseball had changed. I'd been in baseball and out of baseball long enough to know that baseball never changed. It's the "Grand Old Game," a game dependent on its traditions. Baseball never changes, I argued, that's part of the beauty of the game. A bat, a ball, three strikes, four balls, three outs, nine innings, bases ninety feet apart, and an umpire to make decisions and be yelled at. The game was played just as it had been when I left it in 1980, almost as it had been when Abner Doubleday supposedly invented it at Cooperstown, New York, in 1839 and Phil Niekro had made the first pitch.

Baseball changed? The more I thought about it, the more convinced I became that I was absolutely correct. Modern baseball has not changed at all, except for the baseball, the bat, gloves, uniforms, helmets, the ballparks, the field, the strategy, the players—including the influence of black and Hispanic players—the customs, conditioning methods, the way pitchers are used in a game and the pitches they throw, the strike zone, the number of teams and the creation of divisions, the growth and decline of the minor leagues, the methods of obtaining players, the number of players on a team and the creation of the designated hitter, the salaries paid players and the use of agents to negotiate them, the creation of free-agency and the player draft, the modes of broadcasting the game, the means of transportation, the number of games teams play, when they play them, and how long they take to play them, the number of umpires working a game, the use of technology and statistics, the length of the season, the existence of a play-off system, behavior of fans at the game, and even the construction of the bases. But other than that . . .

Baseball is continually changing. I umpired my first game in 1964, and about the only thing in the game that hasn't changed since then is the taste of a ball park hot dog—which is just as stale today as it was then. Everything is different. In the old days—and any time prior to the birth of computers, digital recordings, cordless telephones, nouveau cuisine, and Max Headroom seems to qualify as an old day—a fan would usually take public transportation to the ballpark, which would be located downtown in a major eastern city, in time to arrive before the afternoon game started. The fan would buy his "Annie Oakleys," or tickets, at booths in front of the park, usually asking for seats that weren't behind the poles supporting the stadium. Sometimes the home team would even participate in an archaic rite known as a "doub-ble-head-er," during which the team owner would actually let fans see two games for the price of one game. On rare occasions the team would have a special promotion, known as Ladies' Day, on which all women, including "house-wives"—women who stayed at home during the day—would be admitted to the park free or at a reduced fee, but only when brought by a man.

Once inside the ballpark, which was really still outside in the old day, the fan would see a field covered with actual, green grass, the home team dressed in white flannel uniforms and black shoes, and the visiting team in gray uniforms and black shoes. The players themselves were as white as the home team uniforms. The playing field would be asymmetrical, as it had been built to fit among city blocks, so the distance to the left-field fence might be forty or fifty feet less than the distance to the right-field fence. The scoreboard operator, who was responsible for posting the number of runs scored each inning for that game as well as out-of-town games, might be sticking his head through an opening beneath one of the innings. The outfield fence would be covered with brightly painted advertisements, some of them offering prizes to a player hitting a certain spot on the wall. In Philadelphia's Baker Bowl, for example, a sign extolled the deodorant powers of a certain soap, proclaiming, "The Phillies Use It!" Unfortunately, some graffiti artist had added beneath that statement, "And they still stink!"

Before the game began, players with nicknames like "Moose" and "The Freshest Man in the World" and "Jungle Jim" would be putting on a show for early-arriving fans, playing a bunting game called "pepper," juggling baseballs, throwing balls behind their backs, even taking phantom infield practice. One thing they would not dare do is speak to members of the other team, because of baseball's strict rules against fraternization.

When the game started, the "regulars"—the eight position players who started every game—took the field, while the "scrubbines" sat on the bench. The starting pitcher, who was actually expected to be able to pitch nine innings (nine, count 'em, nine!), would rely on a good fastball and curve and, if he could get away with it, maybe a dab of petroleum jelly on the baseball. Out in the bull pen, wily veteran pitchers who had failed as starters, or young pitchers waiting for an opportunity to prove they were good enough to be a starter, would stay ready in case the starting pitcher, who was expected to pitch nine innings (nine, count 'em, nine!), faltered. Some teams actually carried one pitcher whose only job was to pitch when the starting pitcher failed.

When the home plate umpire, wearing his traditional tie and jacket and, in the American League, using an inflated "balloon" chest protector, called "Play ball," the batter would come to the plate, casually flipping aside one of the two bats he was swinging to loosen up. A real power hitter might even be swinging three bats. The batter might be wearing sliding pads beneath his uniform, or even sliding gloves that went to his elbows, but he would not be wearing batting gloves, wristbands, elbowbands, headbands, patches, or, at least until the mid-1950s, a batting helmet. After spitting on his hands and maybe rubbing some dirt on them to help him grip the bat, he stepped to the plate. Infielders would start "chattering," shouting encouragement to the pitcher. They'd yell things like, "Hum, baby, you can do it!" and "hubba-hubba." Hubba-hubba was very popular, perhaps because it was not difficult to pronounce or remember. Pitchers seemed to understand what it meant, although no pitcher was ever known to say "hubba-hubba" to a fielder.

In the dugout, "bench jockeys" would be trying to steal the other team's signals or shouting derisive remarks at opposition players. If a batter hit a high pop-up, for example, Leo "The Lip" Durocher would scream at him in his shrill voice, "Home run in an elevator shaft!" Leo was considered one of the most clever bench jockeys.

Since it was believed that the heavier the bat the farther the ball traveled, players would use large, thick "lumber" and choke up on the handle. They constantly checked to make sure they didn't hit the ball on the bat label, its weakest spot—although as Yogi Berra once said, "I came up here to hit, not to read." When the ball was hit in the air, fielders, many of them with a "chaw" of tobacco bulging from their cheeks, would actually attempt the death-defying feat of catching a baseball using *two hands at the same time!* Ken "Hawk" Harrelson and Felipe Alou both claim to have popularized the one-handed catch in the mid-1960s. In fact, Harrelson's manager, Gil Hodges, once threatened to keep him on the bench unless he caught with two hands like a "real" ballplayer. I remember watching the great defensive outfielder "Famous" Amos Otis make two errors trying to catch balls one-handed. After the second error I went running out to center field, yelling, "Two hands, Amos, use two hands!"

"But Ronnie," he yelled right back, "they only gave me one glove!"

In baseball's early days, when runs were about as hard to come by as a handout from John D. Rockefeller, a batter reaching base might have tried to advance by stealing, but Babe Ruth changed that. Almost single-handedly, the "Bambino" wiped out the fine art of basestealing. The statistic that has had more influence in baseball history than any other was the fact that a home run is worth four bases, while a player can steal only one at a time. Even then, major league executives were smart enough to understand that four is more than one. (This, of course, went against the mathematics they applied when negotiating annual salaries with their players, at which time they attempted to prove that one was actually more than four.)

If a batter dug his spikes into the ground, or leaned too far over the plate, or if the player hitting before him had hit a home run, the pitcher might attempt to "bruise his breasts" or "brush him back." Rightly or wrongly, the "knockdown" was an accepted part of the game, and the batter knew when to expect to be "dusted."

At the end of the half inning each fielder would gracefully sail his glove onto the grass, where it would remain untouched while his team was at bat—unless a player on the other team playfully stuffed it with grass or dirt or, on occasion, a rubber snake.

Traditionally, the outfielders, second baseman, and shortstop all left their gloves in the outfield, the first and third basemen left their gloves in the respective coaches boxes, the catcher brought his mitt into the dugout with him, and the pitcher left his approximately halfway between the dugout and foul lines. Like many other baseball traditions, it was done this way primarily because it had always been done this way.

Meanwhile, up in the press box, "scribes" would write about "moundsmen" throwing "inshoots," "outshoots," "benders," or "smoke" to "banjo hitters," who hit "cans o' corn" or "daisy scorchers" to the "orchard," where they would be played by "gardeners." If a "gardener," or outfielder, successfully caught the "can o' corn," or fly ball, he would on occasion keep his "rifle" loose by making a practice throw to home plate. Meanwhile, in radio studios all across the state, broadcasters might be re-creating the game from details transmitted by Western Union ticker—and when the ticker slowed down, the player at bat would just keep fouling off pitches until it started again.

Television was to radio what Babe Ruth was to base-stealing. When it became possible to televise games, stations actually hired professional announcers *who had never played major league baseball* to explain it to viewers. Eventually, however, they realized that the ability to hit or pitch was more important than the ability to speak the English language, and they began hiring retired professional ballplayers and umpires to broadcast. Among the most memorable was Dizzy Dean, who told viewers of a Yankee broadcast, "I can describe a ball game well, but when they start statisticing, well, they throw me off the beam." Dean was never deterred by the belief that a broadcaster shouldn't root for the team paying his salary, and once, when umpire Bill McKinley made a call at first base with which he did not agree, Dean suggested, "They shot the wrong McKinley."

In the stands, fans would eat hot dogs, peanuts, and cracker jacks, occasionally taking a sip from the glass bottles of soda pop, beer, or other liquid refreshment they'd carried into the ball park. When something happened they didn't like, they would express their displeasure by razzing the offender with the "old yazoo." The emptied bottles served as an additional means of expressing disagreement with an umpire's call; fortunately, home plate in most ballparks was intentionally situated just beyond bottle range. Fans would throw bottles and fruit and other fans if they were angry; if they were pleased they would throw seat cushions or hats or other fans. All the eating, bottle-throwing, and hurling had to be done quickly, though, because most games were played in less than two hours.

Before 1921, fans were required to throw foul balls hit into the stands back onto the field, and the umpire put the ball back into play. But during a game at New York's Polo Grounds that season, a Giants fan named Reuben Berman shocked the baseball world by catching a foul ball and keeping it. The owners realized that if Berman was permitted to keep his ball the revolution could not be far behind, not to mention the money that they would have to spend to replace lost baseballs, so they took Reuben Berman to court.

It was a fan's natural right to throw bottles at the umpires, they were apparently claiming, but not to keep foul balls.

In perhaps the most significant ruling involving sports fans in America, the court ruled that Reuben Berman could keep his foul ball. Some fans wanted to erect a bronze statue of Reuben Berman outside the Polo Grounds; Giants owners wanted to have Reuben bronzed.

And in those golden days, at the end of the game, the fans peacefully left the ballpark.

The key to enjoying a baseball game today seems to be the guarantee of a good parking spot. The modern baseball fan drives to a modern baseball game in his automobile, so modern ballparks have been built in areas where "adequate parking facilities" can be assured. Cities put up ballparks with space for thirty thousand cars—then build a single two-lane access road to get there. The multipurpose stadium— the only purpose of which is to generate as much income as possible for the municipality—is used for everything from tractor-hauling contests to rock concerts. Usually it is located outside the city, on a site chosen by agreement of all local politicians. These benevolent politicians select the site based on the three basic tenets of stadium construction: convenience for the fans; availability of land; and what do I get out of it?

A day at the ballpark today usually begins at night. The majority of games are now played in the evening, so that fans can attend the game refreshed after a full day's work.

Unfortunately, that also means fans will be driving to the game at precisely the same time everyone in the state is driving home from work. Instead of purchasing tickets at the gate, many fans buy computer-printed tickets at a "ticket outlet." A ticket outlet can accurately be described as "a place having no seats available between home and first or home and third."

Unless a natural disaster strikes, teams play only one game. For the owners, playing two games in front of fans paying one admission would qualify as a disaster. It took the owners almost a full century to understand that they could make almost twice as much money selling two tickets to two separate games than playing two games for the price of one ticket. This economic concept is known as "pleasing the baseball fan, who buys tickets to a baseball game hoping it will be over quickly so he can get back to the traffic jam, and certainly does not want to sit through two long baseball games."

Although most games are played at night, for promotional purposes they are called days. Bat Day, for example, takes place at night. On a promotional day everyone attending under a certain age is given a gift, or some sort of entertainment other than a baseball game is presented. The Yankees, for instance, have Mug Day, on which every fan attending apparently gets mugged. Over the course of a season a fan can obtain an entire uniform, in addition to a bat, ball, and glove, while seeing tightrope walkers, fireworks displays, and my all-time favorite, Captain Dynamite. Captain Dynamite climbs into a box and blows himself up with sticks of dynamite. Surprisingly, he is not an ex-umpire. Jim Fregosi remembers meeting the captain. He extended his hand and said, "Nice to meet you."

"WHAT?" the captain replied.

"I said it's nice to meet you," Fregosi repeated.

"WHAT?" the captain said.

In fact, about the only promotion no longer employed is Ladies' Day. (Readers fill in your own punch line here.)

In cities with domed stadiums, going into the ballpark actually means going into the ballpark. I am pleased to report that after ten years, the retractable dome covering Montreal's Olympic Stadium was finally put into place over the ballpark just in time for the summer of '87. I am less pleased to report that the retractable dome cannot yet be retracted, although engineers claimed they would be able to take the cover off the stadium by winter. Meanwhile, smoking was prohibited in the stadium since there was no means of dissipating the smoke.

The field inside the modern stadium will usually be symmetrical, with the distance to the left-field foul line the same 330 feet as the distance to the right-field foul line. Often the turf will be real artificial grass, which neither grows nor dies and can be painted any color. The most significant problem with artificial turf is that it retains heat remarkably well, meaning the temperature on the field often rises above a hundred degrees. Monsanto Co., the inventor and distributor of Astroturf, investigated the problem in their laboratories and discovered a remarkable method of cooling the turf. "If player comfort becomes an issue in hot weather," they advised, "there is a simple, uncomplicated remedy—*water the (synthetic) grass.*" Proving once again that if the best scientific minds in America work together, even the most difficult problems can be solved.

The outfield walls are no longer painted brightly with advertising; instead they are covered with what appears to be the same type of padding hung behind basketball backboards in high school gymnasiums. A huge television screen on the scoreboard has become an entertainment center— showing statistics, highlight films, memorable moments, replays, and the advertisements that used to appear on the fences. In fact, the only things most modern scoreboards don't provide are inning-by-inning scores of out of town games and replays of every close play in the game on the field—which can only be seen by fans watching the game at home on television. The scoreboard operator has become a "computer engineer," whose job it is to create "enhanced graphics" for the pleasure of the fans.

A recently introduced function of the scoreboard is to order the fans to "Cheer!" at the appropriate time. In some ballparks scoreboards also show fans an electronic device called a "rally meter," which measures the level of noise made by the fans, sort of the way a thermometer is used to determine how sick someone is, and incites them to make even more noise. There are people who see the rally meter as a challenge to scream louder. These people really should be using a thermometer.

Professional and college football teams, basketball teams, even soccer teams use beautiful women wearing skimpy clothing to lead the fans' cheers. Baseball uses a scoreboard and grown human beings dressed up to look like distressed animals and insects to lead their fans' cheers. I think that explains everything about the way baseball is run.

On the field the teams are dressed in form-fitting double-knit uniforms of every conceivable color, as well as some colors that are inconceivable. Before the game begins, players with great nicknames like "Don" and "Fred" and "Jack" take batting practice and infield practice. Players today are permitted to fraternize with members of the other team. In fact, the only thing they are not permitted to do is play pepper.

When the game begins, the left-handed or right-handed platoon, depending on whether the starting pitcher for the opposition is left-handed or right-handed, takes the field, except for the designated hitter in the American League, whom is prohibited by the rules from taking the field. He takes his seat. Of course, many designated hitters couldn't field even before the rules forbade them from doing so. The manager has urged the starting pitcher to try to pitch as many as six innings, at which time the manager can bring in his long reliever or "hold man," who will try to keep the game close until the short man or "closer" is ready. The starting pitcher will rely on a fastball and slider and, if he can get away with it, a dab of petroleum jelly, or a slash in the ball long enough to make Freddie from *Nightmare on Elm Street* proud.

When the home plate umpire, wearing an open-necked, short-sleeve shirt and, in both leagues, using an inside chest protector, calls "Play ball," the batter discards his

lead bat, "doughnut," "wind resistor," or whatever device
he is using to make his bat feel lighter, rubs some pine tar
or other sticky substance on his bat handle or batting
gloves, adjusts his batting glove, wristband, and forearm
band, pulls his protective helmet with its earflaps a little
lower, and finally steps up to the plate. Less preparation
goes into dressing for a formal wedding than for a single
at-bat. Players today wear more decorations than Oliver
North wore when he testified before Congress.

In the dugout, most players are sitting quietly, although
throughout the game many of them will stroll from the
dugout to the locker room, where the game is probably on
television. At least the television is on, although the players
may not be watching the game. And why should they?
They didn't buy a ticket. Instead of cheering from the
dugout, yelling advice like "stick it in his ear," the modern
player puts his hat on backwards, or sideways, or flips up
the brim. This is known as a "rally cap," and supposedly
brings good luck. As far as I'm concerned, that's ridiculous,
wearing a hat some silly way can't possibly bring good
luck—the only things that really bring good luck are talent, hard work, and sitting with your right leg crossing
your left knee, with your arms folded across your chest.

Since it was discovered that the faster the bat speed the
farther the ball will travel, players now use the lightest
possible bat with the thinnest handle and thickest barrel
and hold it at the very bottom. Modern players seem to
believe that "choking up" means getting nervous because
the game is on television. When a ball is hit in the air,
fielders, many of them with a plug of chewing gum in their
mouths, stick up their massive gloves, and any ball within
fifteen to twenty feet lands in it. The gloves are so big, in
fact, that the only time two hands are really needed is to
carry the glove into the dugout after the inning.

If the batter gets on base, the pitcher begins softly tossing the ball over to the base, perhaps once, perhaps twenty
times, just to remind the runner that the pitcher remembers he's there. How could the pitcher forget? The runner
just got there. And what else does the pitcher have to think

about on the mound? The Middle East? Genetic engineering? Quite often though, the runner attempts to steal, and if he is successful, the announcer points out, "He stole that one on the pitcher, who may have forgotten he was there."

If the batter or runner does something positive, he and his teammates show their approval with a new "old custom," slapping each other's open hands as hard as possible. "High fives," slapping palms held high in the air, and "low fives," slapping palms held near the ground, have replaced the age-old custom of slapping each other on the behind, which certainly cannot be shown on television. "Rump-slapping" was far easier on players than "high fives" and "low fives," primarily because they were aiming at a bigger target.

"Curtain calls"—a player coming out of the dugout to acknowledge the cheers of the fans with a wave—are a recent innovation. Old-timers came out of the dugout only to play baseball or fight. The first recorded "curtain call" was taken by Dale Long in 1956, when he homered in his eighth consecutive game, but today some players willingly take more "curtain calls" than Sir Laurence Olivier in *Hamlet*. That may be why these players are known as "hams."

If the batter does dig his plastic spikes into the ground, or crowd the plate, or if the three batters before him have hit home runs, the pitcher may risk throwing the ball as close as the same time zone to the batter. This seems to be justification for the batter and all his teammates, except those players in the clubhouse watching television, to charge the mound and jump on the pitcher. Baseball fights are to fighting what artificial turf is to grass. It looks like a fight and sounds like a fight, but it isn't really a fight. For instance, nobody insults anybody's mother or heritage, primarily because so many of them are related by agent.

Meanwhile, in the pressbox, the team's local free television announcers and paid-cable television announcers and radio announcers, some of whom have not actually been hired by the club but over whom the club has approval, will be broadcasting the game. Some teams carry more announcers than coaches, which makes sense, since no one listens to coaches anyway. The Yankees, for example, have seven regular broadcasters; however, it's important to remember that only five of them are former major league players.

Fortunately, the ability of former players to use the English language has not changed. San Diego Padres' broadcaster Jerry Coleman, for example, told viewers, "Nettles leaped up to make one of those diving stops only he can make," "When you lose your hands you can't play baseball," "Rich Folkers is throwing up in the bullpen," and once admitted, logically, "I never have trouble remembering what I can remember, but I have trouble remembering things I've forgotten."

In the stands, as always, fans are eating hot dogs, peanuts, and Cracker Jacks, as well as popcorn, nachos, kosher corned beef sandwiches, pastrami sandwiches, bratwurst and knockwurst, crabcakes, eggrolls, bagels and cream cheese, ice cream, and just about any other food imaginable, occasionally taking a sip from the plastic cups of soda, beer, and wine they purchased at the ballpark—unless they happen to be sitting in the designated "alcohol-free" section. That means that alcohol is not served in that area, not that alcohol is served free, as some fans believed when they purchased tickets. The modern fan participates in the game by singing popular song lyrics, among them the classic "Nah nah naa nah, nah nah naa nah, hey, hey, hey, goodbye" when they can remember the lyrics, holding up bed sheet banners upon which they have drawn the local television station logo and clever rhymes like "New Hyde Park, New York, loves the Mets and Channel 9," and the ever-popular standing up and sitting down quickly, as well as cheering when ordered to by the scoreboard. With no empty bottles, seat cushions, fruit, or hats to throw, they cleverly manage to sneak beach balls slightly smaller than the state of Maine into the ballpark and throw them on the field. However, in the nonalcohol-free sections, non-alcohol-free fans are still known to throw other fans on the field.

Fortunately, ballpark dining can be enjoyed at a leisurely pace because the pitcher will be very busy tossing the ball to first base to remind the runner that he hasn't forgotten about him.

And at the end of the game, fans can happily celebrate a home team victory by running onto the field and mugging the players or ripping up the field.

2
THE NAME OF THE GAME

The only two pieces of equipment really necessary to play a game of baseball are the bat and the ball. So, naturally, the game is named baseball. When players substitute a stick for the bat, the game is called stickball. If they punch the ball with a closed fist instead of using a bat, the game is called punchball. But if they use a bat, it's called baseball.

The only pieces of equipment that really aren't necessary are the bases. Throw some old clothes on the ground, you've got bases—although it certainly would sound ridiculous to play "old-clothes-on-the-ground ball." But to play the game, you must have something to hit, and something to hit it with.

Everybody knows that a baseball, whose name derives from a game played with bases instead of old clothes thrown on the ground, is a white round object containing a spherical cork and rubber composition core approximately 0.85 inch in diameter surrounded by matching semispherical black rubber sections joined by a hard red rubber band approximately 0.17 inch in thickness, in turn surrounded by a red rubber layer approximately 0.08 inch thick, then wrapped in 219 yards of tightly wrapped blue-and-gray woolen yarn, which is covered with 150 yards of tightly wrapped white cotton thread, coated with a rubber gluing compound, and finally covered with a leather hide cover held in place with 108 red-thread stitches, weighing between 5 and 5¼ ounces with a circumference between 9 and 9.25 inches.

Or maybe it isn't.

The baseball is the single most important piece of equipment in a baseball game. As reliever Tug McGraw once observed, "As long as I hold on to the ball, nothing bad can happen." In fact, as long as the pitcher holds on to the ball, nothing at all can happen.

One of the things that always fascinated me when I was an American League umpire was watching major league pitchers blame their failures on the baseball. They would throw three consecutive pitches outside and immediately ask me for a different baseball, as if it were somehow the baseball's fault that they couldn't throw it over the plate. What they were really doing was telling their manager and the fans that it wasn't their fault they'd made three bad pitches, it was the baseball's fault. They had done everything correctly; the baseball had failed. Bad baseball.

Actually, baseballs are like yuppie stockbrokers—they may all look the same on the outside, but inside they can be very different. At least baseballs can be. In fact, ever since Philadelphia catcher Al Reach and buggy-whip maker Ben Shibe contracted in 1876 to supply the National League with baseballs as much alike as modern science then permitted, baseball players have been complaining about the quality of baseballs they had to play with. Every few years—for example, in 1920, 1926, 1930, 1961, 1968, 1977, 1984, and 1987—knowledgeable baseball people have claimed that a "lively ball," a ball that traveled farther when hit than the ball used the previous year, has secretly been introduced.

And in 1926, 1930, 1961, 1968, 1977, 1984, and 1987, major league baseballs' executives claimed ignorance. Nobody argued that claim. But knowledgeable baseball people still insisted the ball had been changed.

In 1920 they were correct. That season American yarn inside the baseball was replaced by much stronger Australian yarn, making it possible to wind the yarn more tightly, increasing compression, thus making the ball livelier. Batters greeted the new ball with slightly more enthusiasm than flies would greet a field trip to a sugar refinery. Modern baseball really began when the "dead ball" was killed and the new "rabbit ball" was introduced. In 1919, Babe Ruth's twenty-nine home runs had set an all-time record, but only one season later the Babe hit fifty-four homers—and baseball and baseballs would never be the same.

In 1926, a ball with a cushioned cork center was introduced. Although pitchers complained that the new new ball was responsible for the barrage of home runs being hit, J. W. Curtiss, the president of Spalding, the manufacturer of the baseballs, explained the real reason: "[T]he decadence of pitchers, most of them placing their main reliance on the fastball to the exclusion of curves and change of pace. [T]he fact that batsmen have dropped the old-time scientific method of placing their hits by choking their bat in favor of taking a toe hold and swinging freely at all pitches with bats held closely to the handle. The third reason is the premium placed on home run hitting by the magnates themselves, as instanced by the ceaseless exploitation of Babe Ruth as the home run hitter par excellence. . . . So we will probably hear little more of the banal talk about the 'lively' ball."

A year later, Ruth hit sixty home runs.

The 1930 new new new ball may have been the liveliest of all, although Spalding denied it was any different from any other ball. But in 1930 nine *teams* had batting averages over .300, the New York Giants set a team batting mark of .319, the entire National League hit .303, only one team had an earned-run average under 4.00, Bill Terry hit .401, and Hack Wilson knocked in an all-time high of 190 runs. The Philadelphia Phillies had a team batting average of .315, and eight Phillies hit over .300, but the team still finished last, 40 games out of first place, primarily because, according to infielder Fresco Thompson, "Our hitters had no chance to bat against our pitchers."

Not only did Roger Maris hit sixty-one home runs in

1961, when pitchers again complained about the new new new new lively ball, but also Maury Wills hit his first home run after 1,675 at-bats. "Don't tell me it isn't a rabbit ball," Reds' pitcher Jim Brosnan said. "I can hear it squealing every time it goes over the fence." White Sox pitcher Early Wynn concurred, claiming, "Cut the ball open and you'll find a carburetor."

Edwin L. Parker, president of Spalding, claimed, "Today's ball and the one that Ruth hit are identical. Period."

And Mrs. Beryl Gauthier, supervisor of the seventy-five women who actually sewed the covers onto the balls, said succinctly, "Who's Roger Maris?"

Nineteen sixty-eight was the year of the molybdenum ball. Batting averages, slugging percentages, and total runs decreased. Bob Gibson had a 1.12 ERA, and in the All-Star Game twelve pitchers struck out twenty batters. Although some baseball people blamed the lack of offense on the growing popularity of the slider, one fan suggested it was caused by the fact that in 1965 Australian sheep ranchers began adding small doses of the element molybdenum to their sheep feed to help cure a sheep skin disease. Among other things, this fan reported, molybdenum reduces the kinkiness in sheep wool, and it is that kinkiness that gives a baseball its resiliency. So the fact that Frank Robinson, who had hit thirty home runs in 1967, hit only fifteen in 1968 was perhaps due to a lack of kinky sheep.

Spalding replied that it used only wool from domestic sheep, which were known to be plenty kinky.

Domestic sheep farmers then admitted that they, too, were adding molybdenum to the diet of their sheep.

Neither the molybdenum-ball theory nor Einstein's theory of time travel has ever been proven, but to increase offense in 1969 the pitcher's mound was lowered five inches and the strike zone was narrowed, and during spring training baseball began experimenting with the 1-X, a ball that had high seams and only ninety-six stitches. The 1-X supposedly traveled 10 percent farther than the old new ball.

A spokesman for Spalding insisted the new ball was manufactured to specifications.

Pitcher Don Cardwell was one of the first to use the 1-X in a game. After pitching three shutout innings, in the fourth inning he surrendered seven hits and six runs and decided, "I thought the ball began to get livelier in the fourth."

In 1977, Rawlings replaced Spalding as the exclusive supplier of baseballs to the major leagues, using balls that were wound, bound, and sewn in Haiti. Both leagues immediately showed substantial increases in offensive output, and Larry Bowa, who had clobbered four home runs in seven previous seasons, hit two in two months. Players once again began insisting the ball was livelier. "When I got hit in the head," the Brewers' Mike Hegan explained, "the ball rolled all the way to the first-base coach's box. Last year's ball would have gone only halfway down the line."

"I picked one up the other day," Reds' pitcher Gary Nolan exaggerated, "and the darn thing jumped right out of my hand."

"It's definitely livelier," Milwaukee pitcher Jim Slaton exclaimed, "but only when I'm pitching."

"We're not making a rabbit ball," a spokesman for Rawlings claimed, in the days when spokespeople were still spokesmen. "Maybe the other people were making a turtle ball."

When more home runs than ever before started flying out of ballparks in 1984, Texas Rangers' manager Doug Rader believed he had finally figured out the reason. "It's the baseballs. The old ones had former American League President Lee MacPhail's name on them. The new ones have Bobby Brown, and the fewer letters makes them less wind-resistant."

In 1987, once again baseballs began rocketing out of ballparks. Mets' shortstop Rafael Santana doubled his career output of three home runs, hitting three four-hundred-foot blasts in the first three months of the season. Oakland rookie Mark McGwire had thirty-four home runs—by July. "Maybe it's not any livelier," Cardinals' manager Whitey Herzog said, "but tell me why my hitting coach got so much smarter this year and my pitching coach got so much dumber."

"When I was with the Pirates in 1946," Hall of Fame slugger Ralph Kiner remembered, "we played some exhibitions against teams in the colored leagues. They used a ball called the Harwood. That ball flew out of there. This ball sounds like the Harwood we used forty years ago."

Some people had rational explanations for the increase in power production. "It's the bat," Mike Schmidt explained. "It's the batter," Hall of Famer Billy Williams decided. "Guys are just bigger, stronger, and quicker now."

The Dodgers' Phil Garner had a scientific theory: "With the decrease in the ozone layers, we've lost some of the ionized particles, so there's nothing to hold those baseballs back."

Yankee broadcaster Hawk Harrelson had a much more logical explanation: "It used to be that baseballs made in the morning were livelier than ones made in the afternoon, probably because the fingers of the people making them were stronger in the morning and got progressively weaker throughout the day.

"Now every ball is lively. Maybe they put on a second shift."

The Haller Testing Laboratories compared the '87 ball with baseballs manufactured in 1977. "If anything," Haller's president said, "the modern batch is a little deader."

A representative of Rawlings added, "That's just what we've been trying to say all along."

Of course, 1977 happened to be the year Rawlings began manufacturing the ball that players claimed actually had a heartbeat.

Maybe the ball has been made livelier from time to time. But if it has, the thing I want to know is: Who gave the order? This has got to be the best-kept secret in history. The men who've kept this secret shouldn't be in baseball, they should at least be running the CIA.

From time to time there have been publicly announced changes in construction of the baseball. The first lively baseballs were covered with horsehide imported from Bel-

gium and France, but during World War II it became necessary to use Bolivian and domestic horsehide. In 1974 Spalding replaced horsehide with cowhide. Major league players
immediately began complaining that the covers were "soft"
and ripped easily, proving once again that cows simply
cannot hide as well as horses hide.

Spokesindividuals for Spalding claimed that that was
not true.

World War II was tough on baseballs. Not only did the
German occupation of Europe cut the vital horsehide supply line, but the Japanese seizure of Malaya and the Dutch
East Indies created a rubber shortage, and rubber was the
essential ingredient in the core of a baseball.

So Spalding went to war, creating the "balata ball."
Balata was a nonstrategic substance that did almost everything rubber did—except bounce. Spalding substituted it
for rubber at the core of the matter. By the end of the first
month of the 1943 season the New York Yankees and the
St. Louis Browns were tied for the league lead in home
runs: one. No other team had hit a home run.

Spokesmen for Spalding claimed that was not due to the
balata ball, explaining that unexpectedly cold weather and
unusually good pitching were the reasons for the lack of
offense. Within weeks, though, even Spalding admitted the
ball lacked the resiliency of the rubber-core ball and began
breathing some life in the "cement clunker," as the balata
ball had become known. By 1944 it was see you balata for
the ball, as synthetic-rubber supplies became abundant.

Baseball actually has experimented with a livelier baseball in the minor leagues and in spring training several
times. During the 1950s the Southern Association used the
"Old 97," named that because it was determined that anyone over ninety-seven was too old to hit this ball out of the
park. Evidently everyone else could, because just about
every league batting record was broken.

Pitcher Milt Pappas remembers one spring training during which a juiced-up baseball with red and blue seams was
used. "They wanted to see if it would liven up the game.
And it certainly did. When that ball was hit you should

have seen the players diving out of the way. That ball came off the bat so quickly the team wouldn't allow anyone with dependents to play the infield."

That was certainly not the first time anyone had tried to change the color of the baseball. In 1938 several teams experimented with a yellow baseball, believing batters and fans would be able to see the yellow ball better at night. After the ball proved successful, the National League officially approved its use—if managers specifically requested it. None did.

Obviously, if baseball had adopted a yellow ball other sports eventually would have followed, and sports fans would be forced to watch such ridiculous objects as yellow tennis balls.

In the late 1960s Oakland A's owner Charley Finley introduced "The Official Charles O. Finley alert orange baseball" to the world. The world yawned. This came immediately after his fellow American League owners had turned down his request to use green bats.

One rainy night Finley was driving to his home in LaPorte, Indiana, when he noticed that the policemen were wearing orange jackets. "I thought, that's a good idea," he remembers. "They're wearing them so the motorists don't hit them." He reasoned; if policemen wore orange jackets to make themselves more visible thus preventing them from getting hit, orange baseballs would be more visible and thus easier for batters to hit.

"I wanted to introduce it for two reasons. One, a fan can follow the flight of the orange ball a lot more easily than a white ball and, two, the batter can see an orange ball being delivered by the pitcher a lot more easily than a white ball.

"Fans come to the park because they want to see action. The alert orange ball creates more hitting, which makes the game more exciting. They used these things in an exhibition game and we asked people to give their reaction to five innings of white balls and five innings of orange balls. They applauded the orange ball and they booed the white ball."

Of course, these same people didn't realize a baseball

game is only supposed to be nine innings long. I actually umpired two spring training games in which an orange ball was used. The ball wasn't exactly as Finley wanted it, because the entire cover, including the laces, had been painted orange. I don't remember who Oakland played, but I do remember that both games were very well played. There were approximately twenty hits, six or seven strike-outs, and the only error made in the two games was a throwing error.

After the games we were supposed to file a report about the ball's effectiveness with the league office. I spoke to the players: The infielders said they didn't like it because they couldn't see the ball coming off the bat. They didn't make a single error. The pitchers said they didn't like it because they couldn't control it. Only three batters walked in two games. The batters said they didn't like it because they couldn't see the rotation on the ball. They had twenty hits and scored a total of sixteen runs.

I worked behind the plate in one of the games and I loved it. It was much easier to see, although the painted stitches did make it impossible to see the rotation of the ball. But the only thing baseball players willingly change is their uniform.

Oakland infielder Dick Green spoke for most players when asked how he felt about the orange baseball, "I can't even hit the white one."

Baseball did not adopt "The Official Charles O. Finley alert orange baseball," but that did not faze the creative Mr. Finley. He is currently organizing the International Professional Football League, which will play games, natu-rally, with "The Official Charles O. Finley alert orange football."

Through the years people have wanted to change other parts of the baseball besides its color. The Japanese, for example, have invented a baseball covered with artificial horsehide. I guess that proves that artificial horses can't hide any better than real horses hide. In 1875 an inventor pat-ented a waterproof baseball, composed of heart of palm leaf, or other suitable material, wrapped in wool yarn and

covered with vulcanized rubber. Several years later someone else patented a ball with a tiny ball in its center, based
on the theory that the smaller ball rattling inside the baseball would make it easier for the catcher to catch the
larger ball. Another inventor suggested punching holes in
the ball's cover to allow air to escape from inside, helping
the baseball retain its balance longer.

But there are some things about the ball that really
should be left alone. As relief pitcher Tug McGraw said
when asked what he liked best about baseball. "The shape
of the ball. We must never change the shape of the ball."

After spending a quarter century in professional baseball, I think I have enough expertise to say that besides the
baseball, the most important piece of equipment used in
the game is the bat. Ted Williams once said that the most
difficult thing in sports was hitting a pitched baseball with
a bat; well, just imagine how hard it would be to hit a ball
without a bat!

Baseballs come and go, so pitchers never have the time
to develop the kind of deep personal relationship with a
ball that batters have with their bats. Al Bumbry used to
refer to his bat as his "soul pole." Jay Johnstone's bat was
his "business partner." Norm Cash used to talk to his bat.
Once, I remember, after striking out swinging, Norm looked
right at his bat and screamed, "That's it, I warned you.
That's the last time you'll get any pine tar from me!"

Without doubt, the complaint I heard most often throughout my career, besides those about my ability, was that the
wood in bats manufactured today is not as durable as the
wood that used to be used. One day a batter—I believe it
was Duane Kuiper—struck out against Catfish Hunter on
three magnificent pitches on the outside corner. He didn't
swing at any of them. After I called him out on the third
pitch he just shook his head and said, "That's the problem
with these bats today. They're just not making wood the
way they used to."

In the old days a baseball player might go through an
entire season without breaking a bat. Hall of Famer Edd
Roush claimed he played eighteen major league seasons

without breaking one bat. When Bill Terry hit .401 in 1930, he used two bats the entire season. On the pennant-winning 1950 Phillies, Del Ennis and Andy Seminick shared a bat almost the entire year, hitting fifty-five homers with it. Today it is not unusual for a player to go through as many as six dozen bats a season. Orlando Cepeda, for example, would discard a bat after getting a hit with it, believing that each bat had only one good hit in it.

The way major league players go through bats today you would think that baseball bats grow on trees. Well, actually, baseball bats *are* trees. As many as sixty bats are made from a single tree. That means that unless someone has reinvented wood, Bill Terry's bat was made of the same wood used in the manufacture of bats today.

Originally hitters used anything they could swing—wagon tongues, wheel spokes, bedposts, ax handles, tree limbs, newel posts—to bat the ball. When pitchers started throwing curveballs, scientific-minded batters countered with extremely long wagon tongues, wheel spokes, bedposts, ax handles, tree limbs, and newel posts, and finally bats were limited to forty-two inches in length. But in 1884, Pete "Old Gladiator" Browning, a player for the Louisville nine, broke his favorite bed post or ax handle. Bud Hillerich, an apprentice woodturner in his father's shop, turned a new bat for Browning. The next day Browning went three-for-three, and the business of making bats was born. Think of it this way: if "Old Gladiator" had had a bad day, millions of American kids might today be swinging Don Mattingly model bedposts.

The first bats were made of hickory or willow, but today the wood with the best resiliency and driving power is believed to be ash from forty-five-to-fifty-year-old trees that have been grown in New York or Pennsylvania on top of a ridge or that have been exposed to the north and east for proper sunlight. Every player knows that, of course, so often when a player would hit a fly ball just short of the fence I would hear him complain, "Must have come from a tree exposed to the south or west wind."

Think of it this way: The bat that Mark McGwire is

using today most likely came from a tree planted when Ted Williams was a minor leaguer. Companies are continually experimenting with different types of wood, however. In the 1960s Harmon Killebrew used an "Oregon Slammer" made of maple, claiming that a maple bat lasted longer than ash. And in the 1970s the Japanese tried to replace the Louisville Slugger with the Kuboto Slugger, which was made of laminated bamboo. The manufacturer claimed the bat would not chip and guaranteed it for one year.

Players once were so selective about the wood from which their bats would be made that many of them actually went to the Hillerich and Bradsby plant and selected the wood billets, or chunks, that would be turned into their bats. Hugh Duffy, who once hit .438, picked only wood that had a certain ring when he bounced it on the ground. Babe Ruth insisted that the barrel of his bat have knots—actually dark spots where the tree had bent in the wind—in it.

Players cherished good bats as if they were good friends, working on them for hours with bone to harden their surface, constantly oiling them, even taking them home with them at the end of the season. A few players still take extraordinary care of their bats—Don Mattingly, for instance, carries his own bats into the clubhouse after each game, storing them in his locker. A bat with good wood is prized. When Fred Hutchinson was managing the Cardinals, Del Ennis, who must have known that good wood grows on trees, popped out with the bases loaded. Ennis came back to the dugout and dropped his bat in the rack. Hutch grabbed the bat and angrily smashed it against the dugout steps twice. The bat was only slightly dented. Hutch paused, examined the bat, nodded, walked down the bench to where Ennis was seated, and handed him the bat. "Keep it," he said. "It's got good wood."

I saw a lot of bats cracked, broken, and shattered during my career. I once saw Jim Rice swing so hard that, even though he did not hit the ball, the force of his swing broke the bat. But a first baseman named Mike Hargrove had the most shattering experience I've ever seen. Normally, when a bat breaks, a player is left holding a piece of the handle. Maybe even just a little piece. Hargrove didn't even have sawdust. He swung and the bat disappeared. It disintegrated into at least thirty tiny pieces. It was as if it had started snowing wood. The catcher—Darrell Porter, I believe—picked up one of the pieces and examined it. "Damn termites," he said.

More bats than ever before are being cracked and shattered, not because the wood is weaker, but because there is less wood in the bats being used. In the eternal quest for bat speed, which produces more driving force, modern players use the lightest possible bat with the thinnest handle and the thickest barrel. Players used to use long, heavy bats. Edd Roush's 48-ounce bat was perhaps the heaviest ever used in the big leagues. Babe Ruth's bats were 36 inches long and weighed as much as 44 ounces, while Henry Aaron used a 35-inch, 33-ounce bat. The typical bat in the 1930s and 1940s was 36 inches long and weighed 36 ounces. But by the mid-1950s only two sluggers—Ted "The Big Klu" Kluszewski and Bill "Moose" Skrowron—used that big a bat. Today Claudell Washington's 37-ounce bat is among the heaviest in baseball, while Tony Gwynn's 31-ounce, 32½-inch-long bat is about the smallest.

For some players the size of the bat made no difference. Ernie Fazio, a light-hitting Houston infielder, once switched from a 33-ounce bat to a 29-ounce bat, explaining, "The 29-ounce bat is easier to carry back to the dugout."

When Gene Woodling was traded from the American League to the Mets, he used a huge 40-ounce club. In Woodling's first National League game Casey Stengel sent him up to pinch-hit against Sandy Koufax. Bam, bam, bam. He struck out on three straight pitches. He walked back into the dugout and said, "Casey, better order me some 32-ounce bats."

One spring present Red Sox broadcaster Bob Montgomery was trying to make the team as a catcher, so he decided he was going to impress Boston superstar Carl Yastrzemski. He ordered the biggest bat that could legally be used in a game. "That bat was huge. It was 38 inches long, and the weight was irrelevant because it was simply too heavy to control. So one morning in spring training I casually laid it on my shoulder and walked into the clubhouse. I went right over to Yaz's locker and said, 'Carl, I know you're one of the biggest players in the game. I know you've done some big things, but I think this may be too big even for you.'

"Carl and I always got along well after that."

A hitter chooses his bat with as much care as an Old West gunfighter took to select his gun—and both the hitter and the gunfighter lived and died by their choice. Babe Ruth, in fact, even carved notches around the trademark of his bat for each home run he hit using it. "When a bat feels right," Ken Singleton explained, "the balance is so perfect it feels weightless. I spent my whole career looking for a bat that felt as good as the broom handles I used to use playing stickball in the street. I never found one. Sometimes, in fact, I'd end up going up to the plate with a bat that I'm sure God had intended to be a chair leg."

Every bat model is coded with a letter, a number, and the name of the player who either first ordered it or popularized it. Ruth, for example, originally used an R-116, a "Wahoo" Sam Crawford model, which quickly became known as the "Babe Ruth" model. Stan Musial began his career using the Ruth model before going on to Jimmie Foxx, Rudy York, Jimmy Brown, Enos Slaughter, and Walker Cooper models. Ted Williams used a Lefty O'Doul model; Joe Dimaggio spent much of his career using a Bill Brenzel. For a time, Mickey Mantle used a Marv Throneberry. Reggie Jackson, of course, used a Reggie Jackson or, as it has become known in the big leagues, an RJ-288. Players often apply the code numbers to objects besides bats. A woman with bad legs, for example, is a K-12. A K-12 bat has almost no curvature; it looks like a piano leg. Without doubt, however, the most important bat of all was the Honus Wagner model made in 1904. That was the first bat that a player was paid for putting his name on, making Wagner the first player to be paid for endorsing equipment.

Players order new bats during the season based on code

numbers, so that each bat they receive will be the desired weight and length and the handle and barrel will be the designed thickness. Theoretically, each bat will feel exactly like all the others. Once, though, Ted Williams returned an order of bats he'd received, claiming the grip didn't feel right. The bat handles were remeasured: The handles were 5/1000 inch thicker than the ones he had been using. Well of course they felt too thick.

The bat is the player's most important piece of equipment. A player will spend months, even years, determining exactly what length and weight bat he is most comfortable with, how thin he likes the handle, how thick the barrel. He has probably ordered them by the dozens and from those shipments selected only the six or seven that have the proper grain and the right feel, and then lovingly coated those with layers of pine tar and perhaps even "boned" them by rubbing them down with glass bottles until finally the bat is ready to be used. And then, just before he goes to bat, he may casually swing a teammate's bat, decide it feels perfect, and go up to the plate with it. Anyone expecting logic from people who wear bloomers to work has come to the wrong sport. Tommy Agee once had a twenty-two-game hitting streak, for example, during which he used twenty-two different bats. In the 1978 playoff game between the Yankees and Red Sox, Bucky Dent broke his own bat and took one from teammate Mickey Rivers. On the first pitch he hit a dramatic three-run homer to win the pennant. Somehow, for baseball players, the plastic is always greener in someone else's ballpark.

One of the advantages of using your own bat, of course, is that you know what went into making it. When I was growing up in Endicott, New York, we used to have a saying in the neighborhood, "Cheating shows—unless you're very careful." Later I learned that that was also true in the major leagues.

Some batters will tell you that God actually had intended trees to have nails and cork imbedded in them, but forgot. So they volunteered to help out. The best at this, making him the worst offender, was "Stormin" Norm Cash. Any one of Norm's bats would have given a metal detector a nervous breakdown. American League umpires knew never to pick up one of his bats by the barrel because they'd cut their hand. But we never did anything about it because he was such a good guy.

Fixing bats before they break is actually an old major league tradition. Old-time players hammered nails and screws into the barrel, honed one side of the bat to create a flat hitting surface, even sliced grooves into the bat and filled them with transparent wax. When the hitting end of one of Hall of Famer George Sisler's favorite bats began chipping and splitting, for example, a teammate hammered several brads into it. Umpire George "Only One 'I' " Moriarty discovered the nails and ruled the bat illegal. The teammate then extracted the thick nails—replacing them with thin blue Victrola needles and covering the entire bat with tobacco juice. Sisler continued using his finely tuned bat until it cracked completely in half.

During the 1987 season so many players were accused of using bats that had been "fixed" that Commissioner Peter Ueberroth finally had to limit managers to one accusation per game. The bats were all examined but, as was once said of Dizzy Dean's head, "X rays showed nothing." Batters have been cheating probably just as long as pitchers. In the 1970s Graig Nettles and Disco Danny Ford were caught swinging illegal bats. In the 1960s Norm Cash and Hawk Harrelson admitted using fixed bats. In the 1950s Ted Kluszewski hardened his bat with thick tenpenny nails. Notice that it tends to be the strong guys who admit it. Who's going to try to take their bats away from them? Earl Weaver claims that when he was playing on a minor league club in New Orleans every bat on the team was corked. "I hit six homers that season, every one of them in the one month before they found us out. The umpires raided our clubhouse like they were the Untouchables. They destroyed the bats in public, right on the field. I wanted to cry." Well, it's usually the strong guys.

And Weaver spent much of both of our careers accusing *me* of cheating.

In 1974 Nettles hit a routine fly ball to the outfield, and the end of his bat fell off. Six small rubber super-resilient Super Balls bounced onto the ground. Detroit Tigers' catcher Bill Freehan dashed around like someone who has won sixty seconds of free shopping in a supermarket sweepstakes, gathering the bouncing evidence. "I guess he thought they'd put me in front of a firing squad," Nettles said. "I didn't care. I was out anyway."

In the minor leagues Nettles had played with a man who had inserted a tube of mercury in the core of his bat. "The tube was only partially filled. When he held the bat upright, it felt very light. But when he swung it, the centrifugal force of the mercury whipping to the end of the bat made it swing like it weighed a ton. It probably was a great bat, but we never found out—he just couldn't hit the ball with it."

The greatest innovation in bat design since the monumental addition of the little knob at the bottom of the handle was the Japanese "Teacup," a bat that has the end of the barrel scooped out. This supposedly increases bat speed and control. It is also the only innovation. How many things can you do to the design of a bat? In 1972 Hall of Famer Lou Brock became the first major league player to use a teacupped bat, which he'd gotten from Japanese home run king Sadaharu Oh. A few days after Brock, the Padres' Ivan Murrell used a similar bat, and Houston manager Harry Walker immediately protested the game, asserting that there were rules in baseball against Teacups. National League president Chub Feeney eventually ruled that Teacups were legal.

The Teacup was not the only attempt to change the bat, though. John Bennett, creator of the bent-handled tennis racket, bent-handled cookware, and bent-handled hammers, invented the bent-handled baseball bat. Hillerich and Bradsby produced the bat, which had a bent handle, for use in both baseball and softball games, claiming it promoted higher averages. Of course, if you were selling a bat, what other claim could you make? I never saw a wooden version of the bat, but I have seen aluminum bent-handled bats for softball. I never could figure out how to hold it. My first thought when I saw it was that it would be tough to use if you had a hangover.

A chemist invented the checkered baseball bat, a bat in which the handle is scored with a pattern of grooves and protuberances alternating with smooth areas. This supposedly enables the player to get a better grip on the bat.

The little knob at the bottom of the handle was added to help players hold onto the bat when they swung. In baseball's early days crowds often lined the field, and when a bat slipped out of a batter's hands it became a lethal weapon. To avoid problems that would be detrimental to the growing popularity of baseball—like fans being killed at games—the knob, which acts as sort of a brake, was added. Except for the introduction of two-toned bats, that was the only change for half a century. In the 1950s players began coating bat handles with substances like beeswax, elm, resin, and more recently, pine tar, to help them get a firmer grip. Some of today's players adhere to the theory that a bat should be held loosely in their hands as they swing, so they wear batting gloves and coat the handle of their bat with pine tar to improve their grip, then hold it loosely. Inevitably, bats go flying onto the field, into dugouts, and, on occasion, into the stands. Baseball certainly has more fans attending games now than in the past, so it probably can afford to lose a few. Any fan being hit by a thrown bat is usually asked to return that bat to the player who threw it and is given another bat as a souvenir of his near-beheading. Seems to me that that is like giving a mugging victim a replica of the gun with which he was mugged, or giving a new front bumper to someone who was run over.

The distance-throwing champion of the past apparently was Larry Doyle of the New York Giants. Doyle finally attached the bat to his wrist with a string, releasing it gently as he ran toward first.

The present distance leader in the category of unintentional bat-throwing is Dave Winfield. Winfield doesn't need the string; he has a good lawyer.

There are no rules against accidently throwing a bat, so probably the only person ever fined for it was me. When I was working first, third, or the plate and a bat was thrown near me, I would signal fair or foul. The fans always laughed. One Saturday in Boston we were on *The Game of the Week* and I was working home plate. Yaz's bat slipped out of his hand and went spinning like a pinwheel down the first-base line. I leaped out from behind the plate and followed the bat down the line. When it stopped I leaped into the air and made an exaggerated foul call. The fans loved it; the American League office did not. "For conduct unbecoming an American League umpire" I was given a small fine, making me one of the few people to have paid to appear on *The Game of the Week*.

The only truly significant change in the baseball bat since Bud Hillerich turned out the first Louisville Slugger is the creation of the aluminum bat. The first real nonwood bat was manufactured out of Fiberglas in 1962, but that did not prove practical—not unless anyone wanted to see seven-hundred-foot home runs. In 1969, Anthony Merola received the first patent for an aluminum bat. The bat came about as an offshoot of Merola's company's main business, making aluminum pool cues, and immediately became popular. The obvious benefit of the aluminum bat was that it didn't break; the detriments were that it dented easily and didn't sound right. If a player got good metal on the ball, the whack of the bat was replaced by the gong of the bat. Eventually those problems were corrected, and more aluminum bats are sold today than wood bats, saving the lives of several hundred thousand trees a year.

The ball rebounds off an aluminum bat much faster, and travels much farther, than off a wooden bat. That's not dangerous in Little League, softball, and college play, but in professional baseball it could be. Several major league pitchers have said that the only way the aluminum bat would ever be used in the big leagues would be over their dead bodies. They're probably correct about that. "If they used an aluminum bat in the major leagues," Jim Fregosi said, "somebody would get killed. I'm not just concerned about pitchers, I never liked pitchers anyway, but the ball travels so quickly even infielders would be in danger."

Aluminum bats don't break or crack, and they rarely even dent anymore. And they certainly don't burn, which might mean the end of another ancient baseball custom. From time to time hitters have gotten so frustrated that they have piled up their bats and set fire to them. Even Hall of Famer Rogers Hornsby once burned his bats. This, of course, is the classic demonstration of ash to ashes.

3
THE CAST OF CHARACTERS

Baseball's greatest players are elected to the Hall of Fame. The best players are remembered in the record books. Every player and manager who appeared in a major league game is named in *The Baseball Encyclopedia*. And me? I'm a "Character of the Game."

I was watching NBC's *Game of the Week* recently when they paused between innings to show a brief feature titled "Characters of the Game." And there I was, jumping up in the air, "shooting" out Amos Otis at first base, eating a hot dog on the field, calling Mickey Rivers "outoutoutoutout-outout," eating ice cream on the field, wandering to the outfield to try to talk the Tigers' Mickey Stanley out of retiring, eating another hot dog, wiping my brow after making a close call, looking down upon the top of Earl Weaver's head, looking *way* down upon the top of Earl Weaver's head, leaning on the railing behind third base and discussing a call with the fans, eating another hot dog, debating world affairs with Dodgers' third-base coach Tommy Lasorda during the 1974 World Series, and finally, taking a deep bow.

I will never make the Hall of Fame, I'm not in any record books, umpires aren't even listed in *The Baseball Encyclopedia*, and I never appeared on a baseball card, but it makes me feel very good to know that whenever people remember my career, they're going to laugh.

It was the people who laughed at me *during* my career that I minded.

One of the complaints most often heard today is that not only the bats and balls and fields and uniforms and strategy and rules of the game have changed, but also the spirit of the game. The game has become a serious business. Compared to players of the past, today's players are perceived to be about as colorful as a ghost eating a mayonnaise-on-white-bread sandwich in a snowstorm, as unpredictable as an accountants' convention. The different drummer they march to is playing Muzak. Their idea of a wild time is looking at Mike Schmidt's paycheck. In the old days, when men were boys and were known as Dizzy and Bobo and Lefty and Goofy and Casey and Rube, players would do things like run the bases backward, stop the game to watch an airplane fly overhead, hide pigeons under their caps, jump into fountains, eat goldfish, eat baseballs, and boast, as did Dizzy Dean, "My ole' manager, Frankie Frisch, came to me the night before the seventh game of the 1934 World Series and he says, 'Diz, you want to be the greatest man in baseball?' I told him I already was."

Players today, it is generally accepted, are so worried about their multimillion-dollar contracts that they don't have as much fun as the old-timers. Of course, some people believe that multimillion-dollar contracts can be a lot of fun. I suspect that the real difference between today's players and the old-time players might be the difference between the law and the lore. Today's reality often is embellished into tomorrow's myth. Legendary character Rube Waddell once supposedly responded to the taunts of his opponents by calling in his outfield—then striking out three consecutive batters. A true baseball story, even if it probably never happened. "I never would have allowed anything like that," his manager throughout his career, Connie Mack, said, but added, " 'Course, he might have done it in an exhibition game before I got him."

Decades from now, for example, baseball fans might well be listening to wild stories about the crazy antics of zany Steve Garvey. Well, maybe not Steve Garvey.

Characters are born and are made. Doug Radar, a certi-
fied Character of the Game who once claimed that his bats
had been quarantined because of Dutch elm disease, believed, "Being a character is something you work up to.
You have to serve a culprithood." That was not true in my
case. As a child I thought a character was a funny-looking
person who appeared in the comics. It was only after I grew
up that I discovered a character could also be a funny-
looking umpire who appeared in the major leagues.

I did not grow up intending to become a character. The
only person I've ever heard of who simply decided to become a character was pitcher Dizzy Trout, who explained,
"I figured if that guy Dean can get thirty or forty thousand
a year for being a screwball, from now on, call me Diz."

Of course, perhaps you have to be born a character in
the first place to decide to become a character.

As an All-American football player at Syracuse I wasn't
a character. I was the pointer. When there was a fumble, for
example, and everyone else was leaping on the pile to try to
get the ball, I was the player standing and pointing as if we
had recovered it. When there was a measurement for a first
down, I was the one pointing toward our opponents' goal
line as if we had made the necessary yardage. In addition to
pointing, I was also a jumping-in-the-air-and-thrusting-my-
fist-in-the-air-to-celebrate-specialist.

I certainly wasn't a character in the minor leagues and
during my first full season in the majors. I was so nervous
about getting each call correct that I didn't dare do anything even slightly out of character. Or what was later to
become in character.

But by my second season in the major leagues I began to
accept the fact that I belonged there, no matter what the
managers kept telling me, and I began to relax. That's
when I began having fun. I was working first base one day
and the Orioles' Boog Powell was the first baseman. The
batter hit a routine ground ball to the second basemen,
who easily made the play. I was standing behind Powell, so
he couldn't see me. I signaled out, but I went up right
behind Boog and screamed, "Safe!" I don't know why I did

that, but I did. Everybody in the park saw my signal, but only Powell and a few people heard me shout. Boog turned around and started arguing with me. Nobody in the ballpark could figure out what Powell was screaming at, I'd called the runner out on a routine play, and Boog was irate. Even I was enjoying it, because I knew I was going to win that argument. Best of all, there was nothing Earl Weaver could do about it. What was he going to do, come out and argue I'd made the right call? That was the very first time I intentionally did something to entertain the fans. They loved it. And I loved it, too. I quickly grasped the most important lesson I was to learn in the major leagues: When fans are laughing, they cannot be booing.

I had proved I could make them boo. I wanted to make them laugh. Believe me, being laughed at is much better than being jeered. I never planned anything in advance. I suspect planning your moves is against the official rules of characterhood. For example, I first received media attention when I began calling runners "outoutoutoutoutoutout." That started the day Brooks Robinson dived behind third base to knock down a line drive, then recovered quickly enough to pick up the ball and rifle a throw to first base from his knees to just get the runner. Robinson's play got me so excited that my enthusiasm took over. I called the runner "outoutoutoutoutoutout." A play that great deserved more than a simple, "out."

One night in Yankee Stadium I called a runner outout-outoutoutoutout and the fans started applauding me, so I patted myself on my back. Then they started cheering *me*, cheering the *umpire*! Naturally, my partners enjoyed it, too. After the first few times I had done something out of the ordinary during a game, Jerry Neudecker turned to our crew chief, the great Mr. William Haller, and asked, "Bill, what do you think is wrong with Ronnie?" The players liked anything that didn't show them up or interfere with my doing my job. Many players are human beings, too. Only the league office hated it. I had an ongoing correspondence with President Lee MacPhail throughout my career. MacPhail seemed to believe an umpire had done a good job when nobody knew he was there. I am six feet, four inches tall and weigh close to three hundred pounds. How could anybody miss me?

Doing these things changed the game for me. I was still doing my job, but I was having fun and it was obvious that the fans enjoyed watching me. Although I never planned anything, after a while certain things did become calculated. When the score was 6–0 late in a game I began thinking that I'd better do something or the fans were going to go to sleep. So if I was working first or third base and a foul ground ball came near me, I'd pretend to try to catch it. Or between innings I'd go over to the stands and organize a cheer for the umpires.

I never considered my act worth the price of admission to the ballpark, but I was at least as enjoyable as the watered-down soft drinks. And, to paraphrase the immortal Character of the Game Casey Stengel, I couldn't have done most of it without the players.

It takes several years for a "flake" to become a character. I was often criticized by people who claimed I was more interested in making people laugh than in doing a good job. But I was very careful never to let my antics interfere with the job: it's hard to be a character in the unemployment office. So if a game was close I never fooled around. In 1973 the players voted Nestor Chylack and myself the two best umpires in the major leagues, and five years later the umpires selected me president of our association, so obviously I was doing the job.

Being accepted by the fans and the media as a Character of the Game made umpiring a far more enjoyable profession, but toward the end of my career it put additional pressure on me. Fans expected me to perform for them at every game, while the league office made it clear I was not to perform at any game. Looking back on my career, would I have traded that special relationship I shared with the fans, the numerous stories done about me in the magazines, the opportunity to participate in hundreds of television and radio features, the countless letters and gifts I received, and those rare moments when someone told me I had, even briefly, touched their life, for anything in the world? Are mere trinkets worth that kind of enjoyment?

Absolutely. I may have been a character, but I'm not stupid.

Professional baseball has always been rich with characters. Before the turn of the century, a player named John King was being roundly jeered by fans, so he hung a slab of raw beef from the screen behind home plate and loudly suggested, "Gnaw on this awhile, you wolves." They don't make them like King anymore.

Boston's King Kelly, who revolutionized baseball by introducing the slide, constantly took advantage of the few official rules. If it wasn't in the rulebook, it wasn't a rule—and the rulebook hadn't been written yet. He was sitting on the bench one July afternoon in 1889 when a Cincinnati batter hit a high foul pop near the stands. It was obvious Boston's catcher couldn't reach the ball, so Kelly leaped off the bench, shouting loudly, "Kelly now catching for Boston!" and made the catch. They don't make them like Kelly anymore, either.

In the early 1900s Giants' pitcher Bugs Raymond (what a great nickname!) would sneak out of the bull pen during games and trade baseballs for shots of red-eye at a bar across the street. They don't make them like Bugs anymore. Well, maybe a little like Bugs.

Hall of Fame pitcher Rube Waddell was a fire-fighting buff who would leave a game if a good fire was blazing nearby. Once, supposedly, A's manager Connie Mack was admiring the courage of a fireman standing at the very tip of a tower ladder—until someone pointed out that that fireman at the very tip of the tower ladder was his star left-handed pitcher Waddell. They just don't make them like Rube anymore.

In the field, Hall of Famer Rabbit Maranville would stand behind the umpire, mimicking his gestures. At bat, when he flew out, he'd run into the outfield and threaten to punch the fielder who'd caught the ball. He once jumped into the fountain in front of old Buckingham Hotel in St. Louis and proceeded to devour several raw goldfish. In Philadelphia one day, after being locked out of a tenth-floor hotel room poker game, he climbed out the window of another room, crawled around the building on the ledge, and climbed into the game room through the window. Think about this: the man crawled on the ledge on the tenth story to get into a poker game—and people called me a character for eating a hot dog during a game. Obviously it was a lot more dangerous being a character in the old days—except, for the hot dogs in Washington, D.C.; it was pretty dangerous to eat the hot dogs in RFK Stadium. They just don't make them like Rabbit anymore.

Germany Schaefer was baseball's most creative base runner. Not only did he once run the bases in reverse, but one day he decided that the quickest path to third base from first base was through the pitcher's mound and, when the lone umpire turned his back, took that route. But Schaefer is probably best remembered for becoming the only player in baseball history to steal first base. He was on first and another runner was on third. Germany took off for second, hoping to draw a throw from the catcher. The catcher held the ball, and Schaefer made it to second. On the next pitch, Schaefer took off again—this time running back to first. He made it easily. One day Schaefer was in a bad slump when he batted against fast-baller Nick Altrock with a runner on first. Altrock's first pitch was a called strike. Altrock then threw to first in an unsuccessful attempt to pick off the runner. On the second pitch to the plate, Schaefer swung and missed, then walked toward the dugout. "That's only strike two!" the umpire shouted to him. "The hell it is," Schaefer replied. "I swung at the ball he threw to first." They just don't make them like Germany anymore.

Baseball's all-time greatest character, young left-handed-hitting dental college student Casey Stengel, came to the major leagues with the Brooklyn Dodgers in 1912, an event Casey later described as "the greatest thing that ever happened to dentistry." The Washington Senators were also interested in signing him, but owner Clark Griffith decided not to after his scout reported, "Casey Stengel is the world's greatest ballplayer—from the neck down."

Even if Casey had never become a manager, his exploits during his playing career would have earned him character-hood. Ted Williams was often criticized for practicing his batting swing when playing the outfield, but Casey went much farther than that. Between pitches, Casey would scale his glove twenty feet, then practice sliding into it. "I was improving my sliding out there one day," he later remembered, "when the manager told me something that made me stop. 'See that brick house beyond the fence?' he said. 'Well, that's the nuthouse, and if the fellow that runs it ever sees you, he'll come in here and throw a net over you, and I'm not sure it wouldn't be a good idea.' "

In the days before lights were installed in ballparks, games often continued into dusk. Late one afternoon, trying to convince the umpire that it was too dark to continue playing, Casey came to bat wearing a miner's helmet with a searchlight on it.

Eventually the Dodgers traded the popular Stengel to Pittsburgh. When Casey returned to Ebbets Field with the Pirates for the first time, Brooklyn fans gave him a tremendous ovation. Casey responded by taking a deep, sweeping bow and doffing his cap—and a sparrow flew out from beneath it.

By 1923 Casey was back in New York, with the Giants. In the World Series against the Yankees that year, Casey hit .417, and his two home runs led the Giants to their two victories. After the Series though, he was traded to the Boston Braves, causing him to note, "The paths of glory lead only to the Braves." Supposedly Giants' manager John McGraw traded Stengel because Casey had complained that the Giants had hired a detective to trail a teammate of his. "What's wrong with that?" McGraw wondered. "Aren't I good enough to have a detective following me?" Casey asked.

Casey began his managerial career in 1926, when the Braves hired him as president and manager of their Worces-ter team in the Eastern League. When the Toledo Mud

Hens offered him a job as playing manager and the Braves refused to release him from his contract, club president Stengel fired manager Stengel, making him the only manager in history to fire himself.

While managing Toledo one day, he gave his team a two-hour-long, rip-roaring lecture on the proper way for professional ballplayers to conduct themselves. He really got into it, and when he finished he led his charged-up squad onto the playing field—only to discover he had forgotten to put on his pants.

"The Old Professor" returned to Brooklyn as manager of the famed "Daffiness Boys" in 1934. The ineptitude of the Dodgers in those days is exemplified by the classic story of one fan, listening to a radio, yelling to another fan, "The Dodgers have three men on base." To which the other fan replied, "Which base?" Stengel led the team to three second-division finishes. Once, after the team had lost a double-header in Cincinnati, Casey walked into a barber shop and told the barber, "A shave and a haircut please, but don't cut my throat. I want to do that myself later on."

After being fired by the Dodgers, he was hired to manage the Braves. The Braves finished behind the Dodgers. The situation in Boston got so bad that when a cabdriver ran over Casey and broke his leg, a Boston sportswriter voted for the driver for Most Valuable Player. When Stengel was in the hospital, Frankie Frisch sent him a telegram—care of the psychiatric ward. Stengel gleefully informed Frisch that he was mistaken; the hospital was so overcrowded, Casey had been put in the maternity ward.

Even as manager of the World Champion New York Yankees, Casey didn't change. When the White Sox's Bill Veeck installed an expensive scoreboard that detonated fireworks every time a Chicago player hit a home run, Casey retaliated by celebrating a Yankee home run with lighted sparklers.

In 1962 Casey began an entirely new career when the National League expanded to ten teams and he was named manager of the New York Mets. The very first Mets' uniform was made for Stengel, and on the opening day of spring training he filmed a one-minute television commercial for a headache and stomach-ache remedy. It turned out to be apropos—the Mets became the worst team in baseball history that season, losing more games than any team before them. But his "Metsies," as he called them, attracted a large and loyal following, Casey's "New Breed," due primarily to his ability to keep things in perspective. The Mets' first pick in the expansion draft was catcher Hobie Landrith. "You got to have a catcher," he explained, "or you'll have all passed balls." Casey was honest about the Mets ability. "I have a player who is only twenty now," he told sportswriters about a young prospect, "but in ten years he has a chance to be thirty." "My player of the year is Choo Choo Coleman, and I have him for only two days. He runs very good." At the end of the first season, Casey summed up the situation as only he could: "We're damn lucky they didn't expand to twelve teams."

Among Casey's lasting contributions to the game of baseball was the language known as "Stengelese." This was not double-talk; it was more like quadruple-talk. Only he spoke it, which probably was good because only he understood it. There were no interpreters. It was a language he spoke when answering questions, and amazingly he always got around to the answer—although by the time he got there, no one could remember the question. "With this here ball club here," he once explained, "it's actually new, it's men that have played other places, some that haven't had enough experience, others that have had years of experience in which they would sacrifice the thing at their age to get a younger man that's a prospect that because of the drafting, in two years, that young player could be standing by another ball club. So rather than lose 'em by draft, they'd rather play those men and sacrifice the man that has the experience rather than lose the prospect." Make them anymore like Casey they don't just.

One of the very few men who might have been able to converse with Casey was the St. Louis Cardinals' Dizzy Dean, the original and certainly the most dizzy. In the 1930s America was still primarily a rural nation, and Dizzy was the archetypal small-town farmboy who came to the big leagues with a blazing fastball and enchanted fans with his homespun humor. Dizzy had an ego so large that by comparison Muhammad Ali was shy, but he also had the talent to back up his boasts. Certainly part of Dean's original appeal was his naïveté. When he first joined the Cardinals' "Gashouse Gang" in 1930, for example, he rode up to the hotel's seventh floor in the elevator with room-mate Rip Collins. It was probably the first time Dean had ever stayed in a hotel. Collins asked the bellboy to bring some ice, and tipped him when he delivered it. Dean asked Rip why he had paid the bellboy. "That was for the elevator ride," Collins explained.

"They didn't charge me," Dizzy pointed out.

"They know you're with the team," Collins said, "so they just put it on your bill." For the next three days Dizzy climbed the stairs to get to his room.

No one ever had more confidence in himself than Dizzy. In 1933 he set a major league record by striking out seventeen Chicago Cubs and said afterward, "I coulda struck out more, but I didn't know anything about no record.... Shucks, I mighta broke the record for consecutive strike-outs if somebody'd told me what I was doing. I never bothered pitchin' high or low, I just poured the ball in there.

"Never forget the last inning. I had sixteen struck out and Charlie Grimm, the Cubs' manager, sends up a pinch hitter named Jim Mosolf. My catcher, Jimmy Wilson, met this guy and I could hear him say, 'This is a helluva place to stick you in, kid. I wouldn't be surprised if that dizzy guy on the mound throws the first one right at your ear. He don't like pinch hitters.' Wilson'd give me the sign and then he'd straighten up and pound his glove right behind Mosolf's ear and the guy thought sure-n' hell he was gonna get punctured and I just put three Dean specials with smoke curlin' off 'em through there."

A year later Diz was pitching the seventh game of the World Series. "We was leading that ball game 11–0 in the ninth with one out and our manager, Frisch, he sent four pitchers down to the bull pen to warm up. So help me, I thought they must be getting ready for the 1935 season.

"Hank Greenberg was coming up. I already struck him out twice, no trouble t'all, and when he comes out of the Tiger dugout waving those big bats over his head I hollered to Mickey Cochrane, the Detroit manager, 'What'sa matter, ain't you got no pinch hitters?' That Greenberg was my meat. I put two fastballs right past the letters on his uniform blouse, and when he missed the second one I hadda laugh. . . . That Greenberg couldn't hit the next pitch if he'da started to swing when I wound up." If only Ole' Diz had been able to overcome his lack of confidence he might really have been great.

Dean became one of the leaders of the free-spirited Gashouse Gang. One day in St. Louis, for example, the temperature on the field was approaching 110° and the players were complaining about the heat. So Dean and Pepper Martin piled paper and wood in front of their dugout, wrapped themselves in blankets, squatted down "Indian style," and lit their campfire.

After suffering a broken toe when hit by a line drive in an All-Star Game and ruining his arm trying to pitch with that injury, Dean became a radio broadcaster known primarily for his creativity with the English language. Putting it gently, he made me look articulate. After a schoolteachers' association complained that his broadcasts were harmful to the educational process, he replied, "There is a lot of people in the United States who say 'isn't,' and they ain't eating."

In 1947, six years after retiring as an active player, Dean was broadcasting St. Louis Browns' games and complaining to listeners, "I don't know what this game's acomin' to. I swear I could beat nine out of ten of the guys that call themselves pitchers nowadays." On the closing day of the season, he got his chance: General Manager Bill DeWitt signed him to a one-dollar contract. Dean pitched four scoreless innings but left the game after pulling a muscle running to first base. After the game he told reporters, "I still think I can pitch well enough to win, but I ain't agoin' to try." They just don't make them like Dizzy anymore.

Paul Trout was also Dizzy. Like Dean, Dizzy Trout came from a small town, "Sandcut, Indiana, but don't ask me where it is," he said. "I know where it was when I left there, but that don't mean nothing. When you live in Sandcut, you know where you are when you go to bed, but the wind blows so hard in that part of Indiana that it often carries the whole town of Sandcut several miles away and sets it down someplace else from where it was the day before."

Trout pitched 14 years in the big leagues, twice winning twenty or more games. His trademarks were a bright red bandana, which he took out of his back pocket after every pitch ("I wave it at the batters," he explained. "This confuses them.") and a blazing fastball. After beating the Cubs in the 1945 World Series, he reported that his success was due to his atom ball. "Yep, I throw it up to the plate, and the batter hits it right at 'em."

Once, while pitching for the Tigers, he struck out Ted Williams in a crucial situation, and was so pleased that he asked Williams to autograph the ball for him. Williams glared at him but signed the ball. Two weeks later Trout again faced Williams with the ball game on the line. This time Ted hit a long home run and, as he jogged around the bases, shouted to Trout, "I'll sign that SOB, too, if you can find it!"

Trout was a man after my own stomach. He was known to order eighteen eggs for breakfast and invented the popular drink, Scotch and Coke.

Just like the original Dizzy, he became a broadcaster after retiring, and often wound his tales into a knot. Once, for example, he was telling the classic story of umpire George Moriarty. "This fresh busher is up to the plate and Moriarty called a coupla strikes on him," Trout began. "This busher turns to Moriarty and says, 'Say, how do you spell your name?' And Moriarty spells his name like this: 'M-o-r- ... i-r- ... r ... r ... r ...'" Trout paused, then asked his broadcasting partner, "How did Moriarty spell his name?" His partner didn't know, so Trout finished the tale, "Well, anyway, one 'i.' "

Trout also told his listeners about a catcher he had played with: "The curveball and knuckleball got him out of baseball. He couldn't hit the curveball and couldn't catch the knuckleball." And finally, like Dean, he came down from the booth five years after retiring to attempt a comeback. In two brief appearances, his ERA was 81.00. They still just don't make them like Dizzy anymore.

Hall of Fame character Lefty Gomez once came to bat late in the afternoon against a young, wild Bob Feller. As Gomez got to the plate he reached in his back pocket, pulled out a book of matches, and lit one. "Put that out," the umpire directed angrily, "it's not that dark. I can see Feller fine."

"I can see him fine, too," Gomez agreed. "I just want to make sure he can see me." "El Goofy," as he was known, was perhaps the first player to turn his career into a comedy routine. He owed his career, he once said, "To clean living and a fast outfield." His rules of pitching were simple. "One rule I had was make your best pitch and back up third base. That relay might get away."

Unlike many athletes, who get better after ending their careers, Gomez got worse. "I'll never forget one of my earliest experiences as a Yankee. I was in the bull pen. Herb Pennock was leading 2–1 in the eighth and a hard liner knocks him down. They called me in. A lot of thoughts run through your mind when going in to relieve in a tough situation. One of them was, 'Should I spike myself?' Joe McCarthy was waiting on the mound. 'Okay, boss, I told him, this is how I'll pitch to Foxx—' 'What's the matter with you?' McCarthy asked. 'That line drive broke the webbing in Pennock's glove. Give him yours and go back to the bull pen.' "

Like most real characters, Gomez had the ability to have fun on the field. One afternoon, a hard grounder was hit right back to him. Although there was no one on base, Gomez whirled and fired the ball to second base-man Tony Lazzeri. After the play was over a very confused Lazzeri came to the mound and asked Gomez why he'd thrown the ball to him. Gomez explained, "I read an article in *The Sporting News* yesterday that rated you as one of the brainiest infielders in the history of the American League. I said to myself, 'How am I going to test Tony to find out for myself?' So I threw the ball to you, eager to find out what a really brainy second baseman could do with it." They certainly don't make them like Goofy anymore.

No modern character had more nicknames, played on more teams, broke more bones, or had more fun than Bobo Newsom, a pitcher with an ego so big that it was said he could strut while sitting down. "The Great Showboat," "Loud Louie," "Old Buck," or just Bobo, played for nine different teams, some of them several times, during his twenty-year major league career. He was a Senator five times, a St. Louis Brown three times, a Dodger twice, and a Philadelphia Athletic twice. When Washington obtained him for the fifth time, he wired ahead, "Have no fear, Bobo's here," then marched into the city at the head of a sixty-piece band. "This is Bobo's fifth term in Washington," he announced, "which makes Bobo one up on Roosevelt." He won 211 games and in 1941 became the highest-paid pitcher in baseball history. Of course, he also lost 222, which was at least part of the reason he moved around so much.

Bobo referred to himself, as well as everyone else, as Bobo. "Now, listen, Bobo," he once told a sportswriter, "when Bobo says he's ready to pitch, there's nothing to worry about. Because, Bobo, Bobo has a feelin' he's gonna win twenty games this year."

He fractured nine different bones while in the big leagues, once pitching six innings with a broken kneecap. His jaw was broken with President Roosevelt in attendance on open-ing day in 1936 when he got in the way of third baseman Ossie Bluege's throw to first. The trainer wanted him to come out of the game, but Bobo refused, stating, "Whenever President Roosevelt comes to see Bobo pitch, Bobo ain't gonna disappoint him."

He wore number 00 on his size 50 uniform and had more superstitions than anyone in the game: He never tied his own shoelaces; he would stand majestically, arms folded, as someone tied them for him. He always took off his street socks in order, left sock first, then dangled them by their garters and dropped them into his street shoes. At the end of an inning he tossed his glove up in the air so it dropped just in front of him as he crossed the foul line; then he stopped and touched the foul line.

Fittingly, he pitched one no-hitter in his career—and lost it.

Newsom kept pet rabbits in his hotel suite and was considered one of baseball's leading practical jokers. He often substituted a sheet of cardboard for the ham in postgame ham sandwiches and once added Sal Hepatica, a mild laxative, to the Coca-Cola. Lefty Gomez always fantasized about roaring out of the bull pen on a motorcycle, wearing a suit of armor, but Bobo's dream was more elaborate: He wanted to imbed hundreds of ice skates, blades up, into the turf at Detroit's Briggs Stadium, so baseball fans could fasten ice cubes to the shoes and go skating.

There will never be another Bobo, Great Showboat, Loud Louie, Old Buck, any of them.

The major leagues in the days of Rabbit and Lefty and Casey and the Dizzys and Bobo had a legendary cast of characters. "We didn't make near as much money as the fellows today," Dizzy Dean said in the early 1950s, "but we sure had more fun. See, in my days, baseball was something you did without prompting. I'd get to the park at nine o'clock in the morning and put on my uniform, just to admire myself in it. These players today are more concerned with their stocks than the standings."

The introduction of $100,000-plus contracts, the shifting of franchises, the first expansion in half a century, the growing competition from other sports and recreational activities, the emergence of television as a vital factor in baseball's growth, the sale of teams from the families who founded and built them to businessmen and corporations, and the players' disillusionment over the reserve clause that made them the property of one team for their entire career changed the game. More than ever before, the players perceived it as a business. By the '50s the days of the colorful characters were over.

Oh, there were a few exceptions, of course. Even Dizzy would have had to admit that there were a few legitimate characters playing in the 1950s and 1960s. Take Billy Loes— and a lot of general managers wish someone else would've. "I'm hoping fervently that Billy becomes a twenty-game winner this year," a Dodger official said in 1956, "so we can get rid of him."

Like every truly classic character, Loes was one of a kind; it was just that nobody could figure out what kind he was. "He's got a mind of his own," his catcher, Roy Campanella, once said, "but you never know what he's going to do with it." Loes emerged as a character to be reckoned with just before his Dodgers were to meet the Yankees in the 1952 World Series, shattering his first baseball tradition by predicting the Yankees would win the Series in six games. After the Series, though, he protested that he had been misquoted. "What I really said was that the Yankees would win in seven games."

In the sixth game of that Series Loes ensured himself a place in baseball history when a routine ground ball bounced off his knee for a hit, and he explained, "I lost it in the sun."

Loes pitched in the big leagues for eleven years, winning a career high of fourteen games in 1953—which was enough for him. "Why should I want to be a twenty-game winner?" he once asked. "If you win twenty once, they expect you to win it every year and they cut your salary if you don't." After suffering a sore arm and winning only three games for the Orioles in 1958, he announced, "I'm shooting for four wins this year. That will be one more than I won last year, so I'll be improving." Loes won his four in 1959.

"Wily Coyote," as he was called by his Dodger teammates, was never overwhelmed about playing in the big leagues. "I'd like to be a guy making seventy dollars a week, five days a week, Saturday and Sundays off. You got troubles. You're feeling bad. You make mistakes. Who knows it? Play ball and the whole world knows your business."

While playing for the Dodgers one season, he found himself without a roommate. When asked by manager Walter Alston during a team meeting whom he might like to room with, he suggested, "I'd like to room with a guy just like myself." The entire clubhouse erupted in laughter.

Loes was selected by the Mets in the 1962 expansion draft. He appeared in the parade welcoming the team to New York, then retired. They don't make them like Billy Loes anymore, which probably makes a lot of general managers happy.

Whenever someone comes along who plays the game a little harder, who seems a little tougher, who acts a little more cantankerous, he is described as a "throwback to the old days." I've always wondered, in the old days, where did they throw people back to? Numerous players tried to throw Clint Courtney everywhere during his ten full seasons in the big leagues, but he just kept coming back. No one ever played the game quite like "Scrap Iron," who was said to have lost more fights than a punching bag. Clint was ready to fight at the drop of a name. He even had three different fights with Billy "The Kid" Martin, tying him for the record. As Phil Rizzuto once explained, when Courtney put on his uniform he became a different person, "He went berserk."

Courtney ignited one of the great brawls in modern baseball history at Yankee Stadium when he spiked Rizzuto at second base. Umpire Johnny Stevens, who ejected no one because "I would have had to throw out everybody," suffered a separated shoulder. This fight eventually led to a league rule prohibiting fans from bringing bottles into ball parks, because the umpires had to threaten to forfeit the game when fans showered the field with bottles and seat cushions. During the fight Yankee trainer Gus Mauch, trying to protect the fallen Rizzuto from flying spikes, rolled him into the outfield as if he were rolling up a carpet. At the end of the brawl the battered Courtney admitted, "They got a banquet, but I got a sandwich."

Courtney initially gained recognition as the first catcher to wear eyeglasses while playing. His glasses probably kept him out of even more fights—when a fight started other players would knock them off and try to step on them.

It wasn't just modern baseball that Scraps battled, it was the entire modern world. One very hot day in Kansas City he drove up to his team's hotel in a brand new Cadillac he'd just purchased. He got out of the car, and he was drenched. Sweat was pouring from his body. His concerned teammates asked what was wrong. "These damn new cars," he replied, "They don't even give you a window crank. I couldn't put the damn windows down."

Teammate Milt Pappas said quietly, "Scraps, this car has power windows."

Courtney was a fair catcher, but he never actually mastered the art of giving signals to pitchers. Once, for example, Senator manager Charlie Dressen believed the opposition was stealing Courtney's signals when they got a runner to second base. Normally, with a runner on second, the catcher will flash a sequence of several signs, the actual sign being the second or third or whatever number in the sequence the catcher and pitcher have agreed on. Dressen thought the opposition knew that Courtney always used the second sign. "That doesn't make any difference," Scraps told him, "because I always slip it down there when they aren't looking."

When Courtney was still with the Senators, Dressen was upset that his pitchers and catchers were having difficulty communicating signals so he held a meeting in the locker room. After reviewing the signals several times, he told Courtney to get into a crouch and go through a sequence. Courtney did so. Then Dressen asked his pitchers what pitch Scraps had called for. All ten pitchers agreed it was a curveball. "All ten of you are wrong," Courtney announced triumphantly. "I was signaling for a fastball!"

When not fighting, Clint was very well liked by teammates and opponents, who delighted in playing practical jokes on him. Catcher Les Moss often repaired other players' gloves, and one day he was restringing Scraps' catcher's mitt. Early Wynn saw Moss at work and suggested they sew a slice of Limburger cheese into the pocket. "I couldn't do that to an old roomie of mine," Moss said. "Here, give it to me." Moss completed the job, leaving air vents so the odor would come out, then returned it to Courtney.

When Courtney came out to catch, umpire Johnny Stevens crouched over him for the first pitch. Stevens immediately jumped up and called "Time!"

"He was gasping for breath," Wynn remembers. "His eyes were watering, and he couldn't see. He looked into the dugout and saw me sprawled over the bat rack, laughing hysterically. 'Wynn,' he yelled, 'you get out of here! Stay in the clubhouse! If the manager needs you, he can get you!' Meanwhile, Courtney just kept staring at his glove.

" 'John,' I asked, 'what have I done?'

"He was still coughing and choking, but he said, 'I'm not sure what you've done, but we've got nine innings to go and I don't want you doing it any more.' I don't know if Courtney ever even knew something was wrong."

Courtney knew it was time to retire, he said, when he realized "There's just the scrap, not too much iron," and became a minor league manager. They just don't make them like Scrap Iron anymore.

Pitcher Moe Drabowsky was as dizzy as a Dean. Drabowsky, baseball's greatest Polish-born right-handed relief pitcher, pioneered the fine art of bull pen humor during his seventeen-year big league career. While pitching for the Orioles, he called the Kansas City bull pen and ordered them to get pitcher Lew Krausse warmed up. The K.C. bull pen leaped into action, even though starting pitcher Jim Nash was throwing a three-hitter. After four or five minutes, Drabowsky called back and told Krausse to sit down.

Drabowsky worked as a stockbroker in the off-season and often used the bull pen phone to check the latest market quotes. Once he was accused of using the bull pen phone to call Poland. "Absolutely untrue," he responds when asked about that. "I didn't call Poland. I called a Chinese restaurant in Hong Kong to find out if they delivered." He also attempted to call Sophia Loren in Italy.

Drabowsky's years in the bull pen allowed him to perfect one of baseball's greatest traditions: the hotfoot. Properly administering a hotfoot is considered one of baseball's greatest feats, or, in this case, feet. Few things have survived in baseball history as long as the hotfoot. "I owe much of my success in this field," Drabowsky admits, "to Davey Johnson. He taught me the fundamentals. He was quick, but I improved on his methods and carried them to greater glory. At first it was simple: An unsuspecting player would be standing in his locker, he would reach up for his shaving cream or something and, whoosh, he was on fire.

"But eventually one match just wasn't satisfying anymore, so I went to an entire matchbook. One of my favorite targets was a Baltimore writer. He made the mistake of coming into our locker room every day wearing shoes. I'd plant ten matches on each side of his shoe and set it afire. That shoe looked like a World War II battleship going down in flames. Finally he became so concerned about his shoes that he began conducting his interviews looking down—so one day I set his notebook on fire.

"Once Jim Palmer came into the locker room barefooted and started giving an interview. I felt that deserved a major effort, so I abandoned regular matches and went for one of those big wooden babies. Suddenly, in the middle of the interview, Palmer started screaming. The radio station got it on tape and replayed it for weeks.

"Certainly my greatest hotfoot was administered to Baseball Commissioner Bowie Kuhn in our locker room after we'd won the World Series. I placed an entire book of matches under his foot and laid a lighter fluid trail from the matches to the trainer's room. I hid in the trainer's room and lit it. Have you ever wondered how high a baseball commissioner can jump?"

Drabowsky played on nine teams during his career, including the expansion-bred 1969 Kansas City Royals. "They decided to build primarily with young players and wanted a few veterans to stabilize the club. Getting me to stabilize that club was probably a mistake. Joe Gordon was the manager and we got along very well. We used to steal corn from farmers' fields together.''

After a Royals teammate had had a difficult outing the night before, Drabowsky decided to hold a funeral for him in the bull pen. ''We plotted out the grave, the player laid down, and we had six pallbearers, three on each side. I stood at the head of the grave, I cupped my hands, and I started reciting last rites. Unfortunately, I looked up and realized that we were on television. What could I do? I couldn't stop the funeral in the middle. General Manager Ed Short was watching television and was not amused. He called Manager Joe Gordon and asked him what was going on in the bull pen. What could Joe tell him? A funeral?''

Drabowsky did not limit himself to hotfoots. He is the only player known to have put goldfish in the visiting team's water cooler. He also became extremely adept at snake-planting: buttoning a live snake into the pocket of Luis Aparicio's uniform pants in an attempt to discover how fast Aparicio could really run, jamming a snake into the fingers of outfielder Sweet Lou Johnson's glove, which, he estimates, was thrown a hundred feet straight into the air; and finally, while sitting on the dais at an Orioles' old-timers' dinner, planting a three-foot King snake under a napkin in the breadbasket—then handing the basket to Brooks Robinson.

Even if Moe Drabowsky had never dumped a packet of sneezing powder into an opponent's air conditioning system, and even if he had never called a hotel operator, identified himself as a teammate, and demanded she call him every two hours throughout the night so he could take his medicine, ''No matter how much I tell you to cancel these calls,'' Drabowsky would still live in baseball history as one of the craziest men to play the game. Moe Drabowsky once turned down a raise.

''Charley Finley had a policy of rewarding players for individual performances by tearing up their contracts and giving them a raise. I started a game one day and pitched a one-hitter. After the game Charley told me he was going to tear up my contract and give me a five-hundred-dollar raise. 'Thanks very much,' I said, 'but what are you gonna do for the eight other guys on the field?'

"Silence. Then, 'What do you mean, the eight other guys?'

" 'I just threw the ball. The other guys deserve something, too.' Charley refused to give them anything, so I refused his offer. It was the strangest argument anyone ever saw, Charley insisting I accept the raise and me refusing to take it.

"I probably wasn't as good an agent as I should have been."

There absolutely, without doubt, certainly will never be another Moe Drabowsky.

A true test of character, in addition to longevity, is fan appreciation. And few characters have played longer or were more appreciated than Saturnino Orestes Arrieta Armas Minoso. Cuban-born Minnie Minoso apparently got his Minnie name soon after arriving in America, but it took him a while to appreciate it. "I was sitting in a dentist office," he remembers, "and the dentist say, 'Minnie, come here.' I start to get up but his girl assistant walked over to him. I could no believe it—Minnie was a girl's name!"

In 1948 Minoso was playing in the minor leagues, and manager Joe Vosmik gave him the "take" sign, meaning he wasn't to swing at the next pitch. Minoso hit the next pitch for a home run. Afterward, Minnie denied he had missed the sign, claiming, "I see take sign. I think you mean, Minnie, take good swing."

When he was with the White Sox, Minoso occasionally borrowed the station wagon the team used to bring in pitchers from the bull pen to drive to a personal appearance. One day as he sped along, accompanied by Cuban pitcher Sandy Consuegra, he was shocked to see the mileage figures on the odometer. "Twenty-four tousan' miles," he said, shaking his head in disbelief. "I be some sonofagun, you White Sox pitchers are sure no good."

One of the many reasons Minoso was such a hit with

fans in Cleveland and Chicago was his willingness to be hit by a pitch. Minnie set records for being hit by pitches. He survived, however, and when he batted twice for the White Sox in 1980, he became the only man in history to play in the major leagues in five different decades. He anticipates becoming the only player in history to play in six different decades in 1990, although he is already threatening to hold out unless he is paid what he is worth.

They still never make them like Minnie Minoso anymore.

Yogi Berra had a head start in becoming a character. He looked, said Yankee president Larry MacPhail, "like the bottom man on an unemployed acrobatic team." At bat he had a tendency to swing at—and an ability to hit—any pitch thrown within the same zip code as home plate. Yogi is one of the few characters endearing enough to have had a fictional character created in *his* image, the remarkable Yogi Bear.

Yogi was often accused of a lack of intelligence, but he was smart enough to say enough dumb things to enable his popularity to transcend baseball. Honored by his friends from his hometown of St. Louis with a night during his rookie year, for example, Yogi gratefully told everyone, "I want to thank everyone who made this night necessary."

In fact, his "dumb" statements usually contained a great deal of wisdom. Describing left field in Yankee Stadium, a notoriously difficult position to play in the fall because of glaring sunlight and sweeping shadows, he said, accurately, "It gets late early out there." When he went through a long hitless spell at bat, he told reporters succinctly, "I ain't in a slump, I just ain't hitting." When asked if he intended to change after being named manager of the Yankees, he replied, "I'd be pretty dumb if all of a sudden I started being something I'm not." And when he was fired as the Mets' manager he explained, "I got nothing to say and I'm only going to say it once."

It's impossible to separate real Berraisms from those attributed to him by creative sportswriters. Asked by journalists if rookie Don Mattingly had exceeded his expectations, he supposedly answered, "More than that." Once, supposedly, for appearing on a radio show he received a check from broadcaster Jack Buck made out to "Bearer," and complained, "Gee, Jack, I'm disappointed. You've known me so long, and you still don't know how to spell my name?" When describing his audience with the Pope to reporters, Yogi supposedly said, "The Pope must read the papers a lot, because he said, 'Hello, Yogi.' " And when asked how he replied, Yogi answered, "I said, 'Hello, Pope.' " After attending a dinner at the White House, he expressed disappointment because "It was hard to have a conversation with anyone, there were so many people talking," which is reminiscent of his complaint about a popular restaurant: "No wonder no one goes there anymore, it's always so crowded."

Yogi was so popular with fans that when the Mets put him on waivers—meaning that any other team could claim him for a dollar—a seventeen-year-old girl bid for him. "It doesn't seem like anyone else really wants him," she said. "I thought I would buy him." Yogi decided she had him confused with Yogi Bear. Not a particularly difficult thing to do.

Yogi has played, coached, and managed in the big leagues for four decades, and few people understand the game as well as he does. "Baseball," he once declared, "is 80 percent mental and the other half physical." And his oft-quoted philosophy of the game: "It ain't over till it's over" will live as long as the game is played. They absolutely do not make them like Yogi Berra anymore, if they ever did in the first place.

Many characters have been called crazy, but only one could actually prove it. Jimmy Piersall's nervous breakdown was chronicled in the book and hit movie *Fear Strikes Out*, but as someone who watched his antics once quipped, "I still think the count only went to three and two."

A five-time All-Star, Piersall celebrated his mental problems the way other people celebrated Christmas. "Being nuts was the best thing that ever happened to me," he once said. "Nobody knew me until I went nuts." One night, stepping into the batter's box after Yankee pitchers had knocked down the two previous hitters, he told catcher Yogi Berra, "I've got a bat. If you call for a knockdown on me, I'll hit you on top of the head and plead temporary insanity."

Unlike Yogi, it wasn't what Piersall said that defined his character, but rather what he did. At times he batted in a crouch, as if he were Bill Veeck's midget. When a pitch came close to his head, he called time, dropped to his knees, and began praying. Once, after making an outstanding catch, he began applauding himself and, when the fans failed to join him, ran to the infield, stood on the pitcher's mound, held his hands above his head, and led the fans in a round of applause for himself. During pitching changes he would often hide behind the center-field flagpole in Boston's Fenway Park. While waiting on deck he would practice his golf swing rather than his baseball swing.

On occasion he would whistle as he worked in right field, and once he convinced the fans in the right-field stands to join him in a mass serenade, which he led like a conductor. He even held conversations with the fans during the game. Obviously, that had nothing to do with being crazy; from time to time I did the same thing myself. The difference between the two of us was that Piersall continued talking *during* a play, telling his fans while running after a fly ball, "Watch this, watch how easy I do this."

Piersall had a volcanic temper, and his eruptions made it seem as if he had lost his mind. Again. Several times, after being called out by an umpire, he dumped all the bats and balls and much of the equipment in the dugout, including a bucket of sand and the water cooler, onto the field. In Chicago one night, he ended a ball game by catching a fly ball, then turned around and threw it at Veeck's exploding scoreboard. In Baltimore he was arrested for going into the stands to fight a fan who called him crazy.

How crazy was Piersall? Well, he once challenged Moose Skowron to a fight. But as Casey Stengel accurately summed up, "When he hits the ball, he never runs to third base." Although, when he hit his hundredth major league home run, he did run backwards around the bases.

Bob Uecker had a brief but totally undistinguished major league career. In a career marked by no highlights, "Mr. Baseball" remembers his biggest thrill as "The day I saw a guy fall out of the upper deck in Philadelphia."

Uecker established himself as one of baseball's funniest characters while not playing for four big league teams over six seasons. In truth, Uecker didn't have a career as much as he had a long comedy routine. "With Philadelphia, I'd be sitting on the bench and Manager Gene Mauch would holler down, 'Grab a bat, Bob, and stop this rally!' Or he'd send me up to bat and tell me to go for a walk.

"I led the Braves in homers, RBIs, and lies. There were some great moments, though. In 1962 I was voted Minor League Player of the Year. That, unfortunately, was my second year in the majors. And once I received an intentional pass from Sandy Koufax. Sandy got a letter from the commissioner telling him he was damaging the image of the game.

"The fans loved me, though. I never stayed anywhere long enough to earn a ceremonial day, but in Philly they once had a Bob Uecker Day Off in my honor.

"I found out my career was over in a strange way. I was with the Braves and I was getting dressed for a game and a coach came over and told me visitors weren't allowed in the clubhouse.

"I still miss not playing the game. I miss the small events, like coming into the clubhouse after a big game and having your teammates pounding on your back, jumping on you, trying everything to keep you out of the next game."

Uecker retired in 1967 and, as he would admit, baseball's gain became show business's loss. Uecker joined the Brewers as a broadcaster, became the star of the Lite Beer All-Star commercials—which I myself love, even though I have auditioned eleven different times and have never been selected—and has become one of the leading characters on the TV series *Mr. Belvedere.* Uecker might be too embarrassed to admit it, but players as great as Cy Young, who won 511 games, and Babe Ruth, who hit 714 home runs, never had their own television series. And, except for the fact that there was no such thing as television in their lifetime, that remains a remarkable achievement.

Uecker, like Lefty Gomez, saw the humor in his career. The difference between the two of them was that Uecker was as bad as he claims he was. They don't make them like Bob Uecker anymore.

Baseball had a unique vitality in the days of "Scraps" Courtney and Drabowsky and Minnie and Yogi and Piersall and Uecker and Billy Loes and people like Joe Garagiola, who claimed he played with teams so bad that when they were rained out they held a victory party and believed a rally was "two out and a man on first." And Dick "66" Stuart, who hit sixty-six home runs one minor league season and whose first baseman's glove was said to be bronzed— while he was still active. And Bo Belinsky, who pitched a no-hitter his rookie year and ended up engaged to sex queen Mamie Van Doren. And "Marvelous" Marv Throneberry, who missed two out of three bases while running out a triple ("I know he didn't miss third," Casey said, "because he's standing on it."). And umpire Emmett Ashford, who proudly wore cuff links on his uniform. And A's owner Charley Finley, who introduced brightly colored uniforms to baseball and hired the first pinch-running specialist and kept a flock of sheep beyond his outfield fence, who installed a pop-up wooden rabbit to deliver baseballs to umpires, and who paid his players to grow mustaches and brought relief pitchers into the game in taxis and buses and a haywagon and had a mule travel with his team. And people like legendary minor leaguer Billy Scripture, who could break a fungo bat by twisting its barrel with his hands, bite the cover off a baseball in less than two minutes, take a bite out of the bench ("I feel a great release. It has to be cheaper than ulcer surgery."), catch the hardest pitch almost any player could throw—without a glove, and stand in front of a pitching machine and let its pitches hit him in the chest. Baseball in those days had a legendary cast of characters. "Of course, we didn't earn very much compared to what today's players are making," Ron Hansen, a great shortstop and the last man to pull off an unassisted triple play notes, "and money is a great thing, but sometimes it doesn't compensate for the memories. I don't think the players today enjoy playing the game as much as we did."

"We had more fun than they do today," Eddie Kranepool, who played eighteen seasons with the Mets, believes. "We ate together, partied together, drank together. We played the game and had fun afterward. Players today have agents and business managers and worry about their public image, and after the game, instead of sitting around the clubhouse talking baseball, they're off to their business appointments."

The introduction of long-term multimillion-dollar contracts, free agency, agents, no-trade clauses, the growth of the powerful Players' Association that has led to two strikes, the growing influence of television over the game, and the reality of a serious drug problem have changed the game. More than ever before, the players perceive it as a business. The days of the colorful characters have disappeared. Oh, there are a few exceptions, of course. Pitchers throughout baseball history have stood on the mound and talked to batters or to themselves, but only Mark "The Bird" Fidrych spoke to the baseball. Some people believed The Bird had a one-track mind while everyone else was thinking in stereo, but Fidrych played baseball with the enthusiasm of a mosquito in a nudist colony, carefully landscaping the mound by hand, leading cheers for his teammates, celebrating victories, strikeouts, and great plays by leaping in the air, and finally, conversing with the baseball. After winning nineteen games during his spectacular rookie year, Fidrych damaged his arm and was never again an effective pitcher. Based on his dismal performance in his last four years in the majors, if the ball had answered back, it undoubtedly would have said, "Help!" They don't make Birds anymore.

But besides Fidrych, modern baseball just doesn't have the colorful cast of characters of the old days. Well, besides Fidrych and "The Mad Hungarian." The St. Louis Cardinals' organist played Liszt's Hungarian Rhapsody No. 2 when relief pitcher Al "The Mad Hungarian" Hrabosky entered a game. Before each pitch, Hrabosky would walk behind the mound, his back to home plate, psyche himself up like a pressure cooker preparing to explode, and when he was finally ready, slam the ball into his glove, stomp to the pitching rubber, and get ready to throw. "I'm getting myself into a concentrated hate mood," he explained. "I want the hitter to wonder if maybe I am a little crazy." Once, unfortunately, as he slammed the ball into his glove, he missed the glove, throwing the ball into foul territory.

Unlike most pitchers, Hrabosky's real strength didn't come from his arm; it came from his beard and Fu Manchu mustache. So when Cardinal manager Vern Rapp forced him to shave, Hrabosky lost his effectiveness along with his whiskers. "I sincerely believe my appearance had a great effect on my performance and I am a better pitcher when I am myself," he complained. When the Cardinals relented, Hrabosky regained his effectiveness.

Hrabosky knew his on-the-field act increased the pressure on him, but that was his intention. "On the road, I know people pay to see me fail. Nothing gives me more pride than receiving a standing boo."

Off the field, however, he was just as mad. When he was with Kansas City in 1978, the Royals got off to a slow start. So Hrabosky brought a hand grenade into the locker room and told his teammates that if they didn't start playing better baseball he was going to have to blow them up. "The Mad Hungarian" had been, naturally, a weapons demolition expert in the army and had defused the grenade, but he didn't bother to tell anyone. The grenade sat there all season. The night the Royals clinched the pennant, "After my second bottle of champagne, I decided to pull the safety pin. I explained to everyone that as long as I held the safety lever down with my hand there was nothing to be concerned about, but after a few minutes I did suggest they hurry and find a pair of pliers because I'd bent the safety pin when I pulled it out and it wouldn't go back in, and my hand was getting very tired. Finally they got me a pliers and I put the pin back in.

"I came to the park the next morning and was told to

see General Manager Joe Burke. 'I got a very disturbing call about you last night,' he said pleasantly. 'I'm sure there's no validity in it, but I have to ask you. The Kansas City Police Department called and told me you threatened to blow up the ballpark. You have any idea where this could have stemmed from?'

" 'Well,' I admitted, 'I'm not sure. But I did pull the pin on my hand grenade last night.'

" 'Oh,' he said, 'oh.' He thought about that for a moment, then said, 'What?'

"He asked me to get rid of it, but when I went to the locker room my grenade was gone. Soon after I'd left the park, I was told, the police bomb disposal unit had come into the clubhouse and confiscated it. A season later I was gone."

Hrabosky claimed his ultimate ambition was "to become a mercenary. I want to go to Africa and fight evil forces there. I've taken some crash courses on animal behavior, so I'll be able to amass the wild kingdom as my ally." But in fact, he signed a thirty-five-year contract with the Braves, and after retiring in 1982, he became a broadcaster, bought a farm, and raises pure-bred Polish-Arabian horses. They can't afford to make them like "The Mad Hungarian" anymore.

So, except for Fidrych *and* Hrabosky there aren't . . . well, besides Fidrych, Hrabosky, and Doug Rader. "I usually don't make a good first impression," the former third baseman and manager admitted, "or a good second impression. For that matter, I usually come across like a sack of manure." But anyone who played with him, or for him, or met him, or even heard of him, will never forget him. A teammate remembers the night Rader walked into his hotel room totally naked and said, "I'll bet you're wondering where I'm hiding my key." Infielder Tim Flannery struck out three times and made an error in the ninth inning to lose the first game he played for Manager Rader. "After the game he called me into his office," Flannery recalls. "He could see that I was upset, so he told me, 'The reason I've got you in here is to try to talk you out of showing up tomorrow." Infielder Mike Hargrove recalls the day he went on a snorkeling expedition in Hawaii with Manager Rader and a teammate. "One of our mopeds broke down and while we're standing by the side of the road two big guys drove by real close, covering us with dirt and shouting insults. They stopped on the top of a hill and Doug said, 'Let's get those guys.'

"Those guys were huge. When we got closer I noticed the driver had an ice pick in one hand and a big rock in the other. That didn't stop Doug. He ran right up to him, pointed a finger at him, and said, 'You win!' Smartest move I ever saw a manager make."

"This game is based on failure," Rader explained, "and if you took every failure to heart you'd be wearing one of those funny sports coats in about a week. I just try to remember that the idea is to have fun. The things I say just seem to come out. Like when I was in the Army Reserves I went up to my sergeant one day and told him, 'My environment is spasmodic. Every swinging corpuscle in my body is fatigued.' So he told me I'd better lie down."

It was not just what Rader said that provided his character credentials; he also did strange things. After striking out one day, he butted his head against the dugout wall. He was known to take the wrapper off an ice cream bar, eat the wrapper, and stick the ice cream in his ear. He drove a motorcycle into a wall and a golf cart into a lake. Rader invented "Hall Ball," a game in which he tried to run the length of a hotel hallway while everyone else on the team tried to stop him. In college, to protect his amateur status, Rader played semipro hockey under the quite common name of Dominick Bogassio.

When "Mad Dog," as he was occasionally called, announced his desire to manage the Astros, he was asked if he felt his lack of managerial experience would hurt him. "Hell, no," he said sagely. "If experience was that important, we'd never have had anybody walking on the moon."

They don't make them like Dominick Bogassio anymore, either.

But except for Fidrych, Hrabosky, Rader . . . and reliever

Sparky Lyle, whose idea of a wonderful joke was to surprise Yankee manager Bill Virdon by arriving at spring training with plaster casts on an arm and a leg and who often sat naked on birthday cakes in the clubhouse. And Steve "Lefty" Carlton, who supposedly slept on nails and strengthened his arm by swirling it in a barrel of sand. And Tug McGraw, who coined the 1973 pennant-winning Mets' rallying cry "You gotta believe!," replied to a reporter's question about the difference between real grass and artificial turf by explaining, "I don't know. I've never smoked artificial turf," admitted when he received his World Series bonus, "Ninety percent of it I'll spend on whiskey, women, and other good times; the other 10 percent I'll probably waste," and won the hearts of baseball fans in the 1980 World Series playoffs by taking an exaggerated breath and pounding his glove on his heart after a hard line drive went barely foul. They don't . . .

Except for these few players, and maybe vegetarian infielder Pete LaCock, who kept a pet panther, ocelot, and pigeons and married a woman who had her own raccoon. And Mickey Rivers, who once claimed that "George Steinbrenner, Billy Martin, and me are two of a kind," told a reporter that his goals for an upcoming season were "To hit .300, score a hundred runs, and stay accident-prone," complained after rounding first on a base hit and twisting his ankle, "When I rounded the base I couldn't get any friction and I resprung my ankle," and responded to Reggie Jackson's boast that he had a 140 IQ, "Yeah, same as your batting average." And maybe reliever Bob Shirley, who would occasionally chauffeur other relief pitchers into the game. And Bill "Spaceman" Lee, the left-handed pitcher who claimed that Montreal's Olympic Stadium was haunted and once explained, "Your brain has a left and a right hemisphere. The left side controls the right side of your body and the right side controls the left side. Therefore, left-handers are the only people in their right mind." And John "The Count" Montefusco, who owned a racehorse that "Sometimes I would lay down with in the stall and talk to because nobody else would talk to me," often made predictions about his performance (many of which proved to be wrong), and decided he didn't like being a relief pitcher because "When I was a reliever, I came to the ball-park nervous every day. I was losing hair. My arm doesn't mind working every day, but my hair needs four days' rest." And even reliever Charlie Kerfeld, who has a spike haircut, loves punk rock music and slam dancing, wears pink high-top basketball shoes and a "mystical" Jetsons T-shirt, banged his head on the dugout rail trying to run out to congratu-late a teammate and fell back flat on his back, and who signed a contract for $110,037.37 and thirty-seven boxes of orange Jell-O—to match his uniform number, 37, and who replied when asked if he could match Yogi Berra's wit, "I don't think about it much. If I did, I'd probably get massive brain cramps," and, after being sent back to the minor leagues left a message on his answering machine reporting, "I ain't here and I ain't gonna be here for a while, I guess." Except for these few players . . .

   "My career proved to me that baseball fans were starved for color. I see very little emotion out there, perhaps it has to do with the sterile ballparks and high salaries, but I look at the players today and I remember how much fun I had playing the game and, at times, I wonder if these kids have as much fun," said Al "The Mad Hungarian" Hrabosky—whose career ended way back in 1982.

   The balls and the bats and the uniforms and the ball parks and the rules may change, but the game will always have its starring characters. As Casey or Yogi or Dizzy or Kerfeld might have said, "They'll never stop making players like they're not making anymore."

4

RELIEF IS JUST $2.2,000,000 SPREAD OVER THREE YEARS, INCLUDING INCENTIVE BONUSES, AWAY

An essential element in the continuing popularity of baseball has been the ability to maintain the delicate balance between hitting and pitching. For example, batters have been prohibited from using a corked, or otherwise doctored bat, while pitchers have had the pitcher's mound moved back, had to pitch with a livelier baseball, had a new baseball put in play every time the ball in play was slightly marred, were prohibited from applying any substance to a ball or scuffing its cover, and had the outfield fences moved closer to home plate. Batters have been prohibited from applying any substance to a bat more than seventeen inches from the bottom. Pitchers had the pitcher's mound lowered, the strike zone reduced to a size slightly larger than a virus, and have been prohibited from throwing an inside pitch or thinking about throwing an inside pitch. Batters, meanwhile, are absolutely prohibited from stepping out of the batter's box without first requesting permission from the umpire. And pitchers have had the lively ball replaced by a livelier ball, have to pitch to a designated hitter, have to pitch on a plastic infield that turns routine ground balls into missiles traveling faster than a thought, have to deliver the ball within twenty seconds, stop for a second at their waist when pitching from a stretch, and can't even sneak a glance at a base runner without a balk being called. But batters *must* have their uniform shirts tucked in.

Compared to what baseball's rulemakers have done to pitchers, Dr. Frankenstein's monster was loved by the townspeople. The people who claim that pitchers are paranoid are the same people who would have suggested John Dillinger go to the movies.

A story is told about a fan who arrived at the ballpark in the eighth inning and learned that both pitchers were throwing perfect games—no runs, no hits, no base runners. "Oh, good," he said, "I haven't missed anything." That person must have been a member of baseball's management, because almost every significant change in baseball since the turn of the century has been made to increase scoring.

Supposedly, ex-pitcher Babe Ruth's long home runs were the primary reason baseball changed from a pitching-singles-bunting-running game to a power game. Few fans came out to the ballpark especially to see Ruth pitch, but when he started slugging baseballs out of the park, attendance rose significantly. It occurred to baseball's astute mogels that if one home run hitter could increase attendance, a league of home run hitters would create more excitement than a legion of camel-kissing Valentinos. So baseball roared into the twenties with a brand-new lively ball.

In fact, the attack on pitchers had begun long before Ruth farthered the home run. Even before the turn of the century, fastball pitcher Amos "The Hoosier Thunderbolt" Rusie was so dominant that the distance from home plate to the pitcher's rubber had to be increased from fifty feet to the present sixty feet, six inches. And from that time until this afternoon, pitchers have been battered.

Pitchers have not stood still. They couldn't—not with all those line drives and thrown bats rocketing toward them. The job of throwing a baseball has changed so much since Amos Rusie simply reared back and fired his fastball for nine innings that today's pitchers could accurately be called "hurling engineers." Old-time players might laugh at today's pitchers and all their newfangled theories—until they tried to hit against them.

Perhaps the most significant change in the job is the hours. Once upon a time, according to legend and the record books, there was something known as a complete game. A complete game was what it was called when a pitcher finished what he started. "When I came up in 1957," Milt Pappas remembers, "the manager would tell you before the game, 'You're it.' That meant that you were the pitcher that day, the *only* pitcher. Once, when I was pitching for the Orioles, I was beating the White Sox 3–1 in the eighth inning on a boiling hot afternoon. Ted Kluszewski came up as a pinch hitter and hit a three-run homer which would have won the game—but umpire Ed Hurley had called time-out just before I'd pitched, and the home run didn't count. Given a second chance, I got Kluszewski out.

"When I went to the bench I looked at Manager Paul Richards and said, 'God, boss, I'm tired. I can't pitch anymore.' 'Fine,' he said, and brought in a relief pitcher. After the game he called me over and asked if I was still tired. I told him I was. 'Okay,' he answered, 'get your ass outside and run three miles and maybe you'll be able to finish the job next time.' "

Ironically, today's pitchers are bigger, stronger, in better condition, and have better medical treatment available to them than old-timers—but managers expect them to pitch fewer innings and do so with more rest between starts. Most teams today use a five-pitcher rotation, meaning a pitcher starts every fifth game. Teams once had four starters and, in the heat of a pennant race, used only three starters. In 1964, with two weeks left in the season, Philadelphia manager Gene Mauch went to a two-man rotation, pitching Jim Bunning and Chris Short almost every day—and the Phillies blew their 6 ½-game lead. The 1969 Mets were one of the first teams to go to the five-man rotation, and when they won the World's Championship, other teams tried to emulate that success. The big difference is that the

Mets had five outstanding pitchers; most other teams have five pitchers.

Not only were old-time pitchers expected to pitch a complete game, until the mid-1950s they were also required to throw batting practice. The day before Walter Johnson made his major league debut, for example, he pitched batting practice—for both teams. "But he afforded little practice," a newspaper of the day wrote, "as his fastball seemed unhittable." It was in 1955 that the Dodgers' Don Newcombe refused to pitch batting practice, and was denounced, fined, and suspended by the Dodgers for his heresy.

A complete game today is about as rare as a Fourth of July doubleheader. All a manager really expects from his starting pitcher is six or seven good innings. Then his setup man pitches till the ninth when the stopper comes in to finish the game. In the old days starting pitchers hated to be taken out of games. Even before anyone knew the word *machismo*, complete games were considered a test of it. "Being taken out of a game was looked upon as failing," Don Drysdale remembers. "Your teammates looked at you as if you'd let them down, and that's the way you felt. It wasn't that you'd pitched seven good innings, it was that you'd *only* pitched seven innings."

A pitcher who failed to finish felt much the same way I did if I ate only one dessert: We were both left feeling empty.

Starting pitchers fought to stay in the game. Once Al Lopez relieved Early Wynn, and Wynn was so angry he threw the ball away—hitting Lopez right in the chest. Whenever Wynn started for Cleveland, the Indians' clubhouse custodian always made sure the garbage can in the clubhouse was empty. " 'Cause if he got knocked out of a game he'd go back to the clubhouse and kick that can all over the place. So this way I never had a mess to clean up."

Dick Donovan also threw the ball at Manager Whit Wyatt when Wyatt took him out. "What bothered me most," Wyatt said later, "was that he threw the ball at me harder than he was throwing it to the batters." Russ "Mad Monk" Meyer was so upset when he was relieved that he threw his glove into the air in disgust; unfortunately, his glove landed on his head. When Braves' manager Fred Haney went out to the mound to take out Lew Burdette, Burdette glared at him and challenged, "Who you got that's any better?"

"It's not a question of having anyone better," Haney told him, "I just want somebody luckier."

Once Stan Williams refused to leave the mound. Leo Durocher went out to get him and Williams told him, "Dammit Leo, I'm not leaving."

Durocher replied, "That's all right, Stan, neither am I. But here comes (relief pitcher) Sherry, and this mound is getting mightily crowded."

Manager Luke Sewell tried to take out Herm Wehmeier and ended up chasing Wehmeier around the infield trying to get the ball from him, finally catching him in front of second base.

"Only once did I see a pitcher anxious to come out of a game," says Red Sox owner Haywood Sullivan. "I was managing Kansas City in 1965 and Charley Finley had signed Satchel Paige. Officially Satch was fifty-nine years old, but he might have been older. A lot older. It was a promotional stunt, but Satch could still pitch a little. He started against the Red Sox and got them out in order in the first inning. In the second inning Carl Yastrzemski blooped a single over third base; that was the only hit he gave up. Paige batted in the bottom of the second and struck out on three pitches. When he began warming up in the top of the fourth I could see he was exhausted, so I want out to get him. There were thirty-five thousand people in the ballpark, and every one of them was booing me. When I got out there, I said, 'Satch, you had enough?'

"He smiled and asked, 'Man, where has you been?'

" 'All right,' I told him, 'I'm gonna take you out, but don't you leave me standing here by myself. Wait till the reliever gets here, then walk back with me.'

" 'Okay,' he agreed, 'but you better tell him to hurry.' "

There are many reasons that complete games have gone the way of trolley cars, Studebakers, outside chest protectors, *The Saturday Evening Post*, and Reggie bars. As many as five or six dozen balls are used in a game today, but in the early part of the century the home team furnished the umpire with three new balls and these were supposed to last the entire game. The pitcher was allowed to do pretty much anything he wanted to do to the ball. He would start by spitting tobacco juice on it, then get down on his knees and rub it on the grass and gravel, to give it "wings." I suspect if the ball hadn't been dead to begin with, the tobacco juice would have killed it.

By the fifth or sixth inning it became almost impossible to drive the ball beyond the infield. In Detroit one day, for example, baseball's home run king, Nap Lajoie, who had clouted 13 in 1901, insisted after seven innings that the umpire replace the original ball. The ball, which had also been used in the game the day before, was about as hard as an overripe peach but probably couldn't be hit as far. The umpire insisted it was still usable. "You think this league is made of money?" he asked, proving that some things still haven't changed. "This here ball is in play and stays in play."

"Put in a new ball," Lajoie insisted.

"Not while this one's in play."

"All right," Lajoie said, grabbing the ball, rearing back, and heaving it out of the ballpark, "*Now* it's not in play."

Because the peachball was so soft and had been cut up so badly, it had tremendous natural movement, so pitchers could afford to lay the ball over the plate to most batters. They really had to bear down only against their opponents' top two or three hitters. Obviously, this allowed a pitcher like Jack Chesbro to complete forty-eight of the fifty-one games he started in 1904 without turning his arm into spaghetti.

The basic philosophy of pitching—bear down on the hitters who can beat you—remained the same even after the lively ball was introduced. "I didn't do a lot of thinking when those little shortstops who couldn't hit came to bat," the Cardinals' Hall of Famer Bob Gibson says. "I'd just throw them high fastballs, because most of them could have tossed up the ball and hit it four times and they would barely reach the warning track. They'd hit high flies, then shake their heads and complain, 'Just missed it,' and I'd laugh. Sure they did."

Until the early 1960s, pitchers relied on the basic pitches—fastball, overhand curve, or drop—and when the situation called for it, the good spitball or cutball. Joe Nuxhall claims "I pitched in the big leagues for ten years before I learned how to throw a breaking pitch. It'd been nice to have one, but the point is I didn't need it. The theory of pitching in those days was 'go out there and throw it over the plate fast as you can.' " The fastball, overhand curve, change-up, and even the spitball didn't put excessive strain on a pitcher's arm. The introduction of the slider and the other breaking pitches that followed changed the game. Many people believe they are called breaking pitches because they broke a lot of elbows.

In those old days there were fewer major league teams and many more minor league teams, which meant that there was intense competition for spots on the rosters of the sixteen big league clubs, and few pitchers came up to the major leagues until they were twenty-five or twenty-six years old. Tommy Lasorda, for example, was a minor league pitching star in the Dodger organization but never got a real chance to make the Brooklyn team. "I thought I was finally going to make it in 1955, but who was I going to replace? Don Newcombe? Carl Erskine? Joe Black? Billy Loes? Johnny Podres? Even Don Bessent was 8–1. Finally General Manager Buzzy Bavasi called me into his office one day and explained the situation. 'We have a roster problem,' he said. 'We've got to cut somebody. It's a tough decision, there are a lot of outstanding players on this club, so lemme ask you: If you were me, who would you cut?' "

Lasorda didn't hesitate. "Koufax," he said. The Dodgers sent Lasorda to the minors and kept Sandy Koufax. Although Lasorda acknowledges that it took one of the greatest pitchers in baseball history to knock him off the roster, at times he still claims the Dodgers made a mistake.

"Those years in the minors gave us a chance to be bad before we were good," Hawk Harrelson explains. "When people got to the big leagues they had been in the minors for five or six years and had probably been to spring training three or four times. Today any pitcher who can throw strikes is rushed through the minor league system to the majors. I think the last time a minor league pitcher had the chance to win twenty games with one team was in 1966."

Mets' sensation Dwight Gooden was nineteen years old when he made his major league debut, but Joe Nuxhall was only fifteen when the Reds signed him in 1944, making him the youngest person ever to play in the big leagues. "During the war the major leagues were desperate for anyone who could throw hard. Actually, they wanted to sign me when I was fourteen, but I told them I wanted to finish ninth grade.

"I signed at the end of the year and found myself sitting on the bench. One day we were getting beat by the Cardinals 13–0, and Bill McKechnie, our manager, yelled 'Joe!' I was sitting there watching Stan Musial, Walker Cooper, Pepper Martin, and Marty Marion hitting bullets and thinking, 'Man, these guys can hit,' and I didn't hear him. He called me again. This time I heard him. I pointed to myself: 'Yeah, you. Go warm up.'

"I couldn't believe it. Two weeks earlier I'd been pitching to thirteen-year-old kids in junior high school, and they were going to send me out to pitch to Stan Musial.

"I think I was numb when they finally brought me into the game. The first batter grounded to shortstop. I walked the second batter. The third batter popped up. I got two outs and then I got two strikes on the next batter. Suddenly I realized I was pitching in the major leagues. Eight years later I got the third out."

"Stan Musial got the first hit off me. I ended up giving up two hits and five walks. I left the game with an earned-run average of 67.50.

"The Reds sent me to Birmingham. I started one game

there. I got one out in that game. So, in my first year of professional baseball, I pitched one inning, gave up ten runs on three hits and ten walks, I threw three wild pitches, and I had my strikeout.

"I would have to say I probably wasn't ready for the big leagues. I would have to say I was barely ready for tenth grade."

The time spent in the minor leagues gave young pitchers an opportunity to learn how to pitch. "The accent is on youth today," Hall of Famer Don Drysdale explained, "and today you have some people pitching in the big leagues that would be learning in Double-A if it weren't for expansion. I kind of feel sorry for these kids. When they've finished their careers and are sitting in their rocking chairs, will they be able to honestly say, 'I did the best I could'? I doubt it, because they might not ever know how good they could have been if they'd been given the time to grow.

"I watch pitchers working today, and they really don't know how to pitch. For example, they show a batter every pitch they throw his first time up. Why? If a pitcher can get a hitter out with a fastball, why not keep throwing it until the batter adjusts? What happens now, and I see this all the time, is a pitcher gets into a jam in the fifth or sixth inning and would love to have the element of surprise on his side. He'd love to suddenly break off a curve that the batter didn't even know he had that day, but he was throwing the curve in the second inning to just throw it."

In 1987, for example, the Giants' Roger Mason earned a spot in the record books by surrendering home runs to the first three San Diego batters in the game. Marvell Wynn hit a slider, Tony Gwynn hit a fastball, and John Kruk creamed a split-fingered fastball. After the game Mason admitted, "I'm just glad I don't have a fourth pitch."

Young pitchers, it seems, are like blond movie queens— their bodies often mature faster than their minds.

More than any other reason, though, pitchers throw fewer complete games today than ever before because they don't have to. Suppose instead of working a full day, you had to work only six hours, then a telephone call specialist came in to return your calls, followed by a paperwork expert to take care of your paperwork, and finally a desk cleaner who came in to make sure everything was in the proper piles. Or suppose you were in school and after six hours you could bring in an algebra man to get you through algebra and into political science, and if the algebra man faltered in political science, you had a political science specialist come in and finish that class. Or suppose I was working and whenever I had an argument with Weaver or Martin or Houk I could bring in a smart-answer specialist. Who wouldn't take advantage of options like that? That's what being a starting pitcher today is like. Two outs in the seventh inning and a left-handed batter coming to bat? Bring in the two-outs-in-the-seventh-inning, left-handed-batter specialist. Need one out? Call the expert.

The emergence of a corps of relief pitchers is probably the most significant change in the game of baseball in the past quarter century. At the turn of the century, relief pitchers were used in approximately 10 percent of all major league games. By 1980 relievers were appearing in almost eight of every ten games, and I suspect that is now a low figure. The highest paid player in baseball history, including incentives, is relief pitcher Dan Quizenberry, whose 'package' totals $3.5 million per year. How important are relief pitchers? Consider this: Relief pitchers are the only players delivered to their position by a chauffeur!

Until managers began relying on their relief pitchers, a major league pitching staff usually consisted of five starting pitchers, three men who were considered "spot starters" and were available to pitch in relief if absolutely necessary, and *the* relief pitcher. *The* relief pitcher, who was originally known as the "backer-upper" because his job was to back up the starting pitcher, was most often used to pitch the final three innings.

A pitching staff today usually includes five starting pitchers; a "hold man" or "middle man," who is used when a team is trailing early in the game and is expected to hold the other team scoreless until his team can come back; a setup man, who usually enters the game in the sixth or seventh inning to pitch his team into the eighth or ninth; and the star of the staff, the stopper, who then is brought in to finish the game. Some teams have left-handed and right-handed specialists used to face only one or two batters in crisis situations.

I don't think any manager uses a bull pen as well as the Cardinals' Whitey Herzog, who employs a "bull pen by committee." Whitey has his starting pitchers and his stopper—and everybody else may be used at any time in any way for any length. Talk about specialists, I actually saw Whitey bring in a relief pitcher just to issue an intentional walk to a batter. Apparently that was his intentional-walk specialist. Four pitches and out of the game. That's like bringing in Chuck Yeager to start your car.

The "stopper," or short man, is one of the major stars on any successful team. It's the glamor job on the pitching staff, the one that pays the most and usually receives the most attention. But that is a recent development. Being a relief pitcher used to be a source of embarrassment.

With very few exceptions, a bull pen was comprised of veteran pitchers who were no longer effective, young pitchers who hadn't been able to break into the starting rotation, and pitchers recovering from injuries. The bull pen was seen as the place a pitcher was sent to for punishment, much like someone recovering from a bad stomach ache might be sent to a vegetarian restaurant.

"It was all very simple," Jerry Casale, who pitched for the Red Sox in the late 1950s, remembers. "I came up with a sore arm and Manager Pinky Higgins took me aside and told me, 'Go to the bull pen.' Not 'Go to a doctor,' or 'Give it some rest.' Just 'Go to the bull pen.' In those days if you didn't do the job they told you to move over."

Johnny Murphy, one of the first great "stoppers" in baseball history, was a starting pitcher until he hurt his arm. "The Yankees had sent me down to Newark, and I hurt my arm. My manager tried to get me back in shape by working me for an inning or two late in games. I began getting people out, so he said, "Gee, you're doing so well, would you mind staying with it?" I said no, and that's how I became a relief pitcher."

Far more prevalent, however, was the attitude expressed by Hall of Famer Warren Spahn when asked, near the end of his career in the early 1960s, if he would consider pitching in relief. "That would depend on my financial status," he said, "I've got three hundred beef cows to support along with a family. But let me make one thing clear: The matter of pride wouldn't enter into it. If I was broke, I'd wash dishes or dig ditches for a living. However, if I don't have to, I won't. That goes for pitching, too."

Even the rise in the status of relievers hasn't completely eradicated that feeling. When Pirates' manager Chuck Tanner told starting pitcher John Candelaria in 1985 that he was going to put him in the bull pen, the "Candy Man" reacted pleasantly: He kicked his glove over the outfield wall.

Once, the main objective of a pitcher in the bull pen was to pitch well enough to get out of the bull pen. For example, Lindy McDaniel became one of baseball's top relievers in 1959, winning thirteen games in relief. "I don't mind relieving," he said, "just so it doesn't become a permanent thing."

In the World Series that same year, Dodgers' rookie Larry Sherry relieved in four games, winning two and saving two, giving up only one run in 12 ⅔ innings. "Sherry is a better relief pitcher right now than Clem Labine ever was," coach Chuck Dressen said. "Next season, mark my words, Sherry will be a starter."

By the 1980s, however, things had turned around so completely that managers would occasionally try to get a relief pitcher out of a pitching slump by giving him a start. In 1982, in fact, Cubs' pitcher Allen Ripley was pitching so badly in relief that manager Lee Elia had no choice: He demoted him to the starting staff.

Neil Allen pitched in circles. For a time he was a solid starting pitcher for the Mets, but when other teams began bombing him, the Mets moved him to the bull pen. He became an excellent relief pitcher and was traded to the Cardinals. When he lost his effectiveness in the bull pen, the Cardinals made him a starter again. The Yankees have used him as both a starter and reliever.

Charlie Hough, who claims he throws three pitches—a knuckleball, a fastball, and a prayer—failed as a reliever before he became one of the most effective starting pitchers in the American League.

But even more than pitchers disliked relieving, umpires hated to see relief pitchers come into the game. A good game was a quick game. Bringing in a reliever slowed down the game. The reliever had to stroll in from the bull pen, take his warm-up pitches, go over the signs with the catcher, adjust his equipment, adjust his equipment some more, and finally pitch. More importantly, umpires felt that if a relief pitcher was any good, he wouldn't be a relief pitcher. If the starting pitcher couldn't hold the other team, and he was the better pitcher, what could be expected of the relief pitcher? By the time I got to the majors in 1968, that was changing. Young pitchers like Rollie Fingers and Tug McGraw were turning relieving into an honorable profession.

Not every pitcher before that had disliked relieving. "I became a relief pitcher when I was thirty years old," Moe Drabowsky remembers, "and it kept me in the big leagues for seven more years. I liked being a relief pitcher much more than I would have liked being out of baseball. It took me a little while to get used to relieving, but it occurred to me that when I was a starting pitcher I could pitch eight great innings, but give up a home run in the ninth inning to lose the game. And what did the fans remember? That I blew the game in the ninth inning. So as a starting pitcher I had to work more than two hours just to discover I was horse manure that day. But as a reliever, I could come into a game and give up a home run on my third pitch. So as a relief pitcher I only had to work about two minutes to find out I was horse manure."

The superstar of the bull pen is the stopper, the short man. The stopper rarely pitches more than one inning, often facing just one batter, but he usually enters the game with the outcome on the line. Being a great stopper requires much more than pitching skill. He has to have the nerves of the receiver on a circus knife-throwing team, the courage of a photographer taking Sean Penn's photograph, the ability of Charlie Brown to forget a bad day, and the confidence of Sergeant Ernest Bilko.

When the stopper is called into the game, he has to know he can get the batter out. Not think, *know*. One day in 1957, twenty-year-old Cubs' pitcher Dick Drott was in a jam against the Cardinals, and Stan Musial was hitting. Manager Bob Scheffing went out to the mound and advised, "Keep your fastball away from the plate. Make him chase it if you can."

"Skipper," Drott replied, stating a credo that should be inscribed on bull pen walls across America, "Mr. Musial is overmatched."

Every relief pitcher has his own philosophy that allows him to survive the intense pressure of the job. Reliever Bob Miller, who pitched for ten different teams during his seventeen-year career in the majors, wore a T-shirt that read "(Blank) It" and claimed "I just went out there, threw it, and ducked."

As Al "The Mad Hungarian" Hrabosky came into a game, he would remind himself, "I'm the best he's got at this moment. Otherwise he wouldn't be putting me in the game."

Cy Young winner Mike Marshall, who relieved for nine teams during his fourteen years in the majors, claimed he never felt any pressure. "Let's keep it in perspective," he said. "These are baseball games. It's not someone in my family having major surgery. It's nothing that's going to permanently affect my future life."

Probably not unless Billy Martin was his manager, of course.

Before pitching in tense situations, Tug McGraw reminded himself, "It's a round ball and a round bat. According to geometry, that makes it very tough to hit. It's just the batter standing there by himself, while I've got seven guys behind me." Tug also relied on his famed Frozen

Snowball Theory. "Astronomers have estimated that in something like fifty million years, our sun will burn out and then the earth will freeze up and drift through space like a giant frozen snowball. Now, when that happens, who's gonna remember if Willie Stargell hit a grand-slam home run off me?"

McGraw is particularly sensitive about grand slams, having tied the record by giving up four of them while pitching in relief for the Phillies in 1979. "I had a chance to break the record. Houston had the bases loaded and Terry Puhl was at bat. If I was selfish, I would have let him hit a home run so I could have the record all to myself. Instead I got him to hit into a double play. My own fans booed me. They wanted to see the record set."

And finally there was Ron Perranoski, the stopper on the great Dodger teams of the 1960s. "Walter Alston would bring me in and I'd think, gees, if Koufax or Drysdale can't get them out with their stuff, what can he possibly expect from me?"

Relief pitchers are isolated by themselves in the bull pen, much like zoo animals are put in cages, and apparently for many of the same reasons. The bull pen might well be the place where the expression "comic relief" was born, because relief pitchers apparently are willing to do almost anything for a laugh. The Reds' Pedro Bourbon, for example, often bit the heads off grasshoppers to win bets. Obviously that was catching; his teammate Brad "The Animal" Lesley did it free. Lesley, now pitching in Japan, celebrated victories by slapping teammates in the face and banging heads with his catcher. The Phillies' John Boozer would bite grasshoppers in half, claiming that the back half would hop out by itself. Boozer would also spit a wad of tobacco he was chewing straight into the air and try to catch it when it came down. Unfortunately, most of the time he'd miss. Orioles' pitcher Dick Hall supposedly bit the head off a locust, and many pitchers are known for eating spiders. I've often wondered if this is a comment on the mental state of relief pitchers or the quality of ballpark food.

Moe Drabowsky used to organize commando attacks. "After Baltimore traded me to Kansas City, the Orioles' bull pen and the Royals' bull pen feuded with each other. Once, for example, I walked into the Royals' bull pen and discovered that someone had painted the bull pen home plates and pitchers' rubbers black and orange—coincidentally, the Orioles' colors. So the next time we went to Baltimore, naturally I had to retaliate.

"We were playing a night game and I decided to attack the Orioles' pillbox. At twenty-one hundred hours, bull pen time, five or six of us put burnt cork on our faces and loaded up our pockets with rocks and dirt balls. We snuck along the edge of stands, staying in the shadows, until we crawled within range. Then we opened fire, lobbing our mud grenades into their bull pen.

"The next afternoon O's relievers Pete Richert and Eddie Watt decided to launch a counterattack. They put burnt cork on their faces and started crawling along behind the fence. The only mistake they made was forgetting they were attacking during the day. Orioles' general manager Harry Dalton was sitting in the pressbox when he looked into the outfield and happened to notice his relief pitchers, their faces covered with black cork, crawling along in the grass. 'What's going on?' he kept asking. 'Why are my pitchers crawling across center field?' That was one of the worst commando raids in history."

On another occasion Drabowsky decided to stage his own promotion. "I called it 'Firecracker Night in Atlanta.' This was how I found out my career was over. The Braves' mascot, Chief Nok-A-Homa, had a tent in the outfield stands. Every time a Brave hit a home run, he would come out of the tent to do a war dance. I was with the Cardinals at the time, and I brought a bunch of M-80's, large firecrackers, to the ballpark, intending to whip one of them into the chief's tepee and watch him really dance. My method was to put the M-80 in a cigarette, then light the cigarette. The cigarette acted as a delayed fuse, giving me about twelve minutes before the firecracker went off. So I lit the cigarette and I took this thing and I heaved it as far as I could.

"It didn't even clear the outfield fence. It landed in fair territory, in the outfield. I thought, 'That's it, my arm is dead, the career is now over.' But the problem was that this M-80, which was going to explode in exactly twelve minutes, was lying in the outfield. All I could envision was Lou Brock running over to field a ball and have this thing explode in his face. I figured I'd better stop the game and go out and retrieve that thing. Fortunately, my cool prevailed.

" 'Twelve minutes,' I thought. 'Who knows what can happen?' I decided to gamble. I watched the clock, I watched the game. The minutes ticked away. Seven . . . five . . . three . . . one . . . I counted down the seconds . . . four . . . three . . . two . . . BOOM! That thing blew a small piece of turf about twenty feet into the air. It reverberated throughout the ball park. So I did the proper thing under the circumstances: I jumped off the bench and pointed at some people sitting in the upper deck."

Before telephones linked the dugouts and the bull pens, managers used a set of hand signals to indicate which pitcher they wanted to warm up or come into a game. Waving the left hand meant get the left-hander ready, twisting the wrist meant the manager wanted the curveball pitcher, pointing to his head and making little circles meant he wanted Moe Drabowsky. Although Drabowsky popularized the telephone as a weapon, he was not the only player to use it. The Yankees' Whitey Ford once called Kansas City's bull pen and ordered A's pitcher Tom Sturdivant to start throwing. Another Yankee pitcher called his mother in California and asked her to turn on her radio to find out the score of a game being played on the West Coast. But rather than passing along the score to his teammates, he bet them how many runs those teams would score in the next inning. When Yogi Berra was managing the Yankees he picked up the dugout telephone intending to dial 5-3, the bull pen number. Instead of reaching the bull pen, however, he got the short-order cook at the pressroom lunch counter. "Warm up Stafford," Yogi ordered.

"What?" the short-order cook asked.

"Warm up Stafford," Yogi repeated.

"What?"

"Gimme Stafford!" Yogi said loudly.

"All I got here is hamburgers," the cook replied.

Yogi slammed down the receiver, perhaps trying to figure out why a cook was answering the phone in the bull pen.

Relievers will do almost anything to pass time in the bull pen. They have spitting contests: for distance, accuracy, style, how many flies can be downed. They give hotfoots. They play trivia and other word games. In Philadelphia's old Connie Mack Stadium there was a toolshed in the bull pen, and if there were no flies around to spit at, players would entertain women there. Another ballpark had an outhouse near the bull pen. One day, when it was in use, the other pitchers slipped burning newspapers under the door. This is known as a hot-different part of the body.

The games in the bull pen are taken seriously. In 1970, for example, the Minnesota Twins' bull pen crew played a dice game called cover-up. "We used to play in a little shed they had in the back of the bull pen," Ron Perranoski remembers. "Nobody could see us back there. The only pitcher we didn't let play was Tom Hall, so he picketed the game. He made a big sign and walked back and forth in the bull pen complaining that we were unfair to left-handers. Toward the end of the season we had the Ultimate Cover-up Championship. It was during a day game. We even had engraved trophies. It had all the drama of a great checkers match. We were so involved with the cover-up championship that nobody noticed the ball game ended. We celebrated the championship, looked up, and discovered that the ballpark was almost empty."

In fact, sometimes relief pitchers aren't really concentrating on the baseball game. In Toronto the visiting team's bull pen is in foul territory in right field. Royals' pitcher Mike Armstrong was talking to a teammate and turned around just as a ball came bouncing toward him. "I saw everyone else trying to get out of the way and I thought, 'That's funny, the ball isn't hit that hard.' I just assumed it was a foul ball. No one said anything to me, so I caught it on one hop as it caromed off the wall.

"That's about the time I realized it was a fair ball. So I dropped it." The umpires awarded the batter, Armstrong's teammate George Brett, two bases. Normally Brett would have been given a triple, but the umpires penalized him because it was his teammate who had interfered. "George wasn't upset," Armstrong said, "and he shouldn't have been. I could have thrown him out at third anyway."

The most difficult time for a relief pitcher is when he is pitching badly. This is known as Catch . . . well, Pitch-22. Most relievers can't be effective unless they pitch frequently, but they can't pitch frequently unless they're effective.

"I knew I was in trouble when Joe Torre didn't use me for fourteen days," Al Hrabosky remembers. "So I went to Torre and asked him why I wasn't get a chance to pitch. We were in Wrigley Field and he told me, 'You're a fly ball pitcher and I don't want to use you in a small ballpark.'

"A few days later we were home in Atlanta, a big park, and he used almost every pitcher on the staff except me. Some people would consider that a hint. After the game I went to pitching coach Rube Walker and said, 'I'm begging to be used. I don't care about saves, I need the work.'

"Rube looked at me and admitted, 'Al, I forgot about you.'

" 'Rube,' I said, 'tell me anything else, but don't tell me that.'

"Later Rube was talking to Gene Garber and was obviously upset. Gene asked what was wrong and Rube admitted, 'Al's really mad at me. I forgot he wanted to pitch on his birthday.'

" 'His birthday?' Gene said. 'His birthday? He's mad because he hasn't pitched in two weeks!' They told me they couldn't afford to use me because I was pitching badly, but until they used me I had no chance of getting better."

The Orioles' Tom Dukes had a slightly different problem one season. He didn't pitch for seventeen days because the starting pitchers were performing so well. Finally, though, Weaver called him into a game. As he reached the pitcher's mound, Brooks Robinson walked over to him and asked, "You remember where home plate is?"

Dukes looked puzzled. "It is still where it used to be?"

I used to wonder, when I was an active umpire, is it better to be a starting pitcher or a relief pitcher? Or, is it better to pitch more innings less frequently, or fewer innings more often? Or, what I really mean is, would I rather pitch a lot but do it less, or pitch less and do it a lot? I decided I wanted to be the specialist who gets to throw the managers out of the game. Of course, I also wondered if, at six-four, I was too tall to be a short reliever.

As tough as not pitching can be for a pitcher, pitching can be even tougher. The human arm was made for things like hammering in nails, reaching across the table for another portion of roast beef, and throwing players out of the game. It was not made to throw a baseball as hard as possible a hundred or so times every few days. Except for Nolan Ryan, of course; apparently his arm was manufactured precisely for that.

Pitchers have always lived with the knowledge that they are one pitch away from the end of their careers. They just never know what pitch it is. A pitcher with a damaged arm has about as much future as a bald Farrah Fawcett. For that reason pitchers treat their arms as tenderly as they would treat a loved one. Pitchers don't sleep on their pitching arm. In the old days pitchers were so afraid of drafts that they would keep the windows of their train compartments closed no matter how warm it was. Today's pitchers stay out of air-conditioned rooms. Pitchers even refer to their arm in the third person, the way I speak of my stomach. "It likes ice," for example, or "It doesn't like pitching on cool evenings."

Starting pitchers usually have three or four days between games to allow their arms to recover. Relief pitchers often get a few hours. The strain on every pitcher's arm is incredible, but perhaps more so on a reliever's, which is why so many great relief pitchers have lasted only a few years before suffering a serious injury.

"A reliever has to learn how to pitch with pain," Hrabosky

says. "The hardest part of the job is simply to be ready to pitch every day. There were times when my arm ached so badly I literally could not push open a door, but I could go out and throw the ball hard that night because I knew that was my job. That took tremendous pride."

We've had astronauts hit golf balls on the moon, we've invented microscopes powerful enough to find a manager's brain, and we can splice genes carefully enough to create a half-prewashed jean, but we still cannot prevent a pitcher from ruining his arm. Until recently, everything that went wrong with a pitcher's arm was referred to as "a sore arm." Shoulder injuries, elbow problems, strained tendons; everything was a sore arm. Now it is a ruptured medial collateral ligament of the elbow or perhaps an impingement and posterior subluxation (slippage of the humeral head posteriorly causing a chronic capsular irritation), or, simply, a sore arm.

On occasion I've wondered if the precise terminology hasn't added to the length of time pitchers take to recover. "A sore arm" just doesn't sound like an injury that should keep a pitcher out of action for a month or two. But someone who has "a shoulder impingement between the acromion and the greater tuberosity of the humerus that should be treated with brisement" should be out for at least a season. That *sounds* like a bad injury.

In the old days a sore arm often was blamed on bad teeth. "Right after I signed my first contract," Bob Feller remembers, "I had four teeth pulled. And the scout who signed me also wanted me to have my tonsils taken out." In spring training one season, Feller recalls, the Indians sent all their pitchers to a dentist, "and he drilled everybody's teeth, whether they needed fillings or not. When he got ready to drill our last pitcher, the player reached in his mouth and handed the dentist his upper and lower plates."

When Reds' pitcher Lefty Grissom read that the A's Lefty Grove had had three teeth removed after being told they were responsible for his sore arm, Grissom went to a dentist and told him to extract three teeth—any three. It must have worked: Grissom never suffered from a sore arm.

I wonder if anyone at that time remembered that legendary practical joker Casey Stengel had trained to be a dentist.

A trainer's medical equipment, in those days, consisted of tape and liniment. The trainer would stretch the player's arms and legs, give him a pat on the rump, and tell him to have a good game.

In baseball's old days no one really knew what caused a sore arm, how to treat a sore arm, how to repair a sore arm, or how to prevent a sore arm. Heat was considered the proper treatment for an arm, also the only treatment. Every good trainer had his own special "lotion" or liniment or balm, which pitchers were supposed to apply to their arm before and after throwing. "When I was growing up," Jim Kaat remembers, "my baseball coach would tell me before a game, 'Go down there and warm up till you sweat and stink.' And after I'd pitched he'd order me to 'Go home and get under the shower hot as you can stand it.' I'd go home, put a towel on my arm, and stand under that hot shower until my shoulder was beet red.

"When I got into professional baseball in 1958 it was very different. The trainer had this large jar of a homemade brew consisting of wintergreen, omega oil, baby oil, probably some alcohol, and he'd even spit some tobacco juice in it. He'd shake it up and leave it in the corner of the dugout. Before every game we were supposed to dip our hand in it and lather up our pitching arm. It would burn; that's what it was supposed to do. They told you that was the best thing you could do for your arm.

"And after I'd pitched I stood under a hot shower for twenty minutes, or until my arm was beet red."

Those hot lotions actually did seem to make the soreness disappear—they burned so badly it was impossible to feel anything except the fire on your arm. Milt Pappas remembers rubbing his arm with a salve that his trainer used to get from "a secret source" somewhere in South Carolina. "He would wrap my entire arm in this stuff. It was so hot that my arm was burning, my eyes started tearing, and my shorts started smoking."

One of the player's most popular jokes, second only to the hotfoot, consisted of putting a glob of this lotion in a player's athletic supporter, then watching as he put it on. The most difficult part of this joke was not laughing out loud until the smoke actually started coming out of the player's ears. Or elsewhere.

One of the great trainer's jokes in those days was to substitute warm Coca-Cola for liniment without telling the player. That was also the only trainer's joke. The warm soda usually served as well as the liniment, which meant it was either a better medicine than anyone imagined or that the liniment really served no purpose.

In addition to hot balm and the-hotter-the-better showers, the hot wax treatment was popular for a while. In this treatment wax was heated in a tub about two feet deep. The pitcher dipped his elbow into the tub, then took it out and allowed the wax to cool. He repeated the procedure several times. About the only thing that the hot wax treatment accomplished was to create entire teams of pitchers with no hair on one arm.

"Milking" became very popular in the 1950s. The St. Louis Cardinals' famous trainer Doc Weaver realized that every time a pitcher threw a baseball his arm hemorrhaged, meaning that numerous blood vessels were broken or distended. This obviously diminished blood circulation throughout the arm. The proof of this was that after a game, a pitcher's hand often puffs up and turns slightly bluish. "Milking" was a way of restoring normal circulation as rapidly as possible. A pitcher would lay on his back on a table and his arm would be held straight up in the air in a wrist sling. The trainer would then "milk" each finger, much like a farmer milked his cows, trying to force fluid that had gathered in those fingers back to the pitcher's body.

Perhaps the biggest revolution in the care of arms took place in the late 1950s when trainers suddenly discovered that the *worst* possible thing a pitcher could do to his arm after pitching was apply heat. The best treatment was ice.

After only half a century they realized that everything they had been doing was wrong. Heat? Ha! It was as if they said, "Remember mathematics? Forget it." It was as if they had suddenly discovered that garlic actually *attracted* vampires. It was as shocking as if they'd suddenly decided that Canada wasn't a state.

Ice apparently stopped the bleeding in a pitcher's arm. There was resistance to the idea at first, but when Sandy Koufax cut off a portion of an inner tube, filled it with ice, and rested his arm in it, baseball's ice age began. Of course, if Sandy Koufax had decided that having his teeth removed made him as great as he was, half the pitchers in baseball would have been speaking with a lisp.

Not everyone believed in the remedial effects of ice, however, unless it was being used to cool a stiff drink. Bob Feller, for example, suspected that the real benefits of ice were psychological rather than physical, suggesting, "Pitchers might be better off putting ice on their heads."

Heat, ice—some teams and some pitchers believed that nothing was best. Cardinals' trainer Doc Bowman pointed out that Hall of Famers Drysdale, Koufax, and Gibson had begun pitching in the big leagues at roughly the same time and that Drysdale and Koufax, both of whom subscribed to the ice-milk theory, had ruined their arms, while Gibson's sore arms had been temporary. Bowman felt that icing sealed off the tiny veins and capillaries, causing blood to coagulate. He advised letting nature take its course.

So the only thing Hall of Famer Bob Gibson did with his arm after pitching was lift a glass of wine. "My arm ached so much after I pitched that I didn't even want to touch it. Every time. The worst part about it, though, was that I was always meeting somebody who wanted to congratulate me by shaking my hand and squeezing my bicep. These small men would touch me and I'd fall down to my knees and they would think I was kidding. Kidding? They were lucky I didn't hit them. They just didn't understand how badly it hurt. But in two days it would be fine."

"A lot of guys liked to have their arms milked then iced them down," Joe Nuxhall explains, "but I never did. I just let nature take its course. The day after I pitched, I played a little catch and ran. The next day I would throw easy, then rest, and I'd be ready to go again." Gibson pitched seventeen seasons and Nuxhall pitched sixteen in the big leagues, a very strong argument for Ms. Nature.

Milt Pappas tried everything. "I used heat after the game, then I tried ice after the game. My arm still bothered me every time I pitched. I just decided that Mother Nature was going to take care of her own, so I did nothing. I figured that God only put a certain number of pitches in my right arm and when I used them up, it was over. But I always hoped I didn't use up that last one with the bases loaded."

Originally the only machine trainers used to treat pitchers, or any players, was a beat-up heat lamp. Pitchers sat under it and trainers read by it. The first real example of modern medical technology to appear in the trainer's room was the diathermy, or deep-heat, machine.

The prototype diathermy machine was a bizarre contraption that emitted sparks and a blue flame and roared and sputtered. The trainers had to make their own electrodes, the parts that were actually connected to the body, and apply them with soap or jelly. Finding players who would allow themselves to be attached to this machine was like trying to find voulnteers for guillotine experiments. To prove to players that the machine actually applied heat to the muscle without roasting the skin, trainers would hook up a thick roast beef. After twenty minutes the roast beef would be raw on the outside but cooked inside, providing an excellent demonstration of the machine's penetrating abilities. When Cubs' trainer Andy Lotshaw demonstrated the diathermy he didn't have any roast beef available, so he decided to substitute a hot dog. Unfortunately, the hot dog was very greasy, and the machine caught fire. That hot dog was charred to a crisp. Several years later a Cub pitcher first considered using the machine.

Lost in the failure, however, was the historic fact that a hot dog had finally been cooked inside a ballpark.

The diathermy was eventually followed by the whirl-pool bath, which was occasionally used as a particularly shallow diving pool by Jay Johnstone; the ultrasound machine; the hydromassage tank; the infrared baking lamp; the medcollator, the hydrocollator; the supersonic muscle vibrator; the portable pulsator; and many, many others.

Although the machines have many benefits, they probably are about as successful at preventing sore pitching arms as the beat-up heat lamp. "There's only one cure for what's wrong with all us pitchers," Jim Palmer declared, "and that's to take a year off. Then, after you've gone a year without throwing, quit altogether."

On the other hand—or in this case, arm—Lew Burdette, who survived eighteen big league seasons, believes, "A pitcher just has to keep throwing and the soreness will go away."

Sports medicine has become a computer-age science, and doctors usually can determine exactly what's wrong with a pitcher's arm, but they still haven't figured out how to prevent injury. The results of my own scientific study—a poll I called "asking around"—seemed to indicate that even though there are more machines in the trainer's room than in a machine shop, pitchers suffer as many debilitating injuries as ever. "Here is your body and here is the baseball," eminent "Doctor of Pitching" Tom Seaver explained. "You want to put 100 percent of the energy in your body into throwing that ball. How that energy, that shock at the end of every pitch, is absorbed determines whether you have arm trouble. You want to finish your delivery so that the big muscles of the body—the thigh and buttocks—absorb the shock.

"That's why pitchers run wind sprints, to strengthen the large lower-body muscles. If your legs are weak, then you finish your delivery stiff-legged as you get tired, rather than flexible and bouncy, and you end up with a ruined arm."

Alvin Dark was one of the first managers to subscribe to that theory and, in spring training, had his pitchers run three miles every day. Not everybody agreed with him.

I believed that the best way to get in shape for pitching was to pitch, "I couldn't run three miles if I was scared," Bob Miller said. And pitching coach Art Fowler pointed out, "If running won ball games, Jesse Owens would've won forty."

Phil Niekro survived twenty-two seasons in the big leagues without running, but Niekro had his own method of strengthening his legs: polka dancing. He claimed it kept his legs in excellent shape. The polka dancing method does not appear to have caught on with other teams, however.

Texas Rangers' pitching coach Tom House advises his pitchers to strengthen their arms by throwing footballs on the sidelines before the game begins, a technique previously used by the Padres. "A football won't spiral if you throw it wrong," House explains. "The mechanics are the same as those used to throw a baseball. It requires proper positioning of the shoulder and elbow and the perfect weight transfer."

A lot of other trainers believe this is just another fad that will soon be forgotten; in other words, it's just a passing fancy.

No matter what techniques a pitcher uses to strengthen his arm or his body, no matter how much heat or ice or nothing he applies to his arm after pitching, no matter how many hours he sits in the hydrocollator or under the medcollator, (or is it next to the hydrocollator and in the medcollator?), he is still going to have a sore arm. The action of throwing a baseball eventually wears down every arm except Nolan Ryan's. "There was really nothing wrong with my arm," Jim Lonborg said after fifteen big league seasons. "It just doesn't work anymore."

Almost every pitcher has to overcome a real pain every time he pitches—besides the home plate umpire. The great pitchers have the ability to pitch, and pitch well, with that pain. "No one would pitch very much," Tommy John noted, "if you had to be 100 percent every time out. You just learn to pitch with the pain."

Jim Palmer, who was a pain in the neck to umpires, often complained of pain in his arm, even though doctors couldn't find anything wrong. "People were always telling me that I was imagining my arm hurt. When Hank Bauer managed the Orioles he used to say the pain was in my head. I'd say, 'Hank, if it's in my head, how come it's my arm that hurts?"

Earl Weaver claims that Jim Palmer taught him about arm injuries. "He introduced me to the ulna nerve. I thought he invented it. He had so many physical ailments—shoulder, elbow, forearm—that I thought he'd just run out of parts and had made one up when he told me his ulna nerve was bothering him. But I happened to see my own doctor about a problem I was having with my hand, and he told me the problem was my ulna nerve.

"I told him I'd probably caught it from Jim Palmer."

Some pitchers are willing to do whatever's necessary to keep throwing. For a while injections of cortisone, which numbed the muscles, were popular—until it was discovered that cortisone can be bad for the heart and wasn't that effective anyway. Pain-killing pills were also frequently used. "I had four and a half years in the big leagues," Moe Drabowsky remembers, "and I needed five to qualify for the pension plan. I needed ninety days, and I was determined to get them. I went to spring training with Cincinnati and my arm was killing me, but I didn't tell anyone. I pitched as well as I could, but finally it came down to one game: If I pitched well, I made the team; if not, I was gone.

"I went to a doctor on my own and had him inject my arm with cortisone and give me some pain-killers. I didn't know what damage I might be doing to my arm, but I was desperate to make that club. I pitched six good innings and went north with Cincinnati.

"I counted down the days: eighty-four days, seventy-two days. I took those pills every day. I sweated it right down to the wire. In those days when a player got his five years in and qualified for the pension he threw a party to celebrate. It was a big deal. At my party I called our trainer aside and showed him my little jar of pills. 'Watch this,' I said, and flushed them down the toilet. 'If that pain comes back,' I said, 'I'll deal with it on my own.' I was worried about ninety days; somehow I hung on for twelve more years."

There is a difference between a sore arm and a damaged arm. The difference is often called an operation. When a pitcher went "under the knife" in the old days it usually meant his career was over. Today pitchers go "under the laser" or "under the arthroscope" and pitch again.

Before the incredible advances in sports medicine, pitchers used to live in fear of the words "a sore arm." A pitcher who frequently suffered from sore arms had "a glass arm." Pitchers who could pitch often had "a rubber arm." Now that doctors know how to treat most types of arm injuries, pitchers live in fear of new words: "torn rotator cuff."

A torn rotator cuff is the injury that turns pitchers into broadcasters. It usually means that the arm is damaged beyond repair—at least as far as pitching in the major leagues is concerned. Don Drysdale probably was the first pitcher ever to hear those dreaded words. "I'd had a number of sore arms in my career," he explains, "but in 1969 my arm hurt so badly I could barely lift it above my head. The pain was unbelievable. When I tried to pitch I would get my arm over my head and, as I started to bring it forward, it felt as if someone was sticking an ice pick in my shoulder. It hurt so much that my hands started quivering. I went to see Dr. Robert Kerlan, and he made the diagnosis: torn rotator cuff. 'We can operate,' he told me.

" 'That's interesting,' I said. 'Then what happens?'

" 'We tie it together, but after that it's like a piece of elastic that you've resewn. If you keep stretching it, it's going to tear again.'

" 'What does that do to my arm?'

" 'We can operate again.'

" 'And then?'

" 'Well, you might be in the shower one day and you want to wash under your arm, but when you try to raise your arm it won't come up.'

" 'Permanently?'

" 'Permanently.'

" 'Okay,' I said, 'gimme a hammer and nail.'

" 'Why?'

" 'So I can hang up my glove.' I believe that was the day 'a sore arm' became 'a torn rotator cuff.' "

Sports doctors are now capable of doing truly amazing things to repair damaged arms, but one celebrated case stands out. Literature gave us *Frankenstein*. Television gave us *The Six-Million-Dollar Man*, *Woman*, and *Child*. The movies gave us *Robocop*. And baseball gave us ... The Incredible TommyJohn!

Robocop got an entire body; Tommy John got only a new arm. In 1974, the thirty-one-year-old left-hander was pitching for the Dodgers. In the third inning of a game against Montreal, he threw a sinker and "I heard this thudding sound in my elbow, then I felt a sharp pain. My arm felt as if it had come off my body." This was the pitcher's version of a transmission dropping out of a car—the car could still move, as long as it was going downhill. Tommy's elbow had been ripped apart. He might be able to throw a baseball, as long as he didn't try to throw it more than five or six feet. Until the recent advances in medicine, the only thing he could have done was to start accepting invitations to appear at Old-Timers' Games.

In John's case, however, doctors were able to implant a tendon from his right wrist in his left elbow, where it was able to do the job of a ligament. This made him baseball's only right-handed left-hander. Two years later he was again pitching, and winning, in the big leagues. "I know they had to graft a new arm on his body," Pete Rose complained, "but did they have to give him Sandy Koufax's?"

John celebrated his twenty-third year in the big leagues in 1987 as one of the Yankees' leading pitchers. That same year his arm was bar mitzvahed. There are managers who believe that John still pays tribute to surgical skill every time he gets on the pitcher's mound—by doctoring the baseball.

Medical science may have also saved the career of Nolan Ryan. Ryan threw the ball so hard that the friction caused by his release raised blisters on his fingers, preventing him from pitching. After several attempts to cure the problem had failed, doctors suggested a miracle cure: pickle brine. Fortunately, pickle brine is a nonprescription drug that has no serious side effects. Ryan hardened his fingers by soaking them in brine and was never again troubled by blisters. And it didn't even sour his disposition.

Pitchers no longer throw very many complete games, once ridiculed relief pitchers have become the superstars of the pitching staff, the heat lamp and secret hot balm have been replaced by medical equipment even more sophisticated than that found in the most modern television hospital, and pitchers whose sore arms once would have turned them into bar owners are now able to continue pitching. In fact, only one thing hasn't changed since the early days of baseball: When the pitcher makes a mistake, it's still the fault of the home plate umpire.

5
BEFORE THE BALL IS OVER

The very first rule of umpiring is that an umpire must be completely neutral. He must dislike all players on every team equally. Believing that, I have always refrained from taking sides on controversial issues involving players. When asked, I replied that they were all wrong. But I think the time has finally come for me to take a stand. At certain times every man must look deep into his conscience and speak out, no matter what the consequences. And now is such a time. After much soul-searching, after much questioning, I can state without hesitation that I am against the death penalty for pitchers.

Most of them, anyway.

Certainly, many pitchers are not that bright. Some of them, I know, have to be taught how to sweat. But even that is no excuse for the abuses that pitchers have been subject to. The rulemakers have taken away their lands, lowering the mound and moving in the outfield fences. They have violated their constitutional rights, permitting officials to search them without first obtaining a warrant, and merely on the basis of an unfounded accusation. They have supplied new weapons to their mortal enemies, legalizing the designated hitter. They even rearmed those enemies with a new and more powerful baseball. They have greatly reduced the pitchers' primary source of sustenance, the strike zone. And they have even subjected pitchers to unilateral disarmament, taking away the vital brushback and enforcing severe penalties for throwing an occasional illegal pitch.

So who among us can blame pitchers for trying to fight back? As each of these fundamental rights has been eroded, pitchers have bravely attempted to defend their position, resorting at times to such trickery as the spitball, jellyball, scuffball, softball, mudball, knuckleball, slowball, gumball, tobacco ball, forkball, puffball, palmball, slider, splitter, slurve, knuckle curve, the folly floater, and, on occasion, the knockdown.

As a great pitching philosopher once noted, "A baseball that doesn't have movement might also be called 'a home run.' " It's not enough to throw the ball over the plate; the ball has to move up or down, inside or outside. It has to rise or drop. It's got to do something. Anything. Pitchers who throw a ball without movement over the plate are what is known as minor leaguers.

To make the ball move, pitchers may legally change speeds or apply a certain type of spin, causing it to curve, rise, or fall; or apply almost no spin at all—the knuckleball—causing a headache. It's what they may not legally apply that creates one of baseball's biggest embarrassments: the shame of illegal pitches.

One of the few things about baseball that hasn't changed since the turn of the century is the fact that pitchers cheat. They break the rules. They flaunt authority. And worse, they are unsanitary about it.

The "spitball," a euphemistic term meaning the application of any foreign substance to the cover of the baseball, was discovered in 1902 by either Elmer Stricklett, George Hildebrand, or Frank Corridon, each of whom claimed credit. Why each of them claimed credit is something else entirely, as being the first person to spit on a baseball hardly ranks with the discovery of penicillin, contrary to the belief of Gaylord Perry. Hildebrand, incidentally, eventually became an umpire, which is sort of like turning a sinner into a Baptist.

Both the sale of liquor and the spitball were outlawed in the United States in 1919, although major league pitchers then throwing the spitter were legally permitted to continue doing so until they retired. Burleigh Grimes, the last legal spitballer, threw it until 1934. Prohibition, the constitutional amendment against the manufacture, sale, or transportation of liquor, was repealed only one year earlier. Rule 8.02, the rule that banned spitballs, still exists. However, it appears that no one ever took Prohibition or 8.02 seriously, and spitballs became the moonshine of baseball.

Although the myth is that the spitball was banned because pitchers couldn't control it and it was considered dangerous, the reality is that the spitball was outlawed because it was filthy and disgusting. Pitchers believed the wetter the better, and really loaded up the ball. I mean they just slobbered all over it, with big, dripping globs of spit and tobacco juice and other putrid substances. Not only did pitchers load it up, but infielders also drooled over it. And since baseballs were kept in play for several innings before being replaced, after a few innings that baseball looked almost as filthy as my kitchen floor.

It was bad enough that pitchers had to throw it—at least they gained some benefit—but catchers had to catch it, and fielders had to field it and sometimes throw it. It was said that some catchers wanted to have a window installed in their mask. Infielders had difficulties because balls that were loaded up bounced irregularly and, even if they managed to catch it were difficult to throw straight. Additionally, professional baseball was trying to increase attendance by attracting women and children, and part of that effort involved cleaning up its image. And so, if this book were fiction, that would have been the end of the spitball.

This book is nonfiction, however. Anyone who believes that rule 8.02 marked the end of the spitball probably also believes Billy Martin voluntarily resigned as Yankee manager—four times. Even before Grimes retired, pitchers were throwing illegal spitters. Their problem was how to load up the ball without being caught. Dizzy Dean, for example, remembered, "When Frankie Frisch and I were with the

Cardinals, he'd walk over to the mound with the ball to discuss strategy when a tough batter was up. And when he'd hand me the ball it'd be dripping with tobacco juice. That usually was the best strategy."

As time passed, pitchers became more sophisticated in the art of loading up. They improved upon saliva, using Vaseline, K-Y jelly, pine tar, paraffin, mud, anything that would adhere to a baseball that could be hidden on their person. Whitey Ford used a very sticky home brew consisting of turpentine, baby oil, and resin, which he secreted in a tube of roll-on deodorant. Between innings he would put it on both of his hands and all over his uniform shirt. After one game, though, he left the tube on the top shelf of his locker, where Yogi Berra found it. Believing it to be roll-on deodorant, Berra spread it under his arms. His arms literally stuck to his sides. Although some people at first believed Berra was simply doing his famed penguin imitation, in fact, he couldn't get his arms free. Trainer Gus Mauch finally had to cut the hair under Yogi's arms to disarm him.

Ford also admitted throwing a major league mudball, which is not comparable to the amateur mudball made primarily by rolling mud into a ball. A major league mudball is a ball thrown with mud stuffed into its seams, causing it to drop suddenly. Ferguson Jenkins threw a similar pitch, but opposing players called his pitch a dirtball. Is a dirtball more or less sanitary than a spitball?

Probably the most unusual substance applied to the surface of a baseball was employed by Clyde King when he was pitching for the Dodgers. "The Giants' Whitey Lockman always hit me well," King explains. "One day I had two strikes on him with two out in the ninth inning. I knew it was time for my pitch. At that time I threw a pretty good bubble-gum ball. I called Roy Campanella out to the mound and told him what I was going to do, then stuck my gum on the ball. The most important thing in throwing that pitch is to make sure the gum doesn't stick to your hand as you release it. I threw a beauty. As Lockman started swinging the pitch dropped straight down. He missed it by at least a foot. Campy caught it and raced into the dugout. Lockman and the umpire stood at home plate, not knowing what to do.

"When I got to the clubhouse, Campy told me, 'Hey, Professor, you can have this ball, but first you have to get it out of my glove.' "

The biggest problem for a spitball pitcher is where to hide the substance on his body. Often they put it under the brow of their cap, under their armpits, all over their uniform shirt, behind their ears, even somewhere in their glove. Umpire Augie Donatelli once raced to the pitcher's mound and started to search Don Drysdale, who often was accused of throwing wet ones. Donatelli grabbed Drysdale's cap and ran his fingers through his hair. When he finished, Drysdale asked, "Didn't you forget something, Augie?"

Augie looked at him quizzically. "What?"

"Well," Big D explained, "usually when people run their fingers through my hair, they also give me a kiss."

When John "The Wild Goose" Wyatt was pitching for Kansas City, he actually had a syringe filled with Vaseline in the thumb of his glove. If he pressed the ball hard against the thumb, a dab of Vaseline would emerge near the top. Of course, like every pitcher accused of throwing a loaded baseball, Wyatt denied it vehemently, explaining that his mother had raised him to be an honest man. When he told that to a sportswriter one day, the writer asked, "What do you think she'd say about the six jars of Vaseline on the shelf of your locker?"

"She would love it," Wyatt replied innocently. "I have cracked toes, and she always stressed personal hygiene."

Mets' coach Vern Horschiet—"Dad," as he's known to several generations of players—taught his pitchers to cut the inside seam of their gloves and pack it with a mixture of tinture of benzine and resin. The resulting substance is so sticky that a player could dangle the ball from two fingers. Once, I remember, Paul Lindblat had been traded from Horschiet's Oakland team to Texas. When he came in to pitch, "Dad" called me over to his seat in the bull pen and told me to inspect Lindblat's glove because he was cheating. "How can you tell from here?" I asked.

" 'Cause I taught him myself," he told me.

I inspected the glove, then walked back over to Horschiet. "You're probably right," I told him, "but there's no use taking it away from him. He's got two more fixed just like that one in his locker."

Probably the two pitchers best known for spending their entire career "not" throwing the spitter were Lew Burdette and Gaylord Perry. Both Burdette and Perry insisted they never threw the spitball, although Perry probably damaged his claim when he titled his autobiography *Me and the Spitter.* "The spitball is the best pitch I've got," Burdette once explained, "even though I don't throw it."

Pitchers have always contended that they benefit from being accused of throwing the spitball, even as they deny throwing it, because if batters believe they throw it, they start waiting for it. This, theoretically, gives the pitcher an additional pitch, a pitch they claim they don't throw. So the question probably is: Is it better to be accused of throwing the spitball and not throw it, or throw it and not be accused of throwing it? Of course, if they throw it as well as Burdette and Perry, it doesn't matter anyway, because even if the batter knows it's coming, he can't hit it.

Everybody in baseball knew Gaylord threw the spitball. If I knew it, believe me, everybody knew it. When Billy Martin was managing the Yankees, he coated a baseball with about two inches of Vaseline and handed it to the umpire, suggesting he give it to Perry and "Tell him it's ready for him." One day after striking out, Reggie Jackson threw a bucket of water on the field as a symbol of protest. American League president Joe Cronin went so far as having a chemist analyze baseballs thrown by Perry. The chemist found nothing, which is precisely what Perry claimed he was throwing.

One day in Cleveland the Indians asked the umpire to check the ball after almost every pitch Perry threw. Perry supposedly retaliated by filling the resin bag with flour and just pouring it all over the ball, so that every pitch seemed to be coming out of a puff of white flour. "I certainly wouldn't admit that," Perry said, "but if you see me doing a commercial for Pillsbury one day, you'll know why." Was this just another example of not throwing a pitch, or did he really throw it and deny it, or did he not throw it and was simply trying to gain a psychological benefit by admitting he didn't throw it?

In fact, one of the very few pitchers to actually admit throwing illegal pitches was reliever George Frazier, who said proudly, "I don't put any foreign substances on the baseball. Everything I use is from the good old U.S.A."

Actually, the spitball probably isn't even the best of the illegal pitches. Ranking high among baseball's pioneers, along with Abner Doubleday and Alexander Cartwright, who laid down the rules, and Candy Cummings, who is credited with throwing the first curveball, and Branch Rickey, who integrated the game and developed the first minor league system, is Russell William Ford. It was on a rainy spring day in 1910, in Atlanta, Georgia, a day that will live forever in baseball history, that young Russ Ford discovered the scuffball. Ford, trying to make the New York Highlanders that spring, had been forced under the grandstand by a sudden rainstorm. "I started throwing to Ed Sweeney, a New York catcher," Ford later recounted. "One of my pitches carried over his head and struck a wooden post. My next pitch started okay, then sailed about five feet. What was that? I wondered. When I got the ball back, I noticed a rough spot on the cover that had been caused by hitting the post.

"So I decided that what I needed was a scuffed ball, provided I could learn to control it. There was also a problem in keeping it scuffed. At first I used a broken pop bottle. Then I found that emery paper was even better."

Ford quickly learned how to control his "emery ball" and won twenty-six games in his rookie season. When the big leagues made it illegal to deface the ball, his problem became figuring out how to scuff the ball without being caught. Eventually he attached a piece of emery to a length of elastic, which he hid inside his uniform shirt. When he wanted to scuff the ball he drew the emery from his cuff. When he wanted to hide the emery, he released the elastic.

Ironically, Ford disguised his emery ball as a still-legal spitball. "I had been a spitball pitcher," he explained, "and that helped to keep other teams from getting suspicious. I went through the motion of wetting the ball before letting it go."

The scuffball was first used in a major league game on April 21, 1910. An umpire of that time described the pitch almost exactly as umpires today would describe a knuckleball: "Nobody can hit it and nobody can catch it, but we've got to call it."

As soon as other pitchers discovered that by defacing the cover of a baseball they could cause the ball to move even more erratically than they could by spitting on it, they began slicing and dicing and carving and cutting. They grew their fingernails long and sharp and used them to dig nicks into the ball. They sharpened the buckles of their uniform belts and rubbed the ball against it. They stuck phonograph needles in the ball itself. They hid pieces of emery and sandpaper on their bodies. They sharpened the metal ringlets on their gloves. They hid bottle caps in their glove. Some pitchers taped a small piece of a metal grater to their chest and rubbed the ball against it. They forced BB pellets under the cover. St. Louis Browns' pitcher Allen Sothoron didn't bother with any sophisticated shenanigans: He just carried a razor blade out to the mound and sliced the stitches.

Surprisingly, unlike almost every other area of our lives in which technological advances have wrought significant advances, modern pitchers are still using many of the same tried-and-true methods perfected by their ancestral moundsmen. They still sharpen the ringlets on their equipment and glue pieces of sandpaper to their glove or hand. They still let their fingernails grow long and sharpen them. They did have a slight problem for a while when double-knit pants with elastic waistbands replaced belts—have you ever tried to sharpen elastic—but belts are back in style, so belt buckles are being sharpened again. Catchers are still sharpening the screws and bolts and rings on their equipment. There have been a few interesting attempts—certainly John Wyatt tried to be creative with his syringe. And Whitey Ford, pitching's one-man crime wave, did have a ring made for himself that had a tiny piece of a rasp, or file, welded to it. He covered the ring with a Band-Aid, which was appropriate, because he used it only when he needed help. But for the most part, pitchers are in the same primitive stage as Rick Honeycutt, who simply taped a thumbtack to his finger. The reality is that pitchers have not made significant advances in the art of defacing a baseball.

Another thing that hasn't changed is that the umpires are expected to act as baseball's police force. I spent much of my career listening to Gene Mauch and Weaver and Martin and almost every other manager screeching from the dugout, "Check the ball! Check the ball!" Incredibly, it was always the other team that persisted in throwing illegal pitches. No manager's team ever threw an illegal pitch. And any time I checked one of their pitchers they complained, "How come you're always picking on us?"

When Billy Martin was managing Oakland in 1980, for example, nine of the ten pitchers on his staff were suspected of doctoring the baseball. As Joe Garagiola commented, "The Oakland pitching staff must warm up in a car wash." But when Billy was managing Detroit, he once brought a dog to the ballpark and explained to umpire Bill Kunkel that the dog was trained to sniff foreign substances on the ball. Martin planned to have it sit next to him on the bench during the game. Kunkel gave Martin a choice: either he or the dog could stay. Oh, how I wish I could have had a vote.

I hated having to search a pitcher. My mama didn't raise me to be a policeman. Of course, she also didn't raise me to weigh 325 pounds, but that's another story. I wasn't really a cop, but at 325 I was what is known as "an authority figure," so when I asked the pitcher to see the baseball he would immediately bounce it or roll it to me. I'd look at it and, sure enough, it would be a baseball. Sometimes I had to organize an entire search party. The whole umpiring crew would converge on a pitcher and one of us would have to search him physically. As I would always say to Bill Haller in those situations, "You've got the honors."

I have been very fortunate in my life. I've had numerous wonderful experiences. But searching a sweaty pitcher on a humid night is none of them. Some of the pitchers really didn't mind. Gaylord, for example, would tell me, "Look at my left shoulder, but don't look under my hat." Or he'd start giggling, telling me I was tickling him. Once he asked me if I also gave massages.

When Don Sutton was being searched one evening, the umpire found a note in his uniform pocket reading, "You're getting warm, but it's not here."

Tommy John used to warn umpires searching his glove, "Be careful you don't cut your hand on that razor blade."

Some umpires take their crime prevention duties seriously. When Birdie Tebbetts was catching in the 1930s and 1940s, he was known to attach thumbtacks to his shinguards, then cut the ball as he returned it to the pitcher. Umpire Hank Soar knew it, and whenever he caught Tebbetts he acted correctly. "I told him to get rid of them," Soar remembers.

Yankee manager Joe McCarthy also knew what Tebbets was doing, but he needed proof before he could do anything about it. He told his players that if Tebbetts dropped a ball while they were batting, they were to grab it. Sure enough, one afternoon while spitballer Tommy Bridges was on the mound and Joe Gordon was at bat, the ball popped out of Tebbetts' glove. Both Gordon and Tebbetts dived after it and started fighting over the ball. Finally Tebbetts yanked it away and heaved it into the outfield, thus proving Bridges was not throwing the spitball.

Of course, when Tebbetts became manager of the Reds, he had his team take motion pictures of Lew Burdette in an attempt to prove that Burdette was throwing the spitball. Nothing like a born-again manager.

However, Soar did once throw Nellie Fox out of a game for loading up a baseball—unfortunately, Nellie was a second baseman. It seems that he splattered tobacco juice all over the ball.

Umpire Greg Kosc forced Royals' pitcher Vida Blue to change his uniform pants after finding a spot of sticky pine tar, which Blue had covered with white resin. "Before the game I bumped into somebody who had pine tar on his uniform," Blue explained afterward. "In fact, I've been bumping into someone like that for ten years. Since our uniforms are white, and pine tar is dark, I covered it up with resin. When I was with the Giants we had dark uniforms so I could really load up—I mean, bump into the same guy."

In my entire minor and major league career I never caught a single pitcher doing anything illegal, and I called only one balk. And I was wrong on the balk. I didn't want to catch a pitcher for two reasons: one, the American League didn't want me to, and two, the American League *really* didn't want me to. If baseball really wanted to stop pitchers from defacing baseballs, the commissioner would institute a severe penalty and enforce it. That wouldn't stop it, of course, but it would make it seem as if baseball really wanted to stop it.

Occasionally pitchers have been caught. Umpire Doug Harvey—"God," as the players call him—once ejected Don Sutton for throwing a defaced ball. Harvey made it clear that he was not accusing Sutton of actually defacing the ball, just throwing a doctored ball. The circumstantial evidence that Sutton had scratched the ball was overwhelming—Sutton was the only person on the pitcher's mound.

Sutton reacted quite reasonably, immediately threatening to sue Harvey, the National League, and "Whoever runs the umpiring for depriving me of my rights to earn a living as a pitcher."

Umpire Davey Phillips had a similar problem with Gaylord Perry. "Baby Davey" was working the plate, Perry was pitching, and Boston's Reid Nichols was batting. Phillips had warned Perry about throwing questionable pitches in the past. A questionable pitch is a ball that comes in straight for about 58 ½ feet, then drops straight down, as if a lead slab had landed on top if it. Perry had a full count on Nichols and, just before he started his windup, Nichols stepped out of the batter's box and asked Davey to check the baseball. He did. "I looked at the ball," Davey remembers, "and as I turned it around I noticed my hand sliding across the cover. There was a glob of some greasy substance on it—I mean, enough grease that when I touched it I could see my fingerprint.

"I could have ejected him immediately. But he hadn't thrown the ball, so legally he hadn't thrown an illegal pitch. He just had an illegal ball in his possession. So I warned him that if another pitch came in that I thought acted like a spitter, I was going to eject him."

Who could blame Phillips for not throwing out Perry? In fact, if the league had investigated, they would have found only one fingerprint on the ball: Davey Phillips'! Hmmm.

Perry did throw another spitball and Phillips ejected him, the only time in Gaylord's career that he was ejected.

For decades no pitcher was apprehended with the evidence. But recently Rick Honeycutt was caught trying to jettison a thumbtack, Joe Niekro was caught with a piece of sandpaper and a file in his back pocket, and a piece of sandpaper was found in Kevin Gross's glove. Either pitchers are getting more blatant about cheating, or dumber. In their defense, I can guarantee that some of the pitchers I knew couldn't possibly get any dumber.

Perry Mason couldn't have gotten Honeycutt, Niekro, or Gross off. Although there was a rumor that Kevin Gross would claim diplomatic immunity as he was pitching in Philadelphia, that proved false, and each perpetrator received a brief suspension.

Has the apprehension of Perry and Sutton and Honeycutt and the others acted as a deterrent? Let us examine the case of Houston's Mike Scott. After six big league seasons that might charitably be described as mediocre, in 1985 Scott suddenly became one of baseball's dominant pitchers. In the middle of the 1986 season Davey Johnson collected eight baseballs Scott had thrown in a game against the Mets. All eight were scuffed in precisely the same place.

Scott denied defacing the balls, although he admitted he
wanted the psychological advantage of having batters believe he was. Intense surveillance of Scott in action failed
to provide any evidence that he was defacing baseballs. So
were those marks proof that Scott scuffs the ball, or were
they merely psychological scars? Does Scott scuff the ball,
or is the fact that each of them was marked in precisely the
same place the most incredible coincidence since Adam
just happened to bump into Eve?

Are there many pitchers today besides Scott—who at
least throws a psychoball—throwing the spitball or the
sliced ball? Can Wade Boggs hit? Would I like a thick, juicy
steak? Is George Steinbrenner going to fire another manager?

There are several very good arguments for risking the
brief suspension resulting from being caught, among them:
Gaylord Perry won 314 games, Don Sutton has won more
than 300, Tommy John has won more than 270, Whitey
Ford won 236, Joe Niekro has won more than 210, Don
Drysdale won 209, and Lew Burdette won 203.

How important is the illegal pitch? George Bamberger is
acknowledged to be one of the outstanding pitching coaches
in baseball. When Bamberger was with the Orioles in the
early 1970s, young pitcher Ross Grimsley, struggling to
make the team, was having a bad day. Bamberger walked
slowly to the pitcher's mound and supposedly advised
Grimsley, "If you can cheat, I wouldn't wait one pitch
longer."

Not every trick pitch is illegal. Through the years pitchers have resorted to almost every conceivable type of unusual pitch in their never-ending battle against the offense.
The knuckleball, for example, is not illegal—most batters,
catchers, and umpires just consider it immoral. Scientists
recently proved in wind tunnel tests that the knuckleball
actually changes direction twice in midflight. Anyone who
has ever seen a major league knuckleball will find that very
difficult to believe. Twice? No way. Five, six times, at
least. Hall of Famer Hoyt "Tilt" Wilhelm's knuckleball
changed course more often than Long Island's famed Gar-

bage Barge. A batter once claimed that Phil Niekro's knuckleball "actually giggles at you as it goes by."

"After winning my first game in the big leagues," Jerry Casale remembers, "my second start was against Hoyt Wilhelm. In the locker room before the game I kept hearing the guys complaining, 'We got that damn, crooked blankety-blank today.' I kept wondering what was so great about this Wilhelm.

"In those days we warmed up next to home plate. As I warmed up—I was rearing back and throwing bullets—I looked over at Wilhelm, and there he is throwing sort of like a girl. He looked like he was going to fall asleep while he was warming up. Meanwhile, I kept throwing bullets. I couldn't believe Wilhelm was actually a major league pitcher.

"The game started and nobody could hit him. I remembered Ted Williams walking back into the dugout muttering to himself. I was a pretty good hitter, I'd hit a home run in my first start, and I couldn't believe my Red Sox teammates couldn't hit him. I was thinking, 'He throws like a girl, I'll knock the hell out of him.'

"Finally, I got up to bat. Wilhelm threw, his pitch sort of drifted toward me. It was a little outside, then a little inside, then it dropped, then it came at me. I backed out of the way. Orioles' catcher Gus Triandos jumped the other way and blocked it. The umpire didn't know which way to go. I was stunned. I'd never seen anything like it in my life. Never.

"By the third time I went to the plate my goal was to hit the ball. I didn't care where it went, I just wanted to make contact once. I choked up on the bat and tried to push the bat at the ball—and missed it. I batted against Sandy Koufax, Herb Score, Whitey Ford, but without doubt, Hoyt Wilhelm was the toughest pitcher God ever put on the mound. Wilhelm put the fear of death in me. No one else scared me. The thing that puzzled me most was how the umpire called it." Me too.

The knuckleball, or butterfly, or flutterball, or *&!#-@$%!!, is actually one of the oldest trick pitches in baseball. Like some cult religion that barely survives, there has always been at least one but rarely more than five or six devotees throwing the knuckleball in the big leagues at the same time. The pitch seems to have been discovered by Larry Cheney in 1912, when he bent his fingers and dug his fingernails deep into the cover. It was first called a "dry spitter" because, like the spitball, no one could predict the way it would move.

Eddie Rommel followed Cheney. After watching umpires struggle to call his knuckleball for nine seasons, Rommel evidently believed he could do as well, or as bad, because after retiring he became one of baseball's great umpires.

The knuckleball probably gained its greatest popularity when the fastball went to war for the duration. In 1944, the Washington Senators actually had four knucklers on their staff. Naturally, they also had three catchers.

I would hope those catchers had a good mental health plan. "I threw a knuckleball all my life," Wilhelm, who retired after twenty-one seasons at age forty-nine, said, "and it took nothing out of me." Of course not—it was his catchers who had to chase it.

Gus Triandos once exasperated Manager Paul Richards by actually calling for a fastball when Wilhelm was pitching. Wilhelm didn't have a fastball. The batter hit a home run. "Why didn't you call for the knuckler?" Richards demanded.

"Because I can't catch the damn thing," Triandos explained.

For years the record for passed balls in an inning was four, held by the Giants' Ray Katt. Following him with three were Triandos, Joe Ginsberg, and Charlie Lau. All of them were catching Wilhelm. Or, more accurately, not catching Wilhelm.

"One day I struck out Jim Landis on a high third strike," Hoyt recalls, "but the ball leaped up and bounced off the head of my catcher and roomie, Scraps Courtney. He walked slowly out to the mound and drawled, 'Roomie, I jes' wish you'd keep that thing offa my head.' "

"The thing I always told myself when I caught Wilhelm,"

Joe Ginsberg remembers, "is after I miss it, try to keep it in front of me. He would hit you all over. I'd reach down, it would hit me in the mask. I'd reach up, it'd get me in the foot. Once Hoyt tried to help me. 'If I come a little bit inside,' he said, 'the ball will sink.' So the next time I caught him the first pitch came inside, I reached down, and it sailed over my head. 'Let me try to figure it out myself,' I told him.

"Paul Richards, who had been a catcher himself, advised us to keep our eyes above the ball, not that that would enable us to catch it, 'but at least it'll never go over your head.'

"Everybody hated that pitch. I remember once Mickey Mantle was at bat, and he swung and missed at the first pitch. I caught that one. As Wilhelm wound up again, Mickey said, 'I don't know how you guys catch that pitch.' The ball sailed right by me, and as I turned to run after it, I shouted, 'We don't.'

"Umpire Red Foley was an excellent ball-strike umpire, except when Wilhelm was pitching. He'd say things like, 'Ball one I know I missed it don't turn around.'

"Finally, in 1957, Paul Richards created the elephant glove. He knew there were no specifications limiting the size of the catcher's glove, so he went to Wilson Sporting Goods and had them make a giant glove. I was the first one to use it. It was huge, it was heavy, and it was the first flexible catcher's glove, actually the prototype of the gloves catchers are using today. And it worked. Its pocket was so big that by slapping at the area where I thought Wilhelm's knuckleball might show up, I'd catch the ball. The only trouble was, when there was a runner on base, I couldn't find the ball in the glove. I knew it was in there somewhere, and I'd be digging around like a prospector looking for gold, but I couldn't find that sucker, no way. Sometimes I felt very foolish trying to catch it, but at least I had the batter and the umpire looking just as foolish as me."

Catcher Bruce Benedict always conferred with the home plate umpire when Phil Niekro was on the mound. "I'd tell the umpire before the game started, 'Look, I'm probably going to embarrass you because I'm going to be diving all over the place. You'll call a strike and I'm going to be lying flat on the ground and it's gonna make you look bad. But you just do the best you can, hang with it, and I promise I'll never complain.' "

Montreal manager Buck Rodgers, a former catcher, claims he had what is perhaps the most difficult assignment in baseball history. "I was catching knuckleballer Barney Schultz in spring training in Barstow, Florida. There was an advertisement for a Ralston Purina cereal—Checkerboard Squares—on the outfield fence. The entire background was a black-and-white checkerboard, and this pitch was coming out of that. It was absolutely impossible to catch? Catch? I'd reach for the ball and realize I was trying to catch a checkerboard square."

Most knuckleballers adopt the pitch for a simple reason: survival. Hall of Famers Robin Roberts and Warren Spahn used it on occasion late in their careers. Early Wynn, who learned it as a rookie with the Senators in 1944, threw it in difficult situations throughout his career. The leading active knuckleball pitchers are Tom Candiotti, who threw two one-hitters in 1987, winning one of them and losing the second on walks and passed balls, and Charlie Hough. Hough started throwing the knuckleball when he realized "I didn't have a major league fastball. I had a Cal state Fullerton fastball. If a batter was looking for it, I had practically no chance."

Based on Hough's success, the Texas Rangers decided to teach the pitch to four minor league pitchers they did not consider prospects. Within two years, two of them were out of the organization, and only one of the survivors was throwing it frequently. So not only can't pitchers control it, hitters can't hit it, catchers can't catch it, umpires can't call it, coaches can't coach it, and most pitchers can't learn it. The perfect pitch.

There is, however, a pitch even trickier than the knuckleball, a pitch that makes batters look even more foolish when they swing at it and miss than the knuckleball, a pitch so unique that almost every major leaguer who has thrown it has rechristened it. And that pitch is called lobbing it in. Not just "lobbing it in," but throwing it high into the air and having it arch gently over the plate. The blooper, the balloon, the dewdrop, eephus, the folly floater, LaLob, whatever it's called, is a pitch that could be thrown by most girls. In fact, it is the only pitch that could be thrown by most girls.

The lob was first blooped in anger by the Pirates' Rip Sewell in 1943 to the Cubs' Dom Dallessandro. Dallessandro watched it drift passed him, and umpire George Magerkurth called it strike three. "Oh, no," Dallessandro complained, "that's not legitimate. It ain't baseball."

Originally called the "dewdrop" because it dropped out of the sky, it became generally known as the "eephus" pitch. It was named by Sewell's teammate Maurice Van Robays, who explained, "It's a nothin' pitch, and eephus ain't nothin'."

Sewell won forty-two games in two years by adding the lob to his repertoire but probably gained his greatest recognition in the 1946 All-Star Game—when Ted Williams smashed the only home run ever hit off the pitch.

When the Yankees' Steve Hamilton revived the pitch in 1970, calling it a "folly floater," there was some question whether it was legal. Just before Hamilton released his pitch, he hesitated, making some people wonder if that was a balk move meant to deceive the base runner. "Once I step toward the plate, I have to go through with the pitch anyway, so the runner is free to go," Hamilton wrote to the rules committee deliberating the question. "In fact, because the motion takes so much time to complete . . . it's hard to believe anyone could fail to steal second base on it." After an hour's debate, the American League ruled that the pitch was legal—while the National League decided it was not. Hamilton was not going to make a folly of the National League.

The folly floater's finest moment came when he threw it to the Indians' slugging Tony Horton. Horton revved up, waited, waited, and finally swung at it and whiffed for strike three—then got down on his hands and knees and crawled back to the dugout.

I enjoyed working the plate when Hamilton threw the pitch because it was the kind of pitch I usually could call right. The important thing was to wait until it reached the plate before calling it. It took a long time, but I knew it eventually had to go through the strike zone. Most importantly, Hamilton threw it only when the game was settled— either the Yankees were far ahead or far behind—so even if I called it wrong, nobody objected.

A decade later, Dave LaRoche's LaLob ladazzled lafans and Milwaukee Brewers' slugger Gorman Thomas. Thomas was so upset when he struck out swinging on a good LaLob— could there be such a thing as a bad LaLob?—that to prove he could still hit he tossed his helmet into the air and smashed it with his bat. In a semi-classic confrontation during the '82 season, LaRoche threw six consecutive bloopers to Thomas. The tension mounted higher than a climber reaching the summit of a molehill. Thomas fouled off four of them, took one for a ball, then lined a single. When he reached first base he saluted LaRoche appropriately: he stuck out his tongue at him.

Incredibly, unbelievably, impossibly, there actually was a trick pitch slower than the bloop. This was possibly the only pitch I could have outrun. Stu Miller dazzled big league hitters for sixteen seasons with his famed slowball. "The Killer Moth," as he was known, threw a pitch that had four speeds: slow, slower, slowest, and stopped. The key to hitting against Miller was patience. Instead of taking batting practice when he pitched, players used to practice waiting at a bus stop. But Miller once led the National League in earned-run average and twice struck out the three batters he faced in All-Star Games. "It's not so much that it's so slow traveling to the plate," General Manager Frank Lane explained, "it's that it arrives so late."

In an era of baseball dominated by free-swinging power hitters like Mantle, Harmon Killebrew, Willie Mays, and Frank Howard, Miller survived by keeping hitters off balance. "He's the only pitcher in baseball that they time with a sundial," Mantle supposedly said.

"The way it seems to work," Bill Rigney, who managed him with the Giants explained, "is that instead of concentrating on his throwing arm, the batter sees Stu jerk his head, and that's the motion at which he swings. By the time Miller throws the ball, the batter, thinking the pitch is timed with the head movement, is wrenched all out of shape and winds up beating his bat into the ground.

"The only problem I have with him," Rigney added, "is how can I tell when he's losing his stuff?"

Miller retired in 1968. Although he was forty-one, it probably would be inaccurate to say that he quit because he slowed down.

Every few seasons a pitcher starts winning ball games with a trick pitch. Reliever Elroy Face won eighteen games and lost only one in 1959 with a "forkball," a pitch held in his palm between his index finger and middle finger. Burt Hooton's "knuckle curve" was held like a knuckleball and released like a fastball—but it dropped like a spitball. And reliever Bruce Sutter's split-finger fastball is held somewhat similarly to the forkball but is wedged more firmly between the fingers. "It's unhittable," Dick Williams claimed. "It's worse than trying to hit a knuckleball."

The only problem with trick pitches is finding names for all of them. Hooton's knuckle curve, for example, was once simply called "The Thang." Supposedly, a Dodger pitcher in the 1960s threw a combination spitball-slider, which he called a "splider." The newly popular "cut fastball" is a fastball thrown with a stiff wrist and that moves across the plate; it is not a fastball thrown with a cut baseball. The slurve is a cross between a curveball and a slider.

"They've got a lot of names for these pitches now," Pete Reiser once said, "but there are only so many ways you can throw a baseball." True, but apparently they are running out of names before they've exhausted the various types of pitches. Finding new names for trick pitches is getting to be difficult. Montreal pitching coach Larry Bearnarth remembers a young pitcher who held the ball like a forkball but threw it like a screwball. "It dropped straight down and went sideways. A great pitch until his arm went bad. We spent a long time trying to come up with a name for it. For a while we called it a "foshball," but we ended up with just a fork-screwball."

Almost every major league pitcher, at one time in his career, experimented with trick pitches. Bob Gibson, for example, relied on a devastating fastball—most of the time. "I threw one knuckleball in my career," the Hall of Famer remembers. "I threw it to Hank Aaron. He hit a line drive to the second baseman. As he ran passed the mound on his way back to the dugout, he yelled, 'What the blank was that?'

" 'You blank,' I told him proudly, 'that was my knuckleball.' On occasion I'd throw a one-finger curveball. Once in awhile I'd throw a palmball. My real trick pitch was the change-up; the one pitch no one expected me to throw was a change-up. But when I needed an out, there was only one pitch I threw: I just reared back and fired my fastball."

Through the years there have been a lot of names for it: heater, buzzer, smoke, sailer, high hard one, number one, hummer, express, aspirin tablet, pill, pea, lightning, blue streak, high cheese, fog and dead red, but by any name it's still the most exciting pitch in baseball: the fastball. Fastball pitchers are to pitching what home run hitters are to hitting: often not the most consistently successful, but usually the most exciting players of their time. Fastball pitchers are the bridge between generations of baseball fans. When people of all ages start talking baseball, rarely does anyone ask, "Ever see a slower pitcher than Stu Miller?" The discussion is always about "the fastest pitcher . . ." and "the longest home run. . . ."

Fireballers are the legendary pitchers of baseball. The mound was moved back because Amos Rusie simply overpowered batters.

When Walter "Big Train" Johnson broke his catcher's hand with a fastball in the sixth inning, umpire Billy Evans told his replacement, "Try and protect me, will you."

Johnson's first pitch bounced off Evans' chest protector; his second pitch hit Evans on the leg. Evans then wisely called the game on account of darkness.

A batter once walked away from the plate after swinging and missing at Bob "Rapid Robert" Feller's first two pitches. The umpire called him back and reminded him he had one more. "That's all right," the batter replied, "I don't need it."

"Smokey" Joe Wood was the legend to which Walter Johnson was compared. Johnson's fastball became the scale against which Feller's fastball was measured. Feller was the pitcher to whom Nolan Ryan and Sandy Koufax were compared, and Ryan and Koufax became the legends that Dwight Gooden will spend his career chasing. And until recently, until the development of radar detectors capable of timing the speed of a pitch, the only measure of comparison was hyperbole. Amos Rusie was faster than a steam locomotive. Smokey Joe Wood was faster than a car. Walter Johnson, faster than an airplane. Bob Feller, faster than a rocket. Ryan and Koufax threw missiles. And Gooden? Gooden throws laser beams.

National Leaguers who batted against Koufax claim he was the fastest pitcher they ever faced. "I remember pinch-hitting against Koufax during one of his no-hitters," Joey Amalfitano recalls. "I was a good fastball hitter, so I went up to the plate expecting him to throw me a curveball. He didn't. Fastball, fastball, fastball. How fast? How fast is fast? Fast enough, probably faster than that. Strike three, see you later. As I walked back to the dugout I passed Harvey Kuenn, who was also pinch-hitting. 'How's he throwing?' Harvey asked.

" 'Very, very well,' I said.

"Harvey understood. 'Wait for me,' he said. 'I'll be right with you.' "

Catcher Jeff Torborg caught Koufax when he set a major league record by striking out 382 batters, then caught Ryan when he broke the record with 383. Which pitcher was faster? On any given day, both of them. Torborg was crossed up by Ryan one day, expecting a curve and being hit in the back of his hand with a Ryan Express. "It was very sore," he remembers, "but Nolan seemed a little disappointed. 'Your hand's not broken?' he said. 'I must be losing something off my fastball.' "

Ryan was the fastest pitcher I ever saw. Or at least thought I saw. Ryan pitched the only no-hitter I ever worked. It was against the Tigers, and he was just awesome. Mickey Stanley hit a foul ball and applauded himself. Eddie Brinkman remembers that the first batter of the game struck out, walked back to the bench shaking his head, and said, "We'll get them tomorrow, guys."

When Ryan had his fastball *and* was getting his curve over, he was unhittable. Right-handed batters hitting against him would walk back to the bench and cheer, "Come on, you left-handers."

One day, I remember, Ryan was facing the Red Sox. The first two times Rick Burleson batted, Ryan struck him on six straight fastballs. Pure heat. Just overpowered him. Burleson came up again in the seventh inning with a man on third and one out. Ryan's first pitch was the seventh straight fastball he'd thrown him. Strike one. His second pitch was the eighth straight fastball. Strike two. And finally he broke off one of the most beautiful curveballs I've ever seen. Burleson was fooled. Fooled? He was frozen. He never took the bat off his shoulder—strike three! Finally, a curveball. Burleson was furious. He stood at home plate and screamed out at Ryan, "You @#$%$@@!! Why don't you challenge somebody?"

Everybody who has ever played the game has his own candidate for the fastest pitcher ever. And a lot of votes always go to a pitcher who never made the major leagues—the truly legendary Steve Dalkowski, Jr. "I faced Nolan Ryan, 'Sudden Sam' McDowell, Jim Maloney, and Dick Radatz," former Red Sox catcher Bob Montgomery, now a Boston broadcaster, remembers, "and there has never been a human being who threw the ball faster than Steve Dalkowski."

"I had him in Class C one season," Doug Harvey recalls. "I've seen Koufax, Gibson, Juan Marichal, and Ryan.

Dalkowski was the fastest I've ever seen. In one season he broke my bar mask, split my shinguards, hit my chest protector on the shoulder and split the plastic roll on the edge of it, and knocked me back eighteen feet."

Dalkowski was a left-handed pitcher who was as wild as he was fast. "I think the reason he was so wild was that he was afraid he was going to kill somebody," Montgomery says. "He never hit too many right-handed hitters, but left-handed hitters had to stay loose."

The Orioles signed him when he graduated from high school in 1957. In his first four minor league seasons he struck out 665 batters—but walked 726. He also threw as many as six consecutive wild pitches, broke one batter's arm, and severed another hitter's earlobe. He once lost a one-hitter, 9–8. In another game he struck out nineteen and lost 8–3. In a Rookie League game he struck out twenty-four. Dalkowski had started pitching in high school. "When I got the ball over the plate," he told a reporter, "it was fun to watch them swing."

When he did get the ball over the plate he was devastating. In a spring training exhibition game against Cincinnati, he struck out the side on twelve pitches. But he just couldn't get it over the plate consistently. The Orioles tried everything; they let him pitch from a distance of fifteen feet, and when he threw strikes at that distance began moving him back—and discovered that his wildness increased in direct ratio to distance. They erected a large wooden target for him to aim at in the bull pen—he couldn't hit the target. When he finally did, he smashed it to splinters. In one game he threw three consecutive pitches over the catcher's head—and through the protective wire screen.

Doug Harvey remembers a typical Dalkowski game. "We were in Stockton and he struck out the first nine batters. Nine straight, nobody touched the ball. Maybe one batter fouled one pitch. In the fourth inning he was leading 2–0 and pitching a truly perfect game.

"His first pitch in the fourth inning almost cleared the backstop. It was seventeen to twenty feet high. The catcher, a kid named Zupo, just sort of looked up as it sailed over our heads. 'Oops,' he said. I gave him a new ball and he walked out to the mound. 'That's all right, kid,' I heard him tell Dalkowski, 'it could happen to anybody.' A pitch twenty feet high? I'd never seen it happen to anybody before. But that was it. He walked six consecutive batters and left the game losing, 3–2. He still hadn't given up a hit."

Dalkowski never managed to overcome his lack of control and eventually was released.

There was at least one pitcher even faster than Dalkowski, according to former Phillies' owner Bob Carpenter. Carpenter was in Terre Haute with scout Johnny Nee to watch a minor league game. "This pitcher cuts loose with the fastest pitch I've ever seen," Carpenter recalled. "Nee looks at me and says, 'I've never seen a fastball like that—I didn't even see it.'

" 'No wonder,' I told him, 'he hasn't let go of the ball.' He did that five times during the game. He took a big, beautiful motion and threw like hell, he just didn't release the ball. Otherwise, the guy was a tremendous prospect." The Phillies sent this pitcher to medical doctors and to a psychiatrist, but no one could ever help him overcome his problem. He might well have been the only pitcher who truly had nothing on the ball.

There is an old baseball adage, passed down through the ages, that the best pitch in baseball is a strike—and the second-best pitch is a knockdown. Until very recently the knockdown, in all its disguises—the beanball, brushback, duster, message, or purpose pitch—had been an accepted part of the game. Every batter went to the plate knowing that the next pitch might be aimed at his head, and that fear was the pitcher's ultimate weapon. The knockdown was the pitch that maintained the balance of power between the pitcher and the offense. It was the pitcher's enforcer. "If they threw at you in those days," Johnny Pesky explained, "that was a compliment. It meant they respected your ability." Personally, I would have preferred a telegram.

"If they didn't knock me down three or four times in a

series," Hall of Famer Mel Ott, who starred in the 1930s, once told the great sportswriter Jimmy Cannon, "I'd figure I was washed up."

"When I was playing," Hall of Famer Lou Boudreau said of the 1940s, "they threw at you right away to see what kind of man you were. If they thought they could intimidate you, they'd keep coming at you until you blew up or got yourself thrown out. Today's batter gets mad at the first pitch that comes near him."

"When I came up with the Brooklyn Dodgers in 1956," Don Drysdale recalls, "the first question asked at every pregame meeting was, 'Does he like to get knocked down?' If that happened today, I suspect your own players would file a grievance against you."

"The knockdown pitch was an accepted part of baseball in the 1960s," Ron Hansen remembers. "Nobody ever questioned it, no one got very mad about it. We usually knew when it was coming, we expected it. We just got off the ground and got back in the batter's box."

Very rarely did a pitcher try to hit the batter in the head. The purpose of the pitch was to send a message to the hitter or his teammates. The message was that the pitcher was not a happy man. If the pitcher really wanted to hit the batter, he usually aimed at his body. "I knocked down a lot of people," Drysdale admits, "but I can honestly say I never hit anybody in the head."

Bert Blyleven believes, "I've never played with a pitcher who tried to hit a batter in the head. Most pitchers are like me. If I'm going to hit somebody, I'm gonna aim for the bigger parts."

The knockdown was used in many different situations for many different reasons. A primary purpose was intimidation—the pitcher wanted to instill fear in the batter. Few pitchers in recent baseball history were more intimidating than Drysdale. Dick Groat once said that batting against Drysdale was less fun than going to the dentist. Umpire Al Barlick remembered riding up in a Dodger Stadium elevator with Willie Mays. "Gee," Willie said, "I wonder who's gonna pitch for them tomorrow?" When Barlick told him it was Drysdale, he made a face and said, "Goddamn."

"What'sa matter, Willie?" Barlick said. "You're a good hitter."

"I'll tell you what'sa matter," he replied. "I gots to hit him before he hits me!"

Sal "The Barber" Maglie and Early Wynn were the Koufax and Ryan of the knockdown. Legend has it they were so mean that junkyard dogs were afraid of them. Maglie claimed he would have knocked down his grandmother if she tried to crowd the plate; Wynn did knock down his son when the young man stood too close to the plate in batting practice.

"It's my bread and butter," Maglie, the man who taught Drysdale the importance of an inside fastball, used to say. "My job was to protect the plate any way I had to." Intimidation was the basis of Maglie's success. "I never shaved before a game because perspiration made my face sensitive, but the way I looked, with that grizzly beard, the way I pitched, it all helped me. If a hitter was a little edgy when he came to the plate, my job was easier. When a batter got up I'd just stare at him. I wouldn't move, I wouldn't blink, I'd just stare at him. Of course, if he said anything to me, I might scowl. If he said anything else, I'd laugh. Not too many batters dug in too deeply once I started laughing. I think they suspected what I was laughing about."

Early Wynn's scowl was said to be so cold that it intimidated both the batter *and* the on-deck hitter.

In the old days, batters who crowded home plate or got into the batter's box and tried to dig in to get a good foothold were perceived to be sending pitchers an invitation. "I joined the Indians in 1960," Frank Funk remembers, "and the second game I pitched was against the White Sox. Minnie Minoso, then with the White Sox, had a reputation for crowding the plate, but when he came to bat I couldn't believe it. Half his body was over the plate. It was as if he was daring me to pitch him inside. I thought, 'This guy has got to be kidding.'

"My first pitch unbuttoned his shirt—and he took a big

swing at it. 'Well, well,' I thought, 'we'll just have to see about this.'

"My second pitch put him in the dirt. He got up and took one step toward the mound but stopped before he got there.

"It was him or me. The third pitch I threw him was a curveball. He was fooled, he missed it, and threw his bat at it. The bat skittered out toward shortstop. Shortstop Woodie Held picked it up and walked to the plate as if he were going to hand it to Minoso. But just before he got there, he smashed the bat against the ground, cracking it. Then he dropped it at Minoso's feet.

"It really didn't require any mind-reading skills to figure out what was going to happen next. My next pitch decked him. Umpires came at me from everywhere—I think some extras came out of the stands and surrounded me. My manager, Jimmie Dykes, came rushing onto the field, screaming, 'Leave him alone! Get away from him!'

"The umpires were screaming at me, 'We heard about you and we don't go for that in this league!'

" 'What are you talking about?' Dykes was shouting. 'Minoso leads the league in getting hit every year.' Finally Dykes managed to get everything quieted down. The umpires went back to their positions, Minoso started to get back into the batter's box. Then, just before Dykes left the mound, he looked at me and said softly, 'You wanna stick him in the ribs, go ahead, kid. I'll pay for it.' "

When "The Big Bear," Mike Garcia, saw a batter excavating the batter's box, "I wanted to come off the mound and tell him not to bother. He was only gonna have to dig himself a deeper hole after my next pitch."

Batters also knew they might be going down if the hitter before them had hit a home run, or if they had been hitting the pitcher well. Henry Aaron, for example, always hit well against pitcher Stan Williams, so Williams tried to hit Aaron. Williams claimed that he kept a picture of Aaron in his locker and threw baseballs at it for entertainment. Once, while pitching for the Dodgers, Williams accidently hit Aaron in the protective helmet. After the game Williams happened to run into Aaron, and he apologized. "I'm sorry I hit you on the helmet, Hank," he said.

"That's all right," Aaron replied, "forget it."

" 'Cause I meant to hit you in the neck."

Bob Montgomery was on his way up to the majors when he faced aging Sad Sam Jones, on his way down, in the minor leagues. "All I knew about him was that he threw about twelve different types of curveballs and he didn't like a lot of people. The first time I faced him I hit a rocket to right-center field for a double. When I came to bat the next time, the catcher warned me, 'Walk into the box kinda lightly, cause he didn't like what you did to him last time.' I thought he was just trying to make me nervous. All I did was get a hit off the guy. First pitch, right under my chin. That worked: I got nervous.

"Then I went up to the Red Sox. At the end of my rookie year we were facing "Sudden Sam" McDowell. Sam didn't just want to get people out, which he could do by busting his fastball past you, he wanted to make batters look bad. I couldn't hit his fastball if I knew it was coming, but for some reason, with a 3–2 count on me, he threw me a change-up. I jumped all over it. I like to have killed Graig Nettles at third base. It buzzed past him for a hit. I was pretty excited when I reached first base. Hawk Harrelson was standing there, 'Boy, oh, boy,' I said, 'my dad is gonna be happy with me. I got a hit off Sam McDowell.'

"Hawk just looked at me and chuckled knowingly. 'Don't start celebrating just yet,' he suggested.

"My next at-bat I hit a line drive past McDowell's ear for another hit. I was two-for-two off him. That might have been my greatest day in the big leagues.

"A week later we faced McDowell again. My first time at bat he threw me a hard slider, I mean a *hard* slider. When a left-handed pitcher like McDowell throws a slider to a right-handed batter like me, there is no place for that right-handed batter to hide. That pitch keeps curving right at you. I turned my back at the last moment and that pitch hit me right between the shoulder blades. It was one of those pitches that was thrown so hard that it kind of burrowed into my back for a moment, then dropped straight down to the ground. That baby was still hurting me at Christmas.

"Meanwhile, up in the television booth, the announcers were saying, 'He's not going to let him know it hurts.' Of course I wasn't. I couldn't. I couldn't even breathe."

Some pitchers used the knockdown as a means of protest. Scoreboards that "exploded" when a home team batter hit a home run used to infuriate visiting pitchers. "The scoreboard in the Astrodome went off for about a minute," pitcher Claude Raymond remembers, "and that whole time the pitcher had to stand out there getting angrier and angrier. Believe me, nobody wanted to go to bat after that."

When Bill Veeck's scoreboard fireworks went off in Chicago, the next batter almost always went down. That was the pitcher's way of saying, "Go ahead and blow that thing off again."

In some cases a knockdown pitch was thrown for personal reasons. Bob Gibson, for example, always took great pride in his hitting ability. One day he was batting against San Francisco and hit a high pop-up to the infield. Dave Rader, the Giants' catcher, laughed warmly, saying, "Up the old shoot, hey, Gibby?"

Laughing at Bob Gibson is probably not the smartest thing a human being should do. Gibson would have knocked down Sal Maglie's grandmother. Rader led off the next inning—pow! First pitch, right in the shoulder.

Laughing at Gibson was bad enough, but spitting? One night a Reds' pitcher knocked down a Cardinal batter. In the bottom of that inning Pete Rose was the first hitter. Gibson retaliated by dropping Rose into the dirt. Rose got up, dusted himself off, looked at Gibson, and spit twice. Now, that takes both courage and dexterity, because Rose knew he was going to be diving for safety on the next pitch. "The next one I threw was right there," Gibson remembers, "and I don't remember that he ever spit again."

Joe Nuxhall was hit in the knee by a Monte Irvin line drive and had to leave the game. A week later he was on the mound again, and the first batter he faced was Danny

O'Connell. "O'Connell hit a line drive and it hit me on the other knee. My knee turned black; I thought the kneecap was cracked. Eventually I had to leave the game, but while I was sitting out there on the mound, in considerable pain, I looked over to first base and O'Connell was laughing. I thought, 'I'll be damned, it's just not that funny.'

"Coincidentally, both of us got traded to the American League that winter. The following June I was pitching against the Washington Senators, and O'Connell was scheduled to be the lead-off hitter. I told my catcher, 'You might as well stay in the dugout. There isn't going to be anything for you to catch.' O'Connell came to bat; I just reared back and fired at him. I got him in the arm. I'm sure he thought I was crazy, because as he jogged down to first base, I was standing on the mound laughing."

Milt Pappas was traded from the Orioles to Çincinnati in 1966 for Frank Robinson. In those days it was still possible to make major deals without agents, accounting corporations, and law firms becoming involved, and this was a major deal. When the O's played the Reds the following spring, a newspaper photographer asked Pappas if he would pose for a picture with Robinson. Pappas agreed, but the photographer returned and said that Robinson had refused. "That's okay," Pappas thought, "I'll remember that."

Six years later Robinson was traded back to the National League. "We were playing *The Game of the Week* against his new team, the Dodgers. Before the game started I sat down with my catcher, Randy Hundley, and said, 'I'm not gonna tell you why, but when Robinson gets up, just be alive.' Robinson came to bat in the first inning. I knocked him on his ass. Second pitch, same thing. Third pitch, same thing. Then I threw three sliders and struck him out. The next time he came to bat, same thing.

"Finally, after the third time, Robinson stepped out and asked Hundley, 'What's wrong with that guy? Why's he trying to kill me?' Hundley told him he didn't know. I knocked down Robinson every time he got up, and struck him out three times.

"After the game, Hundley cornered me and demanded, 'Now you have to tell me what that was all about.'

" 'Sure,' I told him. 'He wouldn't take his picture with me.' And then I walked away as Hundley muttered 'picture?' "

Probably more knockdown pitches were thrown by a pitcher trying to protect his teammates than for any other reason. "I had my own rule," Drysdale explains. "If one of my teammates went down, two members of the other team went down. If two of mine went down, four of theirs went down. Nobody had to go to Harvard or Yale to do the mathematics. So when I pitched, we never had a lot of guys going down."

"If the ball comes at me," Willie Mays explained, "I just ain't gonna be there. This kind of thing should be kept in the family. If my pitcher takes the situation in hand, it stops."

Few pitchers could stop it better, or more quickly, than Early Wynn. "I wasn't a very good hitter," catcher Joe Ginsberg admits, "but one day I was actually two-for-two. The third time I got up, I got drilled. In those days nobody complained; that wasn't the way it was done. At the end of the half inning I was putting on my shinguards and Early came over to me and asked, 'You think he meant that?'

" 'Early,' I said, 'I'm two-for-two. I'm sure he did."

"The pitcher was the first batter the next inning. Early's first pitch sailed right under his chin, and down he went. *That's* the way it was done."

Wynn was known to have the sense of humor of a parking violations bureau clerk while on the mound. One day the Yankees' "Bullet" Bob Turley pitched him inside. Wynn stepped out of the batter's box and said to catcher Yogi Berra, "You better tell your man Turley to stop pitching me inside. Tell him to pitch me outside. Tell him now, Yogi, because if Turley doesn't start pitching me outside, I'm gonna have to pitch you inside."

"Time!" Berra yelled. From that point on, Turley pitched Wynn outside—way, way outside.

"The thing that kept it from getting out of hand in

those days," Jerry Casale explained, "was that the pitcher always came to bat. There was no designated hitter and much less reliance on relief pitchers. The pitcher batted, so he knew whatever he threw up there was eventually going to come back to him. Once, in the minor leagues, we were playing the Los Angeles Angels in their stadium, a sandbox called Wrigley Field. Power-hitting Steve Bilko was the batter, and you had to pitch him tight in that park. A fastball got away from me and he went down. I hadn't thrown at him. If I'd wanted to knock him down, I would have. I was cocky in those days: If King Kong was crowding the plate, I would have knocked him down. But Bilko was a friend of mine, and the pitch just got away from me.

"Gene Mauch was their manager, and he started screaming at me. Bilko knew I wasn't throwing at him. I came to bat a few innings later and Dick Drott was pitching for them. I could hear Mauch yelling from their dugout, 'Stay loose, you !@#^%$#^&%^&$@#@.' I knew they were trying to rile me up. I thought, 'Drott isn't going to be stupid enough to play on me, is he?' But sure as heck, I looked at him and he was sighting on me. In that split second I knew what was coming. I took it right in the back, and I went down. Our manager, Joe Gordon, wanted to take me out. Was he kidding?

"Dick Drott came to bat for them in the next inning. There was a runner on first with no out, a bunting situation. My catcher, Haywood Sullivan, was pumping signs: curveball, slider. Sure, I was going to throw him a curveball. I thought, 'Lemme see how good my control is. Lemme see if I can get it right in his mouth.' I missed him the first time. As I started winding up to deliver my second pitch, I thought, 'God give me strength to throw this one even harder.' I didn't want to miss that time.

"He turned around to bunt. I hit him in the hand and broke every one of his fingers. I felt like I did my job."

The knockdown wasn't used just to respond to other knockdowns; it was also used to retaliate for any type of dangerous play. The Royals' Hal McRae once slid into Twins' infielder Glenn Borgmann spikes high—it took twelve stitches to close the bloody wound. Pitcher Ron Schueler promised Borgmann he would retaliate. "It took me a long time, but I did," he explains. "McRae was the fifth batter in the inning. I retired the first two hitters, then laid fast-balls down the middle so the next two batters would get hits. I got McRae in the hip."

Sometimes pitchers were ordered by their managers to knock down batters—and were fined if they failed to do so. "I played under nine different managers," Russ "Mad Monk" Meyer claimed, "and only one of them didn't tell me to coldcock somebody."

"Whenever I saw Johnny Bench wiggle his thumb toward the batter," Milt Wilcox said, "the signal to knock him down, I knew it had come from Sparky Anderson."

"When the sign came from the bench, the pitcher would often shake it off," Joe Ginsberg remembers. "The pitcher would tell me he didn't want to knock down the batter. 'If you don't,' I'd remind him, 'we're both fined a hundred dollars.'

" 'Here it comes,' " the pitcher inevitably responded.

Usually managers could order a pitcher to throw at another hitter with impunity—managers didn't have to stand at home plate and become a target. But on occasion players did take action against opposing managers. Leo Durocher, in particular, was known for standing on the top of the dugout steps and screaming, "Stick it in his ear!"

When "Leo the Lip" was managing the Dodgers, a Cub pitcher fired a baseball into the Dodger dugout at him. Cub management then fined the pitcher for missing Durocher. And when Durocher was managing the Giants, Brooklyn's Carl Furillo was hit by Ruben Gomez. Furillo started to trot to first base, then raced into the Giants' dugout. It took a posse of Giants to tear him off Durocher, one of them accidently breaking Furillo's hand during the melee. At least everyone assumed it was an accident.

Like Minoso, some batters tried to intimidate pitchers by crowding the plate. Their intention was to get a hit, or get hit, but to get on base. Those batters often led the league in getting hit by pitches. When Johnny Pesky was with the Red Sox he batted in front of Ted Williams. "Ted would tell me, 'Get on base and I'll hit one off this guy.' Once, I remember, we were in New York in the middle of a pennant race, tied 1–1 in the ninth. Allie Reynolds was pitching for the Yankees, and the count was one ball, two strikes. He came inside with a fastball and rather than backing away, I turned and let it hit me in the shoulder. Boy, it hurt, but I wasn't gonna rub that baby if my arm fell off. I got to first base and Reynolds just stared at me. I looked at the ground. I think we both knew the next time I batted he was gonna put one behind my ear.

"Williams put the second pitch in the bull pen, and we won the game."

Ron Hunt retired in 1974 holding the career and season records for being hit by a pitched ball. Some players stand in front of a mirror practicing their swing. Hunt used to stand in front of a mirror and practice making it look as if he were trying to get out of the way of an inside pitch. One day in spring training he was actually hit three times by the pitching machine. He did everything he could to get hit: Instead of wearing a uniform shirt that fit him, for example, he would wear one several sizes too large, allowing it to balloon out of his pants. Other players talked hitting to reporters; he talked hits. "I guess the best place to be hit is from the shoulder blades to above the waist. The buttocks were probably the best. My legs, elbows, and head were absolutely the worst."

Hunt's record was finally broken, and broken is probably the correct word in this instance, by Don Baylor. I spent much of my career watching baseballs bounce off Baylor. The man was so strong, so tough, that he made you feel sorry for the baseball. Once, I remember, the ball hit him and disappeared. I knew it hit him, but I couldn't find it. He dropped his bat and started trotting down to first base. And when he got halfway there, he lifted his arm—and the ball fell onto the ground. He'd caught it under his arm.

Supposedly, when Don Zimmer was hit in the cheekbone by an outfielder-turned-pitcher, he said something like, "If that's as hard as he can throw, tell him to go back to the outfield." More likely, what he said was, "Munphel, mmmrrrpphh, rrroow." I doubt very much that he could speak at all. Believe me, anyone who has heard the squash of a fastball hitting a skull never wants to hear it again. I was working home plate when Paul Blair was hit in the head, and it was worse than anything I ever saw during my college and professional football career.

Anybody who believes the beanball is a necessary part of baseball either has been hit in the head too often or plays basketball. Only one major league player has ever been killed during a game, but numerous players, from Ducky Medwick to Tony Conigliaro to Dickie Thon, have had their careers curtailed and their lives changed because of a single pitch. The payoff just isn't worth the price.

Players used to have their own means of retaliating— and it wasn't always another knockdown pitch. Moose Skowron remembers being hit intentionally by Ike Delock of the Red Sox. "I thought it was intentional, and I was pretty upset. Gene Mauch was playing second for the Red Sox and Bob Cerv was the batter. I said to myself, 'God, please let him hit a grounder to the shortstop and let them go for a double play. Sure enough, Cerv hits a four-hopper to the shortstop. I got to second just as Mauch got there. I slid into the bag and got his leg. I broke it and that ended his career.

"The next time I saw Mauch he was managing the Phillies. I thought he was going to be mad as hell. Instead he came over to me and said, 'I want to thank you, Moose. You made me a big league manager.' I should have told him it wasn't me, it was Ike Delock."

Since few players were as tough as Skowron, the knockdown was a useful deterrent. But not any longer, at least not in the American League, because pitchers no longer have to come to bat. And the major league rules now allow an umpire to warn both managers and both pitchers after the first close pitch, then eject the next pitcher who, in the umpire's opinion, throws a knockdown pitch. The problem with that, as Leo Durocher pointed out, is that "Theoretically, you could have your pitcher knock down the other team's first batter every day, and the other team couldn't retaliate."

"This new rule says that you can't throw at anybody," Dizzy Dean remarked when it was first passed. "Well, I never tried to kill a batter, but I liked to straighten 'em up once in a while."

"It's a ridiculous rule," my mentor, Bill Haller, believes. "Here's some poor bastard sitting on the bench, he hasn't done a thing, and the umpire's threatening to eject him. Why should he be responsible for the actions of the other team?"

Bert Blyleven claims he is a strong believer in protecting his teammates. "Sometimes I have to retaliate. I believe in that. When I first came up you could throw at somebody and not get fined. Now you come close to a guy and the umpires warn you. So if you try to protect your player, you're out of the game. That's not fair. The result of that rule is that right now, you're better off starting it, because they won't let you finish it."

"I think the rule is going to get somebody seriously hurt," Hawk Harrelson said, "because as soon as the umpire gives a warning the batters feel more secure. They start digging in, they're not prepared to get out of the way. One day somebody's going to dig in and catch one right in the head."

Bob Gibson agrees. "Hitters today have too much confidence that the pitcher is not going to come inside. They're insulted when the pitcher comes inside. Now when a pitcher throws inside, everybody wants to come out and fight. Combined with the fact that pitchers no longer practice coming inside, as we used to, I think there's a real chance that there are going to be some serious injuries."

"The rules have taken the inside pitch away from the pitcher," Jim Kaat points out. "When I came up we were playing the traditional push-'em-back game. Pitchers practiced throwing inside. Wally Bunker and I used to stand there sideways, our gloves at shoulder level, trying to put the ball into the glove. I got to the point where I would say, 'All right, Bunk, show me something. Close your eyes.'

And he would. And I was able to put it in his glove. Today's pitchers don't even throw inside when they're warming up, so if they have to pitch tight during the game, they're liable to hurt somebody."

If any single change symbolizes the difference in the game as it is played today compared to the way it was once played, it is the disappearance of the knockdown pitch. Old-timers defend the way they policed themselves, believing, as Jimmy Piersall said, "They're sissifying the game." Of course, at least one old-timer tried to catch the ball with his eyes closed. Today's players, though, believe there is no place in the game for head-hunting. Me? I'm in favor of anything that prevents injury. Certainly the object of the rules today is a good one: to ensure that today's players will retire a-head of the old-timers.

6

RUNNING THE GAME

Growing up, I was not a very good baseball player. My friends would put me in right field, then make a rule that there was no hitting to right field. I compensated when we played football. The first time my team got the ball, for example, I would yell, "Next touchdown wins!" So the one reminder I constantly heard from my friends was "You can't make up your own rules." It took me a long time, but eventually I proved them wrong. I wrote the first significant change in the rules of baseball since the turn of the century.

I was blamed for many things during my career: strikeouts, errors, losses. Earl Weaver claimed I gave him headaches. But the one thing I deserve to be blamed for, I never am. The Luciano Rule, as we call it in my house, or the Designated Hitter Rule, as it is known by everyone who does not live in my house, was written by me and Lou DiMuro in 1972.

The original rules of baseball were amazingly similar to the rules we used when I was growing up: What can you get away with? At various times, for example, a walk was nine balls, eight balls, seven balls, six balls, and five balls—finally becoming four balls in 1889—while a strikeout was four strikes. That obviously was much better for the single umpire, who was positioned behind the pitcher or in foul territory between home and first, because few pitchers would argue over ball seven. A foul ball caught on one bounce used to be an out, and it wasn't until 1888 that a foul tip became a strike. The rule passed in 1887 that prohibited a batter from calling for a high strike zone or a low strike zone was among the last rules ever passed to benefit the pitcher. Of all the early rules of baseball, my personal favorite warned players that anyone "... who shall use profane or improper language shall be fined 6½ cents for each offense." If they hadn't changed that rule it would have cost Ted Williams a buck just to say hello.

But since 1901, when home plate was enlarged from a twelve-inch square to a five-sided slab seventeen inches wide and an ordinary foul ball became a strike, until the Luciano Rule was passed, the only basic changes in the game were scoring rules. Until 1931, for example, a ball going over the outfield fence on one bounce was a home run at which time it became a ground-rule double. A sacrifice fly was not counted as an official time at bat between 1908 and 1930, when official scorers began counting it in batting averages as a time at bat, only to be permanently reinstated as officially not happening in 1954. So now, if you do nothing, like strike out, it counts as a time at bat, but if you do something like hit a fly ball, it doesn't count. I'd like to meet the man who figured that one out. And I defy any currently living human being to explain accurately the evolution of the save rule for relief pitchers. Does a pitcher get credit for a save if he retires the potential tying run but does not finish the game? What if he finishes the game and does not face the potential tying run? What if the potential tying run is on deck with two out when a relief pitcher comes in and picks off a runner—can a relief pitcher get credit for a save without throwing a pitch? And finally, if you lived in Chicago, would you deposit your savings in a branch of the Ernie Banks?

But my rule, the Designated Hitter Rule, remains the only major change in the way the game is played since the American League was founded in 1901. Truthfully, it wasn't totally my idea. In 1929, National League president John A.

Heydler proposed permitting a permanent batter for the pitcher, complaining that "[O]ne of the dullest things in baseball was a team having a good batting rally stopped by the pitcher coming to bat. . . ." The American League called the proposal "damnfoolery," claiming it was "[S]illy, if not stupid." That's my rule.

But just four decades later the Rules Committee, which itself has often been called "silly, if not stupid," allowed four minor leagues to experiment with variations of the rule. The International League had managers designate a player to hit for the pitcher throughout the game. The Eastern League allowed the manager to substitute a hitter for the pitcher anytime in the game; the hitter would then bat whenever the pitcher's spot in the order came up, while the pitcher could stay in the game. The Texas League permitted a player to pinch-hit as often as the manager desired, but for only one man in a particular inning. The New York-Penn League allowed a designated pinch hitter to bat twice in the game without the manager having to remove the player he hit for. Texas League president Bobby Bragan was an ardent supporter of the rule, asking, "Who wants to see the pitcher strike out? When the pitcher comes to home plate, fans do one of two things: They go to the bathroom, or they yawn." Some really wild and crazy Texans, in fact, probably yawned in the bathroom! So the designated hitter became one of the few rules ever passed at least partially to prevent people from going to the bathroom.

Oakland A's owner Charley Finley was certainly a major force behind the adoption of the rule. "I figured you had to balance out the offense and the defense. In football, eleven players play against eleven. In hockey, it's six against six. In basketball, five against five. But in baseball, a player comes to bat and there are nine players ganged out there against him. One against nine. Then the pitcher has four balls and he only has three strikes. And the pitcher is maybe six-four tall and he winds up and by the time he releases the ball he's right in the hitter's eyes. So I decided to even things up: let's put ten players in there against nine. That's even.

"Who needs the pitcher hitting? The average pitcher couldn't hit my grandmother. And the first time I stood up and explained this at an owners' meeting they unanimously asked me to sit down."

The American League finally adopted the use of a designated hitter for the 1973 season. The National League declined, protesting haughtily that it would continue playing the game the way it was supposed to be played, although I don't see them giving the pitcher nine balls.

Once the American League decided to play ball with ten men instead of nine—the question became how the rule would work. This is where I came in. Literally. The league wanted the rule to be written by someone sensitive to the needs of the game, someone with great understanding of the momentous nature of the change, someone who knew the rules. Failing that, they pretty much wanted whoever was hanging around.

Lou DiMuro and I happened to be visiting the league office, which was then in Boston. The league had already decided to add a designated hitter and had managed to boil the rule down to a neat six pages. Their version covered numerous variations: What happened if the pitcher was moved to the outfield? Could you pinch-hit for the DH? What if a manager wanted to put the DH in the game for defense? Dick Butler, then American League supervisor of umpires, asked Lou and me if we could make it a little more concise. That was like asking us to boil down the U.S. Tax Code to, "Give them all your money."

Lou and I sat down and tried to determine what the intent of the rule was. Whatever it had been, we decided what it should be: Screw the manager. The DH gave the manager a tremendous advantage: we didn't see a need to give the manager an even greater advantage. The DH batted for the pitcher. If the pitcher played another position, the DH was out of the game. If the DH entered the game for defense, the team lost its DH. The DH could be replaced by another DH. We reduced the six pages to a single three-by-

five index card. The following spring our three-by-five card
was adopted as the rule.

As with any significant change, my rule was universally
praised. "It'll ruin the game," Richie Allen predicted. Hank
Aaron decided, "When I can't play in the regular lineup, I'll
quit." But the Desis, or Designated Pinch Hitter, as the DH
was originally called, survived.

Originally, batters resented playing—or, I suppose, not
playing—DH, much like pitchers once resented pitching in
relief. Although the DH went into effect too late to help
players like third basemen Hector Lopez, who was described as having bad hands for a human being, it did
benefit numerous older players like Orlando Cepeda, Tommy
Davis, Willie Horton, Hal McRae, Rusty Staub, Carl
Yastrzemski, Frank Robinson, Harmon Killebrew, Tony
Oliva, Reggie Jackson, Dave Kingman . . . and Henry Aaron,
all of whom had their careers extended because of my rule.
But do I get any thanks?

Actually, a lot of baseball people learned to love the
rule. "I'm a runs-batted-in specialist," said DH Cliff Johnson, who had the defensive skills of the Lincoln Tunnel.
"I'm like the chicken man. I do one thing right."

"I wish the National League had it," Cardinals' manager
Whitey Herzog says. "We've got to be the dumbest league
in the whole world. Every other league and the colleges
have the DH. If the National League had a DH rule, Ted
Simmons would have died a Cardinal. Absolutely. We'd
have buried him on the field the next day."

Initially, no one knew how my rule was going to work.
The first designated hitter in major league history to bat
was the Yankees' Ron Blomberg. "I don't know how I'll
make out as a designated hitter," he said before any DH
had ever batted. "I've never done it before." The rule seemed
to have been passed to aid players like Blomberg, who
could hit but could not field. "I learned to hit by picking
berries off a bush in my front yard in Atlanta, throwing
them up, and hitting them with a stick. But I never had
anyone roll the berries to me so I never learned how to

field." In his first DH appearance, Blomberg walked with the bases loaded, forcing in a run.

Naturally, Billy Martin and Earl Weaver had to be the ones to find the loopholes in my rule. It couldn't have been Ralph Houk, who would have pointed them out to me privately, or Gene Mauch, whom no one would have understood anyway. It had to be the only two men who look for the loophole in a weather report. For example, the American League has a rule that states when a player takes a defensive position without the umpire being notified, he becomes an unannounced substitute. We were in Detroit one day and Tiger first baseman Norm Cash broke the webbing of his glove. While he was fixing it, Gates Brown came out to warm up the infielders. Seeing that, Weaver demanded that Brown stay in the game as an unannounced substitute. Billy Haller explained that that was not the intent of the rule and allowed Cash to take his position. Weaver protested the game.

The very next inning Baltimore catcher Rich Dempsey made the final out, and the Orioles' DH, Ken Singleton, came out to warm up the pitcher. Whoosh—Martin came flying out of the dugout. "Singleton's catching!" he whined. "He's catching! He's gotta catch!" So an asterisk was added to the rule, allowing the DH to warm up the pitcher without entering the game.

In 1979 Weaver listed a pitcher as his DH in his starting lineup twenty-one different times, claiming he didn't want to name his real DH because the opposition might change pitchers before the DH came to bat for the first time, forcing him to make a substitution. Once he put Tippy Martinez in the lineup even though Martinez was attending to personal business in Colorado. Now that's a long-distance hitter. Once again the league amended my rule, requiring the DH to bat at least once unless the opposition changed pitchers.

Even after all this time, the rule is still controversial. Dwight Gooden spoke for most National Leaguers when he said, "The DH is a tenth player. Softball is ten guys, baseball is nine." But American Leaguers like Red Sox owner

Haywood Sullivan point out happily that it has served its purpose by increasing the amount of runs scored and enabled older stars to stay in the game. "With the DH," he pointed out, "Ted Williams could probably still be playing."

It was originally used every other year in the All-Star Game and World Series. When Peter Ueberroth was elected commissioner, he stated that he would end the confusion. He conducted a poll of fans, who turned out to be almost equally divided, so Ueberroth came down squarely on both sides of the issue. And there are people who claim Ueberroth had no political ambitions. So now the DH is used every other year in the All-Star Game but used only in the World Series when the American League club is the home team. I like a strong commissioner not afraid to take a courageous stand in the middle.

Surprisingly, with the exception of the DH, the rules governing play on the field have remained remarkably unchanged since the turn of the century. The few changes usually have resulted from some sneaky player—I know that's redundant—trying to take advantage of the rules. In 1925, for example, pitcher Bill Hubbell intentionally walked several batters by going into a stretch and lobbing the ball to first base. Hubbell was accused of making "a travesty of the game," and the rules were changed to force a pitcher to throw toward home plate. In 1955 the Dodgers had the bases loaded, with Jackie Robinson on second base. Roy Campanella hit a routine ground ball to shortstop, a probable double-play ball. Robinson purposely allowed the ball to hit him. He was ruled out, but Campy was safe at first. The umpires agreed that Robinson had intentionally interfered, but that under the rules then in force they could not anticipate a double play, so they had to allow the play. That rule was changed.

The amazing thing is not that there are loopholes in the rules but that the rules effectively cover such an incredibly wide range of possibilities. One of the wonderful things about baseball is that no matter how many games you've seen, it's always possible to go to a game and see something more ridiculous than you've ever seen before. In

1970, for example, the Pirates and Phillies were tied 1–1 in the seventh. The Pirates were batting with one out, runners on first and third. The batter swung at a pitch and missed for strike three, but the ball got away from the catcher. The runner on third scored and the runner on first was thrown out attempting to go to third for the third out. One run for the Pirates. Right?

Wrong. Phillies' manager Frank Lucchesi screamed from the dugout that the batter had struck out. Hearing that, the batter suddenly took off for first base—but the Phillies' third baseman's throw to first beat him. The umpires ruled the runner was out at third for the second out and that the batter was out at first for the third out. So the run didn't count because the third out was made at first base. Right?

Wrong. An inning later, Pirates' manager Danny Murtaugh came out of the dugout carrying the rulebook. The answer was right there. The applicable rule stated that if a catcher misses the third strike, the batter can run to first only if it is unoccupied and there are less than two outs, or if there are two outs. There was one out when the batter struck out. He became the second out. First base was occupied at that time, so he couldn't run. The out at third was therefore the third out, not the out at first. Legally, the out at first was like a sacrifice fly—it never happened. And because the out at third was the third out, the run counts, right?

Right. It is in the rulebook, although it isn't explained quite that clearly.

Umpires do make an occasional mistake. For example, Big John McSherry, certainly one of the best umpires ever to grace the big leagues, once called an infield fly that didn't exist. "The Mets were playing the Braves," he recalls. "With runners on first and second, a pitch got past Mets' catcher Jerry Grote, allowing each runner to advance a base. The next batter hit a high pop-up, and shortstop Buddy Harrelson circled under it. I called an infield fly, which is applicable when there are runners on first and second, or the bases are loaded, and there are less than two outs. My call meant that the batter-runner was out and runners could advance at their own risk.

"Except there no longer was a runner on first base, so the rule no longer applied. I didn't even hesitate. I immediately started screaming, 'Come onnn, Buddy, catch that ball!' "

Since the rulebook was written it probably has been the basis of more discussions than any other book except the Bible. For example, can there be four legal outs in an inning? It's in the book. And it has happened on the field. Almost. Doug Harvey was working home plate during the 1976 National League play-offs. The Phillies had runners on first and third with one out. The batter hit a line drive to right field. "I saw the umpire at first base signal that the ball had been caught, and an instant later the runner from third whizzed by me. There is no way that that man could have tagged up and scored, so it was obvious to me that he thought the ball had landed safely. The runner at first base also thought the ball was going to drop, so he had taken off for second. When he saw the umpire signal that it had been caught, he tried to get back to first. The outfielder's throw beat him there for the third out. The teams began changing sides.

"The rulebook allows a team to appeal until the next pitch is made or all infielders cross the foul line. The Phillies could have made an appeal play at third base even after the third out had been made. That would have been a legal fourth out, and the run would not have counted."

Once, in an American League game, there was a runner on first base with one out. The batter swung and missed for strike three, but the pitch sailed over the catcher's head and lodged firmly in the umpire's mask. The batter, having just struck out, was awarded first base, and the base runner was advanced to second. It's in the rulebook. Why? Don't ask me, it's not *my* rule. *My* rule is a wonderfully, clearly written rule. But it's there.

Although most of the written rules haven't changed, the unwritten interpretations of some of those rules have. According to the rulebook, for example, for a batter-runner to be called out in a force situation, an infielder must be in contact with the base when he receives the ball. At one time that rule was enforced. But to prevent injury, first basemen and second basemen have been permitted to "cheat," or take their foot off the base an instant before actually catching the ball. The only people who could possibly disagree with that interpretation are the orthopedic surgeons who undoubtedly have lost business.

And certainly the size of the strike zone has changed. The strike zone has decreased in inverse proportion to my weight—as I've gotten larger, it's gotten smaller. So I hereby issue a warning: Unless something is done soon to change this, eventually there will be no strike zone at all. Almost everything in baseball has increased—the size of the players, the size of their gloves, the capacity of the ballparks, the length of a game, the price of admission—everything except the size of the strike zone. Only the strike zone got smaller. The rules once defined a strike as a pitch crossing home plate between the batter's knees and his shoulders. And at one point that is the way it was called. Then the rules were changed and a strike became any pitch crossing the plate between the uniform letters and the knees. The problem with that was that a lot of teams didn't have uniform letters—the Cubs had a logo, for instance. And the rule didn't say from the logo, it said from the letters. So they had to change it again, and in 1968 the strike zone was defined as stretching from the batter's armpits to his knees.

To help us enforce the rule, the rules committee sent us sketches of a player batting, showing us where the strike zone would be on a player standing upright at the plate. The problem was that these sketches were probably done by a police artist who did composites. In reality, no player stood upright at the plate, they all crouched, and the sketches didn't have them crouching.

Legally, the strike zone is still from the armpits to the knees—legally in baseball terminology, that is, as no one has ever gone to jail for calling a pitch at armpit level a ball. But gradually umpires have reinterpreted the meaning of armpits. It's a wonderful job. In what other profession do you have to contemplate the meaning of armpits?

Eventually a strike became a pitch crossing the plate between midchest and lower thigh. Early Wynn once complained that the strike zone had "[s]hrunk like a cheap shirt in a Chinese laundry." And the strike zone he was complaining about was a bit larger than Australia. Until the end of the 1987 season, the strike zone could be found somewhere between the bottom of the player's belt and the top of the player's belt. And a lot of players don't wear belts. I mean, when a player went into a crouch, that thing was hard to find. How hard? Ricky Henderson's strike zone is lower than Earl Weaver. How small? The strike zone is smaller than the twenty-five-dollar entree at a restaurant serving *nouvelle cuisine*. How narrow? The strike zone is even narrower than my handpainted "Visit Florida" neckties. Only on players batting on all fours would it be from the armpits to the knees.

To enlarge the strike zone, prior to the opening of the 1988 season the Rules Committee officially made it smaller. Baseball's new, improved, economy-sized strike zone was defined as "that area over home plate, the upper limit of which is a horizontal line at the midpoint between the top of the shoulders and the top of the uniform pants, and the lower level is a line at the top of the knees." This smaller strike zone means umpires will be calling more strikes because, although baseball now has "high fives," the most recent interpretation of the strike zone has meant there were few high strikes. That will change now, although, as Frank Robinson pointed out, "regardless of any new definition, a strike is what the umpire says it is."

As far as I was concerned, the strike zone was the same when I retired in 1980 as it had been when I first came up to the big leagues, in 1968, just like my bank account. Every umpire knows when a pitch is a strike. A pitch is a strike when he calls it a strike.

In fact, the strike zone has always varied from umpire to umpire. I simply couldn't bend down as low as little Richie Garcia, so the top of my strike zone was higher than his. It used to be said that umpire Ed Runge's strike zone stretched from dugout to dugout, because Runge wanted

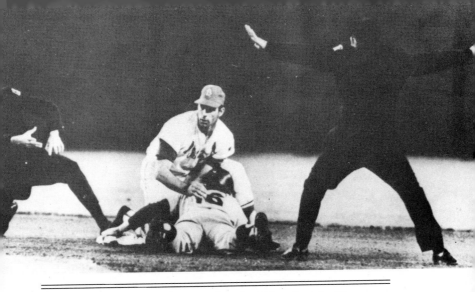

Boxing has split decisions—why shouldn't baseball?
Here, John Kibler calls base runner Bill Sudakis out while
Ed Vargo signals safe. Having seen the replay, I agree
with everybody.   WIDE WORLD

Before the invention of the radar gun, an army
chronograph was used to measure the speed of a fastball.
The pitcher had to throw the ball through the device,
making it difficult for the batter to hit it. Here, Bob
Feller's blows away Atley Donald's world record by
throwing his fastball 98.6 mph.   WIDE WORLD

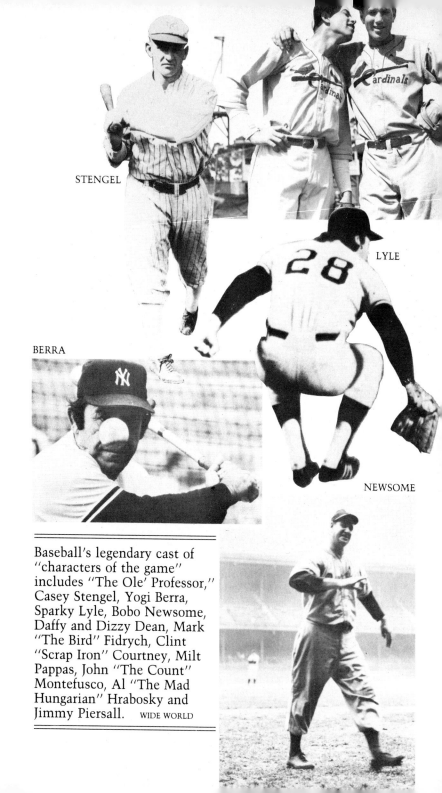

STENGEL

LYLE

BERRA

NEWSOME

Baseball's legendary cast of
"characters of the game"
includes "The Ole' Professor,"
Casey Stengel, Yogi Berra,
Sparky Lyle, Bobo Newsome,
Daffy and Dizzy Dean, Mark
"The Bird" Fidrych, Clint
"Scrap Iron" Courtney, Milt
Pappas, John "The Count"
Montefusco, Al "The Mad
Hungarian" Hrabosky and
Jimmy Piersall.   WIDE WORLD

◁DAFFY AND DIZZY DEAN (DIZZY AT RIGHT)

MARK FIDRYCH

CLINT COURTNEY

MILT PAPPAS

HRABOSKY

JOHN MONTEFUSCO

PIERSALL

Before free agency, players were forced to accept
almost any salary offered by their team. Here, young
Minnie Minoso reacts after receiving his new
contract from the White Sox. The Yankees told Bill
Skowron he couldn't have much money, but he
could keep all the dirt he could eat. After free
agency, salaries escalated into the millions—as
illustrated by Tug McGraw's celebrating after signing
his new deal with the Phillies. WIDE WORLD

MCGRAW

SKOWRON

MINOSO

ELECTRONIC HELMET

SOLARIZED GLOVE

ELECTRONIC GLOVE

CONVERTIBLE HELMET

Equipment of the future includes the electronic glove that enables the catcher or manager or computer to call pitches without signals, a glove with a solarized webbing to eliminate the need for sunglasses, a batting helmet with a built-in sound system enabling the batter to hear the manager or Bruce Springsteen from the bench and the "Bo Jackson Helmet," modeled by Dave Parker, enabling Bo to move between baseball and football without changing headgear. WIDE WORLD

HUMMER

IRON MIKE

WILHELM

Here are three basic types of pitching machines, each able to throw all day, every day, without rest. The popular "Iron Mike" (shown throwing a beanball), the more modern 'Hummer' and the ancient Hoyt Wilhelm, who pitched in more games than anyone in big league history. In this photo Wilhelm is searched by Ghostbusters, who then try to rid mound of the evil spirits that made his pitches move so erratically.   WIDE WORLD

As Ty Cobb proved, baserunning is not that complicated. Even Babe Ruth once stole home against the St. Louis Browns. Until Maury Wills arrived, however, the Dodgers seemed to have problems with the concept, one runner on one base at one time. The Brooklyn Dodgers once had three runners on third at the same time. Here, Jackie Robinson has escaped from a rundown to return safely to third, only to find Carl Furillo waiting there. Unfortunately, Furillo was not there to congratulate him. Proving a move to Los Angeles did nothing to improve baserunning skills, Charley Neal gets back to third and finds recent arrival Frank Howard camped there. WIDE WORLD

TY COBB

BABE RUTH

ROBINSON AND FURILLO

NEAL AND HOWARD

After discovering that artificial turf caused balls to bounce unusually high and often heated up to temperatures above 100°, baseball experimented with something called "natural turf," or "grass," on which balls bounced normally and heat was partially absorbed. However, this "grass" could be ripped and torn and proved to be inferior to man-made surfaces. WIDE WORLD batters up there swinging. Runge was the home plate umpire in the 1967 All-Star Game, when a record twenty-nine batters struck out. Before each game Lee Wyre works at home plate, he uncovers the black border around the plate to increase its width. There are only two things that a player asks from the home plate umpire: first, that he establish what pitches will be called strikes and be consistent throughout the game; and two, that he call everything his way.

The American League actually used to have a larger strike zone than the National League because its umpires used the outside balloon chest protector and couldn't bend down as low, but since the American League adopted the inside protector, its strike zone has become smaller. Ironically, the smaller strike zone hasn't substantially increased the number of walks. By reducing the size, pitchers have been forced to throw more pitches into the batter's hitting area, so batters are swinging at more pitches.

Although the rules governing play on the field are basically the same as they have been since Babe Ruth was a pitcher, other rules of baseball have been changed. For example, games called because of poor weather still become official after the team that is trailing has at least five complete at bats, but until recently the score always reverted to the last inning completed before the umpires stopped play. That meant that any runs scored in an uncompleted inning didn't count. Now, if a team ties the score or goes ahead before the game is called and the inning is not completed, the game is suspended and must eventually be finished from that point. I'm sure I think that's the way the rule presently reads.

Every umpire was in favor of that change. There are few things as irritating as watching a manager who is sitting warm and dry in the dugout, stalling while you have to stand outside in the rain. The old rule encouraged managers to change pitchers, pinch-hit, have conversations on the mound, signal for pick-off attempts, serve dinner, and start arguments. Prolonged arguments. The subject matter was always the same: How much rain is too much rain? The definition of enough rain depended on the score. Ducks might be floating around second base, but the manager of the trailing team would complain we were trying to get him. But when that same manager's team was winning, he wanted us to call the game when someone used the water fountain. Even today, when I'm taking a shower, I expect to hear some manager screaming at me that it isn't really wet.

I hated working in a rainstorm. It's my philosophy that the only people supposed to work in the rain are grounds-keepers and umbrella salesmen.

There are several things I don't understand about base-ball besides the fact that a player can hit a fly ball and not be charged with a time at bat, but a player who misses the ball is. For example: It wasn't until protective batting hel-mets became mandatory that baseball outlawed the knock-down pitch. A batted ball that lodges in the roof of a domed stadium is called a ground-rule double when it should be called a roof-rule double. And in the days before lights were installed, day games would often start at three-thirty in the afternoon so people could attend after work, while today, with lights available, day games usually start at one-thirty.

Except for electrical blackouts and games played in Chi-cago's Wrigley Field, ball games no longer are called on account of darkness. Umpires in the old days often had to determine the difference between daylight and no light. The accepted rule was to use their own judgment, although the major leagues once investigated using a photographer's exposure meter and setting arbitrary standards.

Night baseball certainly is one of the significant changes in modern baseball, and naturally baseball officials imme-diately saw its benefits. "There is no chance night baseball will become popular in the major leagues," Washington Senators' owner Clark Griffith stated flatly in 1935. "The game was meant to be played in the Lord's own sunshine." That year the Cincinnati Reds had paid General Electric $50,000 to install lights, and the National League permit-ted them to play seven night games. Any more than that, it was felt, would be disastrous. The American League re-jected the concept of night baseball, calling it "bush."

The first night game was played under artificial lighting

in 1883 and minor league teams began playing regularly scheduled night games in 1930. In 1932 the Cardinals had drawn ten thousand fans for a night exhibition game against the bearded barnstorming team, the House of David, featuring pitcher Grover Cleveland Alexander. But people took such a dim view of night baseball that Hall of Fame umpire Bill Klem refused to commit himself to work the plate during the first official night game until the lights had been turned on and he had an opportunity to see what he could see. Only after President Roosevelt had thrown a switch in Washington to turn on the lights in Cincinnati (that must have been some long extension cord!) did Klem agree to work the game.

Night games were such an immediate success that it would take only thirty-five years for baseball to begin playing most World Series games at night, when baseball fans were at home to watch them.

Baseball's dark ages ended in 1947. The Red Sox and Tigers became the final big league teams to install lights, with the exception of the Cubs, and games no longer had to be called on account of darkness. Except once in a while. In Washington one night George Kell was at bat when the lights suddenly went out. "The count was two-and-two and the pitcher was in his windup when they went out," Kell recalled. "I quickly dived into the dirt. I must have laid there for a minute. Then I began to feel foolish and started to get up. Just as I did, the lights came on again. It was quite a sight. Every outfielder and infielder, even the catcher, was flat on the ground. The only player standing was the pitcher—of course, he was also the only player who knew who had the baseball."

Although the rules of play have remained relatively stable, the business rules of baseball have been changed more frequently than Wilt Chamberlain has threatened to come out of retirement. For many baseball fans, for example, the brief interleague trading period, when American League teams could make trades with National League teams, was the highlight of the winter Hot Stove League. Of course, these are probably the same people who plan months in advance to attend the big Arbor Day parade. And, for a while, I was fascinated by the concept of putting players on waivers—

I thought they were putting players on wafers. Alas, those days of high adventure, those sleepless nights wondering if a certain player would "clear waivers," have ended. Baseball has pretty much adopted the business rules of Wall Street: We can do anything we want anytime we want to do it.

"We've had so many rule changes that we can't keep track of it ourselves," Mets' brilliant vice-president Joe McIlwayne explained. "We have to have a resident expert on the rules. The waiver period is a classic example of how confusing it has gotten. Twice we've gone ahead and done something and we didn't know we had to have waivers on the players to do it. They've changed the waiver period. There are three waiver periods in the season now, so if you're gonna get waivers on somebody to do something, you got to have it three different times during the year. The dates used to be June 15; now it's August 1. Then there's the waiver period at the end of the season; then another one comes. Then December 10, I think, is a cutoff, or when another period begins."

It seems to me that what McIlwayne is really trying to explain is that the interleague trading period, which used to be only from January to December on days ending in "y," is now all year, unless it has been changed, assuming the player has a valid contract and does not have a no-trade clause and his agent agrees to the trade and the other club is willing to pick up a portion of the long-term contract.

The best thing about these rules is that nobody knows what they are, which is why they work so well. As long as nobody knows them, nobody can complain that another team has broken them, which is why those rules will continue to be enforced. Only when somebody tries to understand them will there be problems. "One man really can't control the whole thing anymore," McIlwayne points out.

Although the rules by which the game is played haven't changed significantly, the way the game is played has: The game is now played on plastic, by ten men, who are hitting a ball that should be banned under the disarmament agreement covering medium-range missiles. Rosters have been reduced to twenty-four players, starting pitchers throw complete games about as often as Rocky Balboa loses a fight, and home runs are about as rare as a cold day in December in International Falls, Minnesota. These changes, as well as numerous others, have forced managers to use more different strategies than ever before.

Once there was something known as *The Book*. *The Book* didn't actually exist, but managers always played the game by it. This book that didn't exist contained the entire body of baseball wisdom and strategy that had been gleaned over decades of seasons. Managers followed it religiously, because it informed them in what situations it was proper to bunt, hit and run, steal, and change pitchers. A good manager always went by *The Book*, which was subtitled, *How to Play Inside Baseball*. There was a good reason for this. More than anything else, *The Book* had one significant purpose: It helped managers keep their jobs. As long as they managed "by *The Book*," the players could be blamed for failure. Only when a manager went against *The Book*, and his strategy failed, was it his fault.

The guiding principles enumerated in *The Book* were: Play for one run at a time, never embarrass the other team by padding a large lead, never bunt in the ninth inning to tie a game if you're the visiting team, never pinch-hit for a starting layer before the seventh inning, never intentionally walk the batter who becomes the potential leading run, and put your best eight regular players on the field every day.

The Book has been completely revised. Managers now use two players where they used to use one, even though they have fewer players on the roster. Basestealing has once again become an important part of the game. And inside baseball—playing for one run—no longer exists. Remember bunting? Remember when a Cadillac cost forty-five hundred dollars?

The fundamental principle of baseball today, the source of all managerial decisions, the very nucleus of strategy, is that players batting from the side of the plate opposite the arm with which the pitcher throws will do better than batters hitting from the same side. Managers will do almost anything to gain the statistical advantage in the continuing battle of lefty vs. righty.

A perfect example took place in 1983. The Expos' Bryan Little, a switch-hitter, was batting against the Giants' right-handed pitcher Fred Breining with a runner on first in a late inning of a close game. Breining's first two pitches were balls. Giants' manager Frank Robinson then brought in left-handed relief pitcher Gary Lavelle to face Little. Little, who had been batting left-handed, turned around and batted right-handed against Lavelle. Little tried to bunt twice and fouled off both pitches. Montreal manager Bill Virdon sent in Jim Wohlford to pinch-hit for Little. Wohlford flew out.

That's more specialists for one at-bat than are found in a doctors' country club. Two batters and two pitchers for one fly-out? A lot of batters could have done that against one pitcher.

Using right-handed or left-handed batters based on who is pitching for the other team is known as platooning. Platooning is best described as the science of dividing one position between two players. Once there were two types of major league players: the regulars, who were in the starting lineup every day, no matter who was pitching for the other team; and the substitutes, or "scrubs." The job of the scrubs was to be ready to play in case of injury or earthquake. Other than that, they were rarely used. Originally, second-string players were derisively called "muffins," and they were often so bad that misplayed balls became "muffs."

Casey Stengel is given credit for popularizing platooning as manager of the Yankees from the late 1940s until 1960. Casey won ten pennants and seven World Championships in twelve seasons, supposedly by juggling his lineup. During the 1953 season, for example, he used 101 different starting lineups. But the reality is that in 1953, and in most of those seasons, the Yankees had so much more talent than their American League rivals that it didn't matter who played. It was like having to choose between gold and diamonds. Other teams, seeing how successful the Yankees were, tried to emulate them. Unfortunately, in many instances, these teams were limited to choosing between soup and water.

Casey may have popularized it, but he certainly didn't invent it. In 1889 Pittsburgh player-manager "Foxy Ned" Hanlon, a left-handed batter, substituted a right-handed hitter for himself when the opposing pitcher threw with his left, or "fork" hand, and platooning was born. A true

platoon system was first installed in 1914 by George Stall-
ings, manager of the "Miracle Braves," who used what
became known as "interchangeable outfields" depending on
who was pitching against his team. In 1920 Cleveland
Indians' manager Tris Speaker was severely criticized for
platooning players at three positions en route to winning
the World Championship. Some sportswriters warned that
Speaker's "constant substitution of players . . . is unwise and
has gone to such lengths that it has become an abuse which
threatens the popularity of the game and the impairment
of its dignity." And I thought Howard Cosell was tough.

Platooning eventually became so prevalent that American League president Ban Johnson supposedly considered a
rule to limit the number of substitutions, finally deciding
against it. But Speaker continued to be ridiculed for his use
of the strategy. "Speaker is looking for a second trainer," a
Detroit News columnist wrote. "The guy who is doing the
work now is a right-hander and he does very well with the
left-handers on the club, but the right-handers are suffering
and Speaker will have to get a left-handed trainer for them.

"Cleveland has two groundskeepers of equal ranking.
One is a right-hander and the other pulls dandelions with
his left hand. The ticket-sellers and ticket-takers work in
relays, right-handers on Mondays, Wednesdays, and Fri-
days, and left-handers on other days.

"Cleveland fans are also carefully arranged. The right-
handed bottle-throwers are on the right side of the field. . . .
Playing baseball in Cleveland is a cinch. A player works
only half-time and gets paid for full-time."

Platooning probably reached its zenith in the seventh
game of the 1924 World Series, when Washington Senators'
manager Bucky Harris started a right-handed pitcher, forcing New York Giants' manager John McGraw to use his
left-handed lineup. Harris removed his starter after he had
faced one batter and brought in the left-hander he'd secretly been warming up. This was considered either brilliant strategy or terribly unsporting, depending on which
team you were rooting for.

Only forty years later, many baseball purists were still
against platooning. "I don't like this business," Pirates'

manager Danny Murtaugh said before winning the World Championship in 1960. "I believe I should go with my best players every day because when you platoon you substitute the second-best."

Tigers' manager Bill Norman agreed, explaining, "I put up my lineup in the dugout and that's it."

Most managers followed the lead of the Dodgers' Walter Alston. Throughout the 1950s he played the same lineup almost every day. Of course, that lineup included Roy Campanella, Gil Hodges, Jackie Robinson, Pee Wee Reese, Carl Furillo, Duke Snider, and Jim Gilliam. But as those players retired Alston began platooning. When the Dodgers failed to win the pennant in 1961, critics blamed Alston for his platooning. "Just give me another Campy, Robinson, and Pee Wee," he responded, and "I'll play them every day."

Gradually every manager started platooning. The reason was simple: to keep his job. If a left-handed batter fails to hit against a right-handed pitcher, it's the player's fault; but if a manager had played the same left-hander against a left-handed pitcher, it became his fault. Managers still claimed to like a set lineup; in fact, they claimed they liked it so much they had two of them: one when right-handers were pitching and another when left-handers were pitching.

Unlike most people, who would love the opportunity to play half the time and make just as much money, most players hated being platooned. "I had played every day with the Yankees," right-handed hitter Bill Skowron remembers, "but I eventually ended up with the White Sox playing only against left-handed pitchers. The problem was that I could always hit right-handers better. Left-handers started jamming me with that slider inside and I thought, 'Gees, please gimme those right-handers.'

"I finally went to see the manager, Eddie Stanky, and said, 'I want to play. I don't want to sit on the bench. Believe me, when I can't play, I'll be the first to know it.'

" 'Moose,' Stanky said, 'who I play is my prerogative.'

"I said, 'I don't even know what the hell that word means, but if it means I'm not going to play, I'd like to get traded.' So it was because of platooning that I learned a new word and got traded to California."

One of the complaints most often heard about platooning is that it damages the confidence of young players. Stengel, for example, supposedly destroyed Clete Boyer by pinch-hitting for him when the opposition changed pitchers very early in the game on several occasions. In fact, he hurt Boyer so badly that Clete was able to play only sixteen seasons in the big leagues. Fred Lynn was platooned his first big league season, "and I didn't like it too much. The first game I ever started was in Milwaukee. I hit a home run my first time up, a double the next time, and the third time I came to bat, Manager Darrell Johnson took me out for a pinch hitter. I thought, 'This is some tough league.' "

Unlike Lynn, though, who became a regular, some players spent their entire careers being platooned. Left-handed hitter Art Shamsky, for instance, had more chance of batting against Bigfoot than a left-handed pitcher. "Somewhere along the line, some scout in the stands makes a judgment on you which affects your whole career. He puts a label on you and that's it. My label was that I was a platoon player.

"I had played every day in the minor leagues, but when I came up with Cincinnati they had Vada Pinson, Frank Robinson, and Deron Johnson starting in the outfield, and Pete Rose played a little out there, so I could understand not playing every game. I hit left-handed, so I played mostly when right-handers were pitching. Well, because I only played against right-handers, people began to believe I couldn't hit left-handers. Of course I couldn't hit them: I never batted against them. It was ridiculous. I didn't play against them, so people believed I couldn't hit them; because people believed I couldn't hit them, I never got to play against them.

"Once I hit four consecutive home runs over two games: one in my last at-bat one day, and three more in my three at-bats the next day. The Hall of Fame called and wanted my bat. They told me if I hit five in a row they wanted my uniform, my locker. I don't know what they would have wanted if I had hit six in a row. Anyway, I'd hit four consecutive home runs, and the next day I was benched because the Dodgers were starting a left-handed pitcher.

"I just . . . I really couldn't believe it. Dave Bristol was the manager. 'Dave,' I said, 'I can't believe I'm not playing.'

"He explained it quite clearly: 'Well, they got a left-hander pitching.' I pointed out that one of the three home runs I'd hit the previous game had been against a left-hander. It didn't matter. That label was stuck on me and there was nothing I could do about it.

"A few years later I was with the Mets, platooning in right field with Ron Swoboda. One day we were playing the Cubs in Wrigley Field. I was three-for-three, I had a home run, a double, and a single with four runs batted in, and the wind was really blowing out. The game was tied in the eighth inning when I came to bat, and the Cubs brought in a left-hander. Our manager, Gil Hodges, took me out for a pinch hitter. Three-for-three and he pinch-hit for me. No way. I went back into the locker room and I can remember sitting there with my hands on my knees and thinking, 'What am I doing? I'm never gonna have any pride in my ability because they've taken it away from me. I'm never gonna make any real money because I'm never gonna get a chance to put any real numbers up.' I began to think I was wasting my time.

"I was thirty years old when I retired after the 1972 season. I think I probably could have played a few more seasons, but they just took the fun out of it for me."

Platooning has made a roster consisting of regulars, pitchers, and scrubs outmoded. A roster is now made up of regulars; platoon players; utility players who can play several positions—none of them well enough to play regularly; pitchers; relief pitchers; and role players. Role players are the scrubs of yesteryear. In the old days, for example, defensive replacements inserted into the game in late innings were known as "caddies," players who "picked up" the last few innings for the stars. "Caddy" was sort of a demeaning word. Caddies drove Fords. Today they are role players.

Role players are defensive replacements, third-string catchers, pinch runners, and decoys. Role players are very important. There are twenty-four players on a major league roster, and if you didn't have role players, you'd probably have only twenty-three or twenty-two players.

The defensive response to platooning is the relief pitcher. If one manager's lineup is loaded with right-handed batters, when the other manager has to bring in a reliever, he will undoubtedly use a right-hander, forcing the manager of the first team to respond by substituting his left-handed batters, in which case the manager of the second team will try to put a left-handed reliever in the game as soon as possible.

The only thing that prevents this strategy from continuing into eternity is the player limit and the rule stating that when a pitcher is brought into the game he must face at least one batter. So quite often, late in the game, the manager of the team at bat sends a decoy up to bat. The decoy is a role player, whose primary skill is that he bats from the opposite side of the plate than the arm with which the pitcher is throwing. His job is to come out of the dugout, swing weighted bats over his head cleverly enough to make it appear that he actually is going to hit, and be announced into the game. The manager of the defensive team responds to the decoy by bringing in a pitcher who throws from the same side, forcing the first manager to pinch-hit for the pinch hitter. The first pinch hitter officially has played in the game, although he never actually came to bat or played in the field. If that's playing, I hereby claim I've dated Linda Evans, although I've never actually met her or spoken to her.

In this era of specialization, the decoy is the ultimate specialist: He does nothing. So here is my question: If the decoy's mother asks him, "Did you play yesterday?" what is the correct answer? And how does a player prepare to be a decoy? How many seasons must a player spend in the minors practicing to look like he's coming up to bat before he's ready not to play in the big leagues?

Coinciding with the acceptance of platooning has been a reliance by managers on statistics. To know which lineup to use, a manager must know how a player performs in specific situations. Statistics once consisted of "What'd he hit last year?" The statistics available to a manager today can tell him how a particular player hits against left-handed pitchers in day games following night games with runners in scoring position after the seventh inning when the temperature is seventy or above. In fact, about the only statistic not readily available is how many different statistics are kept.

The Brooklyn Dodgers' Branch Rickey probably was the first executive to recognize the value of performance records. In 1947 he hired baseball's first club statistician to keep track of stats no one had bothered compiling before— for example, how many pitches a pitcher threw during a game, or what percentage of base stealers a catcher throws out during a season.

In 1954 Rickey ushered baseball into the computer age— well, actually in this case it was the adding machine age. "An electronic calculator was fed a wealth of baseball statistics today," IBM boldly announced, "and when it had digested them a few seconds later, it came up with the names of the fifty top offensive stars in the National League last season, based on their ability to get on base and to score." Compared to what statistics are now available, this was similar to launching the space age by letting the air out of a balloon.

Rickey used the calculator to figure out a new statistic he called "on-base average." Rickey believed that "A player's ability to get on base, whether it be by getting a hit, being walked, or being hit by a pitch, and his power to hit for the extra base, are important considerations in evaluating his effectiveness." According to IBM's Type 650 Magnetic Drum Data Processing Machine, the top five offensive players in the National League in 1954 were Willie Mays, Duke Snider, Eddie Mathews, Stan Musial, and Ted Kluszewski. Wow! Who would have guessed? Imagine who Rickey might have come up with if he didn't have IBM.

As platooning became more popular, managers began to rely on statistics more and more. By 1961, for example,

Dodgers' manager Walter Alston was constantly referring to two sets of index cards during games. The blue set told him how well each Dodger had hit against the opponent's pitcher in 1959, 1960, and lifetime. The red set told him how well the opponent's batters performed against the Dodger pitchers.

Among the most significant advances in the use of statistics since then has been a change in the colors of the index cards. Earl Weaver, for example, used white cards.

Baseball, as in almost every other area, has only reluctantly accepted the importance of statistics. In 1975 the Elias Sports Bureau, baseball's official recordkeeper, began marketing reports that analyzed every player's performance: how he performed against other teams, how he did against specific pitchers or batters, and how he did in specific situations. These reports showed, for instance, the chances of Dave Winfield hitting safely while facing a left-handed pitcher with a runner on second base. Seems to me that this is potentially important information. It was the first time this information was compiled for every player in baseball. And the reaction from the clubs was unanimous: Not one team wanted it.

Certain managers, though, have long recognized the value of statistics. "I never played for a manager who relied on them," Whitey Herzog, one of baseball's most successful managers, says. "When I was playing, Cleveland had two great relief pitchers: Ray Narleski, a right-hander, and Don Mossi, a left-hander. I was a left-handed hitter, but for some reason I could always hit Mossi and I couldn't hit Narleski. It was amazing. But none of my managers figured that out. Invariably I'd go up to bat against Narleski, Cleveland would bring in Mossi, and the manager would pinch-hit for me. Well, goddamn, if they'd kept any kind of stats, they would have known I could hit him. Maybe there were seventy-six other guys in the league I couldn't hit. But if they'd kept stats they'd have known I could hit Mossi."

As a manager, Herzog rarely relies on computerized statistics. "I got them in my head," he explains. "Ask me about anybody in the National League, I'll tell you where he hits the ball or how he matches up against my pitchers. I'm not against computers, we use them to keep a running tab of the players, but if I just look at a computerized sheet I'm not going to absorb as much information as I will if I do the charts myself. Every day, after every game I've ever managed, I've done a master chart of every pitch, where it was, and what happened. So I'll get some idea of what my players are capable of doing."

Herzog neglects to mention that he does those charts from memory. Cardinals' broadcaster Mike Shannon claims Herzog has the best memory of anyone in baseball. "What he sees on the field he does not forget. Ask him about a game in 1963 and he'll tell you the weather, the count on the batter, the pitch he hit, and where it landed."

It's sort of amazing. Whitey Herzog remembers a pitch in the second inning of a game twenty years ago. I have to make a list to remind myself to put gas in the car. That's not fair. When I was working, the biggest problem I had was remembering the count. I learned early not to rely on the scoreboard, which was usually wrong. Sometimes, if a pitch was fouled off, I'd forget to click my hand counter. Inevitably, every time that happened, a pitch later the batter would ask me for the count and I'd have to take a vote. The catcher would tell me, " 'Member? He fouled off the second pitch." The second pitch? I couldn't remember the last pitch.

Earl Weaver always relied heavily on statistics. "When Weaver came back to manage the Orioles in 1985," Steve Hirdt of the Elias Sports Bureau and one of the authors of the *Baseball Analyst* remembers, "the O's public-relations director called me and said, 'Weaver came in today. The first thing he said was hello, and the next thing he said was call Steve Hirdt and get the up-to-date batter-pitcher statistics."

Weaver and his little cards used to drive us crazy. Two out in the ninth inning, the tying run on second, he would send up the batboy to hit. Everybody in the ballpark knew it was a ridiculous move. But the batboy would get a hit. Either Weaver was the luckiest man I've ever known or one of the best managers. And if he was really that lucky, he wouldn't have had me in his life.

Some managers don't need statistics to know how their players perform. "One of the things we were wondering about one day in 1985," Steve Hirdt said, "was which batters make most of their outs on ground balls and which batters flew out the most." (I myself rarely wonder about such things, but that's what those wacky guys at the Elias Sports Bureau do.) "So we programmed every single at-bat in the major leagues since 1975," Hirdt continued. "It was an extensive project. We created a program and finally ran it, and we discovered that the Mets' Wally Backman had made more outs on grounders than anyone else and Cincinnati's Gary Redus had flown out more than anyone else.

"Sometime later I was talking to [Reds' manager] Pete Rose. When you're talking to Pete it does not take long for the subject to get around to stats. I told him about our project and then asked him if he could guess who, of everybody who'd played in the big leagues the previous ten years, had made the most outs on fly balls.

"He thought for a minute, then asked, 'Is he a regular?' I told him that the minimum we'd used was a thousand at-bats. 'Oh, okay,' he said, 'Gary Redus.'

"I was astonished. He knew it from observation. I felt like I was the first person to land on the moon and I'd opened the door and found some old beer cans lying around."

Can managers count on statistics? Some managers I knew couldn't count on their fingers. Obviously, some statistics have more meaning than others. For example, it would be accurate to say that during my first year in the big leagues, 5 percent of all American League umpires were named Ron Luciano. It would also be accurate to say that I worked games in which less than half of 1 percent of all the decisions I made were wrong—of course, that doesn't tell you that all of the decisions I got right were on balls and strikes and the only one I got wrong was calling the winning run safe at home plate.

The difficulty in using statistics is knowing when to

use them. Unfortunately, no statistics enable a manager to make that decision. For example, in 1986, the Angels were one strike away from winning the American League Playoffs. Reliever Donny Moore was pitching for California and Dave Henderson was batting for the Red Sox. Henderson had been terrible in clutch situations, or "late-inning pressure situations," as they are now called, most of the year. Something like one hit in thirteen at-bats. Obviously, Boston manager John McNamara should have pinch-hit for him. But in an eerily similar situation a year earlier, Henderson had been playing for the Mariners and had hit a game-winning home run off Moore. So perhaps Angels' manager Gene Mauch should have replaced Moore.

Neither manager made a move. Once again, Henderson hit a game-winning home run off Moore.

Sometimes the numbers collide. With the score tied in the ninth inning, Mets' reliever Jesse Orosco, who had pitched almost three seasons without giving up an extra-base hit to a left-handed batter, was facing the Padres' Tony Gwynn, statistically one of the best clutch hitters in the game. Which statistic prevails? If you were the manager, what would you have done? Besides get a drink of water. Walk Gwynn? Pitch to him?

Gwynn hit a game-winning home run.

And sometimes statistics are not reliable, although there also are no statistics to determine how often that happens. In fourteen career at-bats, for example, Terry Pendleton had never gotten a hit off Orosco. But in a clutch situation early in 1987, Whitey Herzog let him bat. Pendleton's clutch hit led to the game-winning rally.

I think if I were Orosco, I'd throw out my computer.

"Some people believe a manager should be a slave to statistics," Steve Hirdt explains. "I'm not one of them. They are a factor and should be considered along with such things as what will it do to a player's psychology if I bench him against a particular pitcher? Will it tell him I have no faith in him? Is winning this game so important that I might damage a player for weeks? Is the player on a hit streak? Is he slumping?"

Mets' manager Davey Johnson has an extensive knowledge of computers but claims that before he makes any managerial decision "I try to figure out what [broadcaster] Tim McCarver is saying, then I do it."

Baseball is really just beginning to understand how to make use of advanced technology, like computers and fax machines, both on the field and in running team business. Front offices are just now beginning to explore the possibilities. Personally, I've always been intrigued by computers. When I opened my sporting goods store in Endicott, New York, for example, I put my entire inventory on a spreadsheet. It was a tremendous help: By pressing a few buttons I could determine how many blue sweat suits we had in stock, how many indoor shot puts we'd sold in the past month, how many canoe oars we had on order. My computer was so helpful, in fact, that when the store went out of business, I knew within minutes how much money I'd lost.

The introduction of the livelier ball in 1920 was as important to baseball as the invention of brakes was to the automobile industry. That season the New York Yankees became the first team in baseball history to have more home runs than stolen bases, initiating a fundamental change in the way the game was played. Until that year it was about as easy to score a run as it was to win a large Kewpie doll at a carnival ring-toss, so baserunning and basestealing were among the most important aspects of the game. The advent of the home run made it easier to score runs, and the stolen base became as rare as a good stock tip during the Depression. Only recently has the stolen base reappeared as an important offensive weapon, once again causing fundamental changes in baseball strategy—as well as causing a significant increase in managerial ulcers.

Ty Cobb was the Picasso of the basepaths—sometimes he did things that didn't seem to make sense to anyone else, but in the end it turned out to be art. No base runner was ever more feared than Cobb, and his record of ninety-six stolen bases in a season stood for decades. "Tighten your belt," Germany Schaefer used to warn catchers about Cobb, "or he'll steal your pants."

Cobb used to arrive at spring training with lead slugs sewn into the soles of his shoes and removed them at the beginning of the regular season to increase his speed greatly. Casey Stengel recalled that Cobb was the only player he ever saw who could consistently score a runner from first base on a simple hit-and-run play. "It was a remarkable thing," Casey said. "He'd hit the ball to right field and never stop at first base. He'd go right to second. And where's the right fielder going to throw the ball? He's got to throw it to the shortstop covering second base. So when the throw goes into second and Cobb slides in on his backside and wraps his legs around the fella, how's he gonna throw the ball to home, which is where the other runner is going because he didn't stop at third base?"

Teams used to install special plays just to stop Cobb. In spring training one year the Indians plotted a way to trick him. Supposedly, when Cobb attempted to steal second, the catcher was to throw the ball intentionally into center field. The center fielder was to field the ball on one bounce. "There's no way we'll nail him at third," Cleveland manager Jim McGuire, who devised this play, explained, "so the center fielder has to bobble the ball. When Cobb sees that, he won't stop. The center fielder throws home and Cobb is out by thirty feet." The Indians practiced the play over and over, and early in the season they played Cobb's Tigers for the first time. When Cobb got on first, they tried the play. Everything proceeded exactly as planned— except that Cobb easily beat the center fielder's throw to the plate. Although McGuire was disappointed, he didn't give up. "Cobb is fresh now," he explained. "We'll try it again in September. He'll be tired then."

Very few players in baseball history could disrupt a pitcher by getting on base as well as Cobb, but Jackie Robinson was one of them. Robinson's brilliance on the basepaths was not based on his speed, although he was "faster than you could say Jack Robinson," but on his instinct. "Jackie was better in a rundown than anybody I

ever saw," his teammate Hall of Famer Duke Snider says.
"I've got a photograph at home of Jackie caught in a rundown between third and home, and there were six Phillies
surrounding him. The surprising thing about that is not
that there were six players there, but that there were only
six players there. And still he got out of it—he ran into
their pitcher, Russ Meyer, and the umpires called interfer-
ence and allowed him to score."

Robinson's presence on the bases so dominated the action that television invented the split screen just to cover
him. NBC's Harry Coyle directed television coverage of the
1947 World Series, in which the Yankees and Dodgers
played. "Robinson caused us to try to figure out how to
show two things at once. At that point we didn't have the
technology to split the screen; we barely had the technology to broadcast the game. So what we did was use two
cameras and split their lenses. In other words, instead of
completely turning the lens, in one camera we showed
only the left half of the picture—the batter—and in the
other camera we showed only the right half—Robinson on
first base. Although both halves were semicircles, we put
them both up and invented the split screen."

Fortunately, for me, television had already invented the
wide-angle lens when I came along.

Running right after Robinson were players like Hall of
Famer Luis Aparicio, Maury Wills, Hall of Famer Lou Brock,
Rickey Henderson, and Vince Coleman. Like Robinson,
each of these players had the magical ability to make the
one base gained on a steal seem to be as valuable as the
four bases represented by a home run. When they were on
base, pitchers worried more about them than Pinocchio
worried about Dutch elm disease.

In the new vernacular of baseball, runs scored by these
"rabbits" are said to be "manufactured," which means, I
guess, that eventually we're going to be importing some great
Japanese base runners and paying them less. Runs are manufactured in various ways. I remember watching Vince Coleman in a game against Montreal. He chopped a high bouncer
into the Astroturf and was standing on first base before

the ball came down. Expos' pitcher David Palmer threw over to first base one dozen times trying to keep Coleman close. Finally, he threw his first pitch to the batter, Willie McGee. And it was a pitch-out.

Would you say that Coleman had disrupted Palmer's concentration? Would you say the game was going to last four hours?

On the second pitch, Coleman stole second. Watching Coleman steal a base is like watching milk blend into coffee. Coleman took a lead off second; Montreal's shortstop and second basemen both made feints toward the base to try to keep him close. Palmer whirled around once and faked a throw. The Cardinal fans in the stands immediately started screaming, "balk!," which the rules say that fans must do whenever the opposition pitcher fakes a throw to second. Before throwing his second pitch, Palmer whirled again. This time he threw the ball into center field, allowing Coleman to go to third.

Coleman had hit a high infield bouncer and was on third. At that point, if looks could kill, Palmer would have been arraigned on a manslaughter charge. But any juror who has ever pitched, or umpired, in a situation like this would have to agree that Palmer had grounds for justifiable homicide.

Finally Palmer threw his third pitch. McGee hit a slow roller to second base, scoring Coleman. And he beat it out. Before throwing another pitch, Palmer made *nine* pick-off throws to first base. And when he finally pitched, McGee stole second base. Isn't that kind of treatment illegal under the constitutional prevention against cruel and unusual punishment?

But this is exactly the kind of thing that a great base runner can make happen. Basestealing has become such an important part of the offense today that, unlike the old days, teams continue to run when they have a big lead. In the old days there was a tacit agreement that a runner would not attempt to steal when his team had a five- or six-run lead. If he did, the pitcher was then entitled to try to make the batter eat the baseball. "We didn't want to embarrass the other team," said Ed Brinkman, whose fifteen-year major league career ended in 1975. "So when you got a certain number of runs ahead, and every team had a different number—three, five—then you'd close it down. Today they just keep going. The belief today is, if the other team agrees to stop hitting home runs, we'll stop running."

The ironic aspect of that is that the home run forces teams to keep running. With the lively ball, no lead is safe. If Sandy Koufax had a six-run lead, they could turn off the lights and go home. But in 1987, for example, '86 Cy Young Award winner Roger Clemens blew a nine-run lead *in one inning*.

Players like Henderson, Coleman, McGee, and Willie Wilson make baserunning look simple. But to many others it's about as simple as trying to solve Rubic's Cube in the dark while being tickled with a feather. Theoretically, it is easy: All you do is run directly from first to second to third to home. At times, though, that journey has seemed more perilous than Indiana Jones' vacation. As recently as 1985, for example, those same baserunning daredevils, the Cardinals, were leading the Cubs with nobody out, Andy Van Slyke on first base, and Jack Clark on second. Batter Terry Pendleton's line drive was caught by first baseman Leon Durham. Durham threw to second, but shortstop Chris Speier wasn't on the base, so Clark got back safely. Speier saw that Van Slyke was caught off first, however, and threw back to Durham. His throw hit Van Slyke in the helmet and bounced away. *That* was when it started getting complicated.

Van Slyke took off for second. Clark stood there. Van Slyke reached second base and stepped past Clark. Umpire Charlie Williams immediately called him out for passing a base runner. That was the second out. Unfortunately, when Van Slyke arrived at second, Clark wasn't sure who was entitled to the base. "We were both standing there," he explained, "so I thought I ought to go to the next base." And so he took off for third. He got caught in a rundown and was eventually tagged out—by center fielder Bob Dernier.

"It was just your routine triple play," Speier said after the game.

"To be quite honest," Clark later admitted, "I still don't know what happened on the play."

Once, Tony Oliva hit a gigantic home run onto the roof in Detroit. Oliva trotted around first base—right past base runner Cesar Tovar, who was waiting to tag up. Tovar said he didn't think the ball was going out. He must have meant out of the solar system.

And then, of course, there was the great Willie Stargell. When caught in a rundown, he desperately looked at the umpire and screamed, "Time out!"

Giants' pitcher Roger Mason probably should be playing in the American League, where he wouldn't have to come to bat. Actually, it's not the batting he has difficulty with, it's the running. In a game against the Cubs he was thrown out at first base by right fielder André Dawson. Of course, he had a logical explanation: "I was running into the wind."

Lou Piniella must have at least tied a record when he was thrown out at every base one night in Kansas City. But in 1983, Piniella actually scored from first base on a single, running right past third base coach Don Zimmer, who was signaling him to stop. After the game Lou told reporters he doesn't use a third-base coach. A few days later, though, he was thrown out trying to stretch a single into a double, causing Graig Nettles to suggest, "I guess he doesn't use a first-base coach, either."

Incredible as it seems, in 1931 Yankees Lou Gehrig and Dixie Walker were both tagged out at home plate on the same play by catcher Luke Sewell. And only half a century later two other Yankees, Bobby Meacham and Dale Berra, were tagged out at the plate on the same play by catcher Carlton Fisk.

When Jimmy Dykes was player-manager of the Chicago White Sox he was continually frustrated by his team's ineptitude on the bases. The day after one of his players had been picked off second, he lectured his team, telling them, loudly, "There's no excuse for a man to get picked off second because he has the entire play in front of him.

Only a lunkhead could get picked off second." Predictably, during the game against the Tigers that day, Dykes reached second. As he took his lead off the base, Tigers' catcher Rudy York fired to second. As Dykes tried desperately to dive back, Charlie Gehringer tagged him. "I got back!" Dykes yelled at umpire Bill Dinneen.

"I know it," Dinneen agreed as he called him out. "But where have you been?"

There are several reasons for the basestealing revival: the pitcher, the catcher, the runner, and the equipment. "It's the pitchers," Jim Kaat believes. "Pitchers have not made a conscious effort to learn how to hold base runners on, and that's why the running game has been so successful. When I first came up in 1959, the baserunning game in the American League consisted of Luis Aparicio. He was it. We really didn't have a lot of speed burners. Today the groundskeeper can run.

"I had to learn how to hold runners on later in my career. I knew that it took me .9 second to deliver the ball from a set position, and an average catcher can throw to second in 2 seconds, that's 2.9 seconds, and there isn't a runner alive who can run from first to second in 2.9 seconds. The problem is that most pitchers with big leg kicks, take 1.5 or 1.6 seconds to release the ball. If those pitchers would learn how to hold runners on, they could help shut down the runners."

"It's the catchers today," former catcher Jim Fanning explains. "When I was playing, everybody caught with two hands—Walker Cooper, Del Crandall, Campy, Yogi—and as soon as the ball was caught, we had it in our hands. The flexible glove used today is so good that catchers catch everything with one hand. If you catch a ball with one hand, it's got to take you some time to grab it with the other hand, and you lose that split second."

I think it's the players. One of the most obvious changes in baseball since I've been involved is the contribution made by black and Latin players. They arrive in the major leagues with great speed and good baserunning fundamentals. Sliding, for example. Everybody slides head first today, but when I first came up they slid the traditional way, leg outstretched toward the bag. I remember one night in Minnesota when Rod Carew tried to steal second. "I'd never gone head first before," he recalls, "so I thought this time I would. Unfortunately, it had been raining, and the infield was mud. When I dived I just stuck in the ground. I was about ten feet from the base, my arms stretched straight out, not moving. Mostly, I looked like an airplane."

To me, the ironic thing was that as the players got faster, the game got slower. The more they ran, the longer pitchers took. In fact, players got so quick, the games all take more than three hours. I'm afraid that if players keep getting faster, the games might never end.

New uniforms and bases also have helped base runners. By the end of a game in the old days, the woolen uniforms would be soaked with sweat and weigh as much as seven or eight extra pounds. Compared to that, running in lightweight doubleknits is like weight-lifting a cloud.

One thing I've never understood is why, when a pitcher gets on base, the first thing he does is put on his jacket. Seems to me that's like putting a saddlebag on a racehorse. The thing that would really make sense would be taking off his shirt.

Bases, or sacks, were once canvas bags filled with sawdust, hair, and cotton, padded with foam rubber, and held in place by leather cross-straps slipped through a metal spike in the ground. By the end of a game they were packed down flat, and runners often slid right over them. Usually they tried to grab ahold of the straps as they whizzed by. Bases today have a hard plastic shell three to five inches high, are filled with a bonded polyester padding, and are secured in the ground with long aluminum pegs. Believe me, it would be easier to shoplift a destroyer than to move one of those babies. Because they are so solid, players not only grab them as they slide by, but also are able to push off them with their foot as they round the bases, enabling them to make much sharper turns than ever before.

One of the first people to recognize the strategic importance of baserunning was Charley Finley. In addition to the

designated hitter, Charley also wanted the American League
to adopt a designated runner. When he was turned down,
he simply added his own. It was really a pinch runner
rather than a DR, meaning he could be inserted into the
game only once. "The Panamanian Express," Allan Lewis,
was the first DR, but Finley actually permitted him to bat
on occasion. On rare occasion.

In 1974, Finley replaced Lewis with sprinter Herb Washington, "The World's Fastest Human." Washington, who
had been working as a radio sports reporter when Finley
offered him the job, had last played baseball his junior
year in high school. He had been hoping to play pro football. Although he claimed he owned a glove, he never had
an opportunity to use it. Over two seasons, Washington
played in 104 games, stole 30 bases, scored 33 runs, and
never came to bat. Not only didn't he bat during games, he
didn't even hit in batting practice. While the rest of Finley's
A's were hitting, he was running around the bases.

A lot of A's didn't know how to accept a player who did
nothing but run. "I suppose if he breaks his leg," first
baseman Pat Bourque decided, "they'll have to shoot him."

The 1974 World Series was the only one I ever worked.
That was the most boring Series since "My Mother the
Car" eloped with "Mr. Ed." The highlight of that Series
took place when Oakland manager Alvin Dark inserted
Washington in a clutch situation—and Dodger reliever Mike
Marshall picked him off.

The rules of baseball have continually evolved, but the
game really hasn't changed very much. The pitcher pitches,
the hitter hits, the fielders field. But to someone who has
never seen the game played before, it can be as complicated
as playing Scrabble with hieroglyphics. During World War
II American soldiers in the Far East introduced baseball to
the Chinese. Unfortunately, the Chinese didn't quite understand the rules. To them, it seemed, the game was
simple:

   1. You wave your bat around fiercely and the pitcher
       has to hit it with the ball.

2. If he does, you are punished by having to run like hell to four bases, where four of your friends try to stop the man who catches the ball from hitting you with it.

3. They attempt to catch the ball before you are hit.

4. If you think your friend may miss the ball, you slide under him and take cover.

5. Nobody may throw the ball at you while you are on base.

6. If, while on base, another bat is hit by the pitcher's ball, you are again punished by having to run like hell.

7. The catcher, who is your friend, wears a hideous mask to further disconcert the pitcher's aim at the bat.

8. If the ball fails to touch the bat in three swings, cheers of *Ding how!* are heard, meaning the batter is shifty, fast, and good because the pitcher didn't hit the bat.

9. If the player is foolish enough to be caught unaware by the pitcher and is hit by the ball, he is disgraced and is not allowed any more chances at bat, but must go to first base, in his crippled state, and run like hell when the bat of the next player is hit.

As the legendary Max Asnas, proprietor of New York's famed Stage Delicatessen used to say, "It doesn't sound like much, but from this they make a good living."

7
THE RULERS OF
THE GAME

I've always thought athletic slogans were clever. Not necessarily meaningful, or true, but clever. For example, "When the going gets tough, the tough get going." Does that mean that when the going gets tough, they leave? In fact, it may not mean very much, but it sounds like it does. Or, "It's not the size of the boy in the fight, it's the size of the fight in the boy." Great, but if the gentle six-seven Frank Howard had fought the feisty five-five Freddie Patek, I'd still take Howard. And then there is my favorite slogan of all: "Winners never cheat and cheaters never win." I'd like to meet the person who wrote that one. I've got a sporting goods store to sell him.

Who are they kidding? Anyone who believes that also believes that the insurance company is really concerned about his or her welfare. Winners do cheat; cheaters do win. In fact, you can read the rulebook from cover to cover and not find the word "cheating" mentioned once.

The major leagues have a long and dishonorable tradition of cheating. The rules have not just been broken, they also have been mashed, smashed, mangled, and spiked. Compared to some of the things that have been done, minor infractions like scuffing baseballs and doctoring bats are crimes about as serious as jaywalking in Times Square on New Year's Eve.

Long before the turn of the century, the Baltimore Orioles were renown for their chicanery—and that was even
long before Earl Weaver. In sacrifice-fly situations, for example, the lone umpire had to keep his eye on the outfielder to ensure that the ball was caught. While the attention
of the umpire was occupied, third baseman John McGraw
would grab the base runner's belt and hold on to it until
the umpire turned to look in his direction. In their home
park, Orioles outfielders hid baseballs in the dense outfield
grass. When a drive hit by an opponent got past them they
substituted one of the previously hidden balls for the actual
ball in play. One day, though, Joe Quinn of the St. Louis
Browns rocketed a hit into left-center field. Left fielder Joe
Kelley picked up a planted ball and threw to third to nail
Quinn. Unfortunately, center fielder Steve Brodie caught
up to the real ball and threw that one to third. The game
was forfeited to St. Louis.

On the bases, Oriole runners took advantage of the fact
that the single umpire couldn't watch everything by occasionally cutting across the infield to get from first to third.
The Orioles were not the only team to do this, though, and
usually there was nothing the umpire could do about it.
Once, however, legendary Irish umpire Tim Hurst called a
runner safe on a close play at home plate, then immediately turned around and saw the base runner who had been
on first standing calmly on third. Hurst called that runner
out for cutting across the infield.

"You didn't see me," the runner, Bill Lang, argued.
"You can't call me out."

"I can't?" Hurst replied. "It is true, William, that I
didn't see ye cut across second base. But neither did I see ye
touch it. You just arrived too soon."

At one time a caught foul tip was an out, and Connie
Mack—sweet, honest Connie Mack—took advantage of that
by clucking his tongue and imitating the sound of a foul tip
to fool the umpire. Ty Cobb used to teach catchers to pick
up a handful of dirt and, just as the batter was concentrating on the pitch, flip it onto their hands or feet. Casey

Stengel used to try to distract hitters by screaming at them just as the pitcher delivered the ball.

Even in those grand old days the home field advantage meant much more than having the local fans there to cheer for the team. The tricks teams played to gain an advantage over opponents were worthy of a presidential candidate. Before stadiums had permanent seats in the outfield, for example, teams were permitted to erect temporary bleachers or simply put up a rope if a large crowd was expected, and any ball hit into that area was ruled a ground-rule double. When Ty Cobb was managing the Tigers and a power-hitting team was visiting, he would have the groundcrew set up the bleachers, turning balls that might otherwise have been home runs into doubles. And if the crowd wasn't large enough to justify putting up the seats, Cobb would have the groundcrew sit in those bleachers so the umpire would not order them removed.

In Chicago, Cubs fans standing behind the outfield rope would push forward toward the infield when the home team was at bat and back up several steps when the visitors came to bat. And for many years Cubs outfielders were instructed to "lose" balls hit into the ivy covering the outfield brick wall, turning potential triples into ground-rule doubles.

When Bill Veeck—who, in fact, planted that ivy in Chicago—owned the Cleveland Indians, he moved the outfield fences in or out depending on the lineup of the visiting team. When the league finally passed a rule prohibiting that, Veeck compensated: He would go out to the ball park at night, dig up home plate, and move it a few feet forward or backward.

Kansas City's famed groundskeeper George Toma once complained "The groundskeeper is the dirt of the organization," but long ago teams realized that a properly prepared infield can be worth several victories each season. When Cobb was playing for the Tigers, for example, a body of water known as "Cobb Lake" magically appeared between the pitcher's mound and home plate in Detroit, allowing

Cobb's bunts to stop rolling and making it difficult for visiting pitchers and third basemen to move quickly. When Maury Wills was stealing bases for the Dodgers, other teams would put so much water on their basepaths, according to columnist Jim Murray, "that instead of coaches, lifeguards should be stationed on the bases ... that an aircraft carrier wouldn't have run aground ... that instead of double plays you had synchronized swimming ... that when the One Great Scorer says 'he died at third,' he'll mean by drowning," and writer Mel Durslag noted that the Giants' infield "had enough water to run a hydro-electric plant."

Infields have often been tailored to help pitchers as well as hitters and runners. When I first came up to the majors, for example, the White Sox had the offensive firepower of, say, Monoco. The team was totally dependent on their pitching, and several of their starting pitchers threw sinkers. The grass on that infield was so long and the dirt was so wet that we used to refer to Comiskey Park's infield as Camp Swampy. I remember seeing several balls hit straight into the muck in front of the plate—and stick there.

For more than a hundred years teams have adjusted the slope of the ground near the foul lines depending on whether they wanted bunts and topped grounders to roll fair or foul. Teams with several fast runners usually want those balls to stay fair; power hitting teams want them to roll foul. Some teams that depended on speed even painted their foul lines with several coats of thick whitewash rather than chalk, creating a slight ledge to keep balls in fair territory. Slight ledge? In Kansas City poor little Freddie Patek used to have to hurdle the foul lines to get to his shortstop position. I think baseball has thus far been very fortunate that no one has been seriously hurt falling off a foul line.

Some teams raise or lower the pitcher's mound to conform to the needs of their pitching staff. For example, a team with fastball pitchers usually has a high mound.

Usually you can tell which teams those are when visiting pitchers start hammering pitons into the ground to climb to the top of the mound. In some cities they don't actually raise the pitcher's mound—they just make sure it is a different height than the mound in the visiting team's bull pen. That forces the reliever to adjust when he comes in the game.

One season the American League was determined to standardize the height of all pitcher's mounds, so they sent each umpiring crew a tape measure, a stick, and a level. We were supposed to put the stick on the rubber, use the level to make sure it was straight, then measure the height of the mound from the edge of the grass. Who figured that one out, Frank Lloyd Wright? I came close; I measured the stick. Excuse me; I happen not to like heights. With my ability, I always had plenty of things to argue about with managers, I didn't need anything else. Of course, that was another one of those rules that everybody violated so nobody could complain about it.

When teams played "inside baseball," as opposed to playing baseball inside, as they do now, and each run was important, sign-stealing was considered as much an art as bank-robbing. Teams often had players or coaches hiding somewhere in the outfield stands reading the catcher's signals with high-powered binoculars and relaying whatever information they gathered to the hitter. Various methods were used to communicate the information. In 1910, a Philadelphia Athletics player stationed on a rooftop beyond the outfield turned a weathervane north to indicate the pitcher was throwing a curveball and south when a fastball was coming. In Detroit, a sign painted on the fence included the letter "B." An open slot in the top half of the "B" indicated a fastball was coming; an open slot in the lower half meant it would be a curveball. In Cleveland, the eyes of an Indian painted on the fence moved left or right to tip off the pitch to the batter. The Cubs had someone in an apartment building overlooking Wrigley Field pull the window blinds up if a fastball was coming and lower them

if it was a curveball. Of course, if Dizzy Dean was pitching, it was curtains anyway. Milt Pappas remembers serving as an undercover operative in Chicago when he was
with Cincinnati in the early 1960s. "Our manager, Dave
Bristol, was convinced someone was stealing our signs, so
when I wasn't scheduled to pitch he'd have me dress in
street clothes and sit in the center-field bleachers, searching for someone with binoculars. I never found anyone.
However, when I was traded to the Cubs I asked if anyone
had been relaying signs from the bleachers. Absolutely not,
they told me; he had been relaying signs from inside the
scoreboard."

When Alvin Dark was managing the Giants he was
certain the Reds and Braves were using binoculars to
steal his catcher's signals, and decided to draw attention to
the problem, thus forcing the National League to do something about it. So he armed a coach with high-powered
binoculars and a white towel and put him in the outfield
stands. When he showed the white towel, a fastball was
coming; when the towel was not visible, the catcher had
signaled for a curveball. Dark's ploy was so clever that
nobody on the Braves noticed—but Willie Mays hit four
home runs.

Players used to complain to me that the Milwaukee
Brewers' mascot, Bernie Brewer, who sat on a platform in
center field and slid down a pole into a "vat of beer"
every time a Brewer hit a home run, was transmitting
signs by wearing white gloves when a fastball was coming
and taking them off to signal a curveball. I tried to watch
him, and I had excellent eyes in those days—I could barely
see Bernie Brewer. That platform was 450 feet from home
plate and about 60 feet high. Gloves? Who could tell if he
had clothes on? But the players were convinced he was
helping the Brewers cheat. Obviously he didn't help them
enough— they finished in the second division almost every
season.

The major leagues started using electronic devices to
relay signals long before the CIA did—in fact, long before

there was a CIA. Actually, it was almost before there was electricity. In Philadelphia in the late 1890s signals were relayed from the center-field clubhouse to the third-base coach's box on a buried telegraph wire. The third-base coach stood directly on top of a steel plate, and a player in the clubhouse would buzz one, two, or more times to indicate the catcher's signal to the coach. The coach would then transmit the information to the batter. The wire was discovered when an opposing third baseman tripped over what he thought was a vine and pulled it up—and watched much of the outfield come up with it.

After the Giants' Bobby Thomson hit the most famous home run in baseball history to win the 1951 National League pennant, rumors spread that Thomson had been tipped off to Dodger pitcher Ralph Branca's pitch by a buzzer system that ran from the clubhouse in deep, deep center field in the Polo Grounds to the Giants' dugout. That charge was denied, of course—but by the Dodgers' catcher, Rube Walker, who explained, "If Thomson knew what was coming, he'd never have been in the batter's box. I signaled for a knockdown pitch."

Baseball's cheaters have always attempted to utilize the latest advances in electronics. In the 1950s, for example, the White Sox supposedly not only wired their third base for sound, they also installed a transmitter in pitcher Early Wynn's cap so manager Al Lopez could talk to him on the field.

Skulduggery became far less complicated with the invention of television . . . and television cameras. Long lenses in center field enabled a spy to stay in his own clubhouse and steal the catcher's signals. When my good friend Billy Martin was managing the Texas Rangers, he supposedly had a closed-circuit camera installed in the outfield. Ranger coach Jim Fregosi was assigned to monitor the television set in the clubhouse and communicate the information to Martin in the dugout by walkie-talkie. Believe me, if I had had that kind of intelligence setup when I was in school, I probably could have even passed chemistry.

"We used to have a camera set up in center field at

Wrigley Field," former Cub coach Charlie Metro remembers, "and one day against the Cardinals we stole every pitch called by the St. Louis catcher. It worked fine. It didn't matter, though: We were so bad that we lost a doubleheader."

In 1985 the Indians were so sure that the Orioles were stealing their signs from TV that Cleveland pitcher Tom Waddell, slightly confused about his own catcher's signs, decided he would "just look into the Orioles' dugout to see what pitch I was supposed to throw."

Unless someone was able to decipher the meaning of the signals, however, knowing them was about as valuable as stealing air out of a tire. For example, if the catcher puts down two fingers, then one, then three, then one again, which number in the sequence are the pitcher and catcher using, and what pitch does that number indicate? In some cases that was extremely difficult to figure out, although not when Clint Courtney was concerned. In 1961 Scraps was catching for Baltimore. In the eighth inning of a close game against the Yankees, Mickey Mantle doubled. Normally, when a base runner gets to second, the catcher and pitcher change their signals to prevent the runner from relaying the pitch to the batter. So Courtney walked slowly out to the mound and told his catcher, "I'm gonna flash three signs, but the only one that counts is the first one. The other two are to fool Mantle."

The pitcher nodded. Courtney squatted behind the plate and very carefully put down one, one, and one. The pitcher shook his head as if he hadn't seen right. Courtney ran through the signals again: one, one, one. "Time," the pitcher called, and Courtney once again trotted out to the mound. "What'sa matter?" he asked.

"I don't think you're fooling anybody," the pitcher said. "You gave me the same sign three times."

"I did?" Courtney said. "Oh, well, let's change it to two, then. Two's the indicator." So Courtney trotted back to home plate, squatted, hesitated for a moment, then signaled two, two, two.

The problem with depending on a stolen signal is that

there is always the danger of being wrong. Being wrong
when a baseball is being thrown at your head is very different from guessing incorrectly that Prince Charles starred in
Purple Rain. The results can be disastrous. Once, Chuck
Dressen, acknowledged to be one of the greatest espionage
agents in baseball history, believed he had stolen the catcher's sign and told batter "Ducky" Medwick to expect a
curveball. Medwick waited too long before trying to get out
of the way of an inside fastball. His skull was fractured,
ending his career.

"I loved knowing what was coming," Moose Skowron
remembers. "Bob Turley was great at figuring out what the
pitcher was going to throw. I'll bet he must have given
Mickey Mantle fifty home runs. But in those days *everybody*
used to try to steal signs. When I was with the Dodgers we
were in Milwaukee one day and Lew Burdette was pitching
against us. Our batboy, *the batboy*, told me even he could
pick up what Burdette was throwing. I told him that if
Burdette was going to throw a fastball, say, 'Come on,
Moose,' but that if it was a curveball, say nothing. I hit
two home runs off Burdette and tipped the batboy fifty
dollars.

"When I was traded to the White Sox they told me that
they had someone in the scoreboard with binoculars. I
thought that was great. First time I came to bat, I looked
down to coach Tony Cuccinello—fastball. Great; I dug in.
The first pitch was a curveball. Hmmm. Cuccinello got
five out of six pitches wrong. He could have done better by
guessing. That was the last time I took a sign from anybody."

While some players were praying that they would get
the other team's signals, pitcher Al Worthington was doing
just the opposite: A born-again Christian, he objected on
religious grounds to using binoculars to steal signs. When
he was with the Giants in 1959, Worthington told Manager
Bill Rigney that he refused to play for a team that cheated.
And the next year, when Worthington was with the Red
Sox, he told them the same thing, and that same season,
when he was with the White Sox, he told them the same

thing. And the following season, when he pitched for Cincinnati . . .

For many players, the real mystery was not the meaning of the other team's signals, it was understanding their own team's signs. There have been many major league players who had difficulty understanding the little picture on a men's room door, much less figuring out a set of signs as complicated as, oh, a traffic light. Zeke Bonura, for example, was an excellent hitter with the White Sox in the 1930s, but signals eluded him. "He just couldn't remember the signs," his teammate Luke Appling recalls, "no matter what we did. Finally, one day he came over to me and told me he'd figured out how we could work the hit and run when he was on base and I was at bat. 'How's that?' I asked. 'It's like this,' he explained. 'I get on base, and when I run, you hit.'

"Eventually we had signals just for him. When Manager Jimmy Dykes wanted to hit and run when he was on base, he would wave a handkerchief at him. Once when I was at bat Dykes started waving that handkerchief. Forty thousand people in the ballpark saw Dykes standing on the top step of the dugout waving that thing, but Zeke didn't run. I got a base hit to right field, and he was thrown out easily trying for third base. Cost us the game. Afterward, Dykes went up to him in the clubhouse and said, 'There were forty thousand people in the stands, and every one of them saw me waving this handkerchief at you. How come you didn't see it?"

"Oh, I saw it, Papa Dykes," Zeke said, then explained, "but I thought you all was just kidding."

The first time the White Sox played Washington after Bonura had been traded to the Senators, a player asked Dykes if he was going to change the signs because Bonura knew what they were. "Not necessary," Dykes explained. "He couldn't even remember them when he was with us."

Dick "Dr. Strangeglove" Stuart had so much difficulty reading his team's signs that one day he suggested to a coach, "How about if when I get on, you just point to the base you want me to go to?"

Not only do batters and base runners have difficulty communicating with their coaches, sometimes pitchers and catchers understand each other about as well as Ricky Ricardo and Rhett Butler. Lefty Gomez, for example, would throw whatever pitch he felt like throwing. He thought it was nice that catcher Bill Dickey kept signaling because it gave Dickey something to do, but he just threw the pitch he wanted to throw anyway. Gomez used to drive Dickey crazy, but there was nothing the catcher could do about it. Dickey long remembered a game in which Lefty was getting blasted and called him out to the mound. "I think I know what the problem is," he said. "I think they're wise to our signals."

"Wise to our signals?" Dickey replied in astonishment. "Wise to our signals? If I don't know what you're gonna throw, and you don't know what you're gonna throw, how in the world are they gonna figure it out?"

During the classic 1975 World Series between the Reds and Red Sox, Cincinnati's Hall of Fame catcher Johnny Bench remembers a situation in the late innings of a tie game in which Boston had a runner on first, Denny Doyle on third, Fred Lynn at bat, and nobody out. "Will McEnaney was pitching, and we'd used the same signs all year. I gave him three signs; the third sign, a slider outside, was the pitch I wanted. I got ready outside and I'm getting set to catch the ball and all of a sudden I realize it's a fastball inside and I know I'm not going to be able to reach back. At best, I hoped to be able to get a glove on the ball and knock it down. But the runner on third was probably going to score.

"Lynn swung and popped it up to left field. George Foster went into foul territory to catch it, and as he did, I heard Red Sox third base coach Don Zimmer screaming 'No! No! No!' to Doyle, meaning, 'Don't tag up and run.' But Doyle must have thought he was screaming 'Go! Go! Go!' because he took off for the plate.

"Foster made a perfect one-hop throw, and I tagged out Doyle to complete the double play. It took two missed signals, but from a passed ball, a run in, and a runner on second, we ended up with two outs and a runner on first.

"I went out to the pitcher's mound and told McEnaney, 'You crossed me up,' and went through the sequence I'd signaled.

" 'I guess I did,' he agreed. 'Well, sometimes those things work out, don't they?'

"Just then the home plate umpire came out to the mound and saw us laughing. He clapped his hands and said, 'Let's go, let's go. What are you guys talking about?'

"I just looked at him, shook my head, and said, 'You wouldn't understand.' "

Sign-stealing is another casualty of the long ball. The game has gotten so complicated that teams rarely bother trying to steal signs. At one time all the scrubs would sit together in the dugout, trying to pick up the other team's signals. But on several teams today the players move freely back and forth between the dugout and the clubhouse during the game—and often, instead of watching the ball game on the clubhouse television and trying to pick up signs, they're watching Vanna White trying to figure out how to turn over two letters at the same time.

"We never bothered trying to steal signs when I was with Baltimore," Earl Weaver claimed. "It just got too complicated. Most pitchers call their own games now anyway; they add or subtract a pitch from the signal the catcher gave by rubbing a part of their uniform with their glove. How is a runner on second gonna see that?"

Richie Zisk, who played thirteen seasons in the big leagues with five different teams, remembers, "Not one of those teams emphasized it or even mentioned it. At bat we were on our own."

Finally, there was that master of signals, Tommy Byrne, who pitched for thirteen seasons, mostly with the Yankees. It wasn't necessary to try to steal his signals; he gave them away. Byrne would stand on the mound and tell the batter what pitch he was going to throw. "Hitters hated him," Phil Rizzuto says. "He'd tell them, 'fastball,' and you know they had to be thinking, 'He said fastball, so that means it's got to be a curve,' and he would throw the fastball past them. It was the most distracting thing I ever saw on the field."

Byrne and I had a lot in common: Our strategy was to try to keep the ballplayers confused. Of course, if talking was all it took to be successful, I should have made the Hall of Fame.

Managers and ballplayers steal and cheat. But when they get caught, who gets blamed for it? Hint: not their mothers. Another hint: not their teammates. Answer: the umpire. Consider the plight of the umpire, who comes to work ready to do his job, armed only with the rulebook and his own integrity and ability. Aligned against him are at least forty-eight players, several coaches, and two managers, each one of them willing to break the rules to win. And when one of them, just one of them, does something illegal, who does the other team scream at? Not the player. Not the manager. The umpire. Numerous times in my career I had managers shouting at me, "How can you let him get away with that?" How can *I* let him get away with it? First they complain I can't see a pitch six inches away, then they yell at me for not being able to spot a man with a pair of binoculars in an apartment building outside the ballpark.

When I was an active umpire I used to fantasize about what the world would be like if there were umpires or officials in everyday life. Wouldn't it be nice if every time someone in another car cut you off, he was thrown off the highway? And how nice it would be if every time you got mad at somebody because of your own failure, there was someone right there for you to yell at to relieve your anger. And when things did not go your way, wouldn't it be wonderful to have someone to blame? Of course it would.

Many people would describe that fantasy as paranoia. Anyone who has umpired would realize it was optimistic. Soon after General Douglas MacArthur returned from Korea, for example, he attended a game at the Polo Grounds at which he told reporters, "I'm glad to be here and enjoy the privilege of booing the umpire in our great American tradition." And that was before the game had started! Imagine what the tradition might be if the umpire had actually made a mistake. I knew we were fighting tyranny for many reasons, I just hadn't realized that the right to boo me was one of them.

There have been as many changes in the job of the umpire as there have been in every other aspect of the game. When the National League was founded in 1876, the single umpire, whose uniform often consisted of a suit and stovepipe hat, sat between home and first on a stool tall enough to allow him a sweeping view of the entire field. The league had no umpiring staff. On the day of each scheduled game, the home team provided a list of three candidates. The three names were put into a hat and the manager of the visiting team picked out the name of the man who would umpire that day. The umpire would be paid five dollars for the game.

As the old Orioles proved, the umpire couldn't see everything that happened on the field, so the rulebook suggested, "Should the umpire be unable to determine whether a catch has been fairly made or not, he shall be at liberty to appeal to the bystanders and to render his decision according to the fairest testimony at his command." That meant that the umpire could actually ask the fans to rule on a play, sort of an early version of the instant replay. That rule had two purposes: one, to determine the outcome of a close play; and two, to save the umpire's life.

Almost everything about the job has changed since then: the number of umpires on the field, the equipment and uniforms, the application of the rules, and the working conditions. But one thing really hasn't changed very much: the relationship between the players, the managers, the fans—and the umpires. One of baseball's most popular early stars was Arlie Latham, nicknamed "The Freshest Man on Earth." That didn't mean he was new, it meant he was nasty. Newspaper stories of games in which he played detailed his latest battle with the umpire even before giving an account of the ball game.

When Hall of Famer Bill Klem first joined the National

League in 1905, veteran umpire Jack Sheridan warned him to be careful which newspapers he read. "The sportswriters blame everything on the umpire," he told Klem, "including their wives' cooking." Sheridan gave him a list of which papers he should read in seven of the eight National League cities. Klem examined the list and realized that it included no St. Louis papers.

"When you're in St. Louis, Bill," Sheridan advised, "don't read."

Klem thought he was kidding until he made his first trip there. The day after he had called three St. Louis runners out at the plate to cost the Cardinals the game, a St. Louis newspaper headline declared, "Umpire Klem Kills Innocent Fan." The story that followed blamed a fatal heart attack suffered by a fan on Klem's calls at home plate.

The Cubs' Heinie Zimmerman was thrown out of so many games for his abusive attitude toward umpires that in 1913 a supposedly anonymous fan sent half of a torn hundred-dollar bill to the *Chicago Tribune* and promised to send Zimmerman the other half of the bill if he could go two weeks without being ejected from a game, a feat many people believed to be as impossible as flying across an ocean. With most of Chicago—and certainly every umpire—rooting for him, Zimmerman made it. He was presented with the other half of the bill at home plate by an umpire, and that, as he might have said, probably was the only time in his career that an umpire ever gave him anything. Eventually the newspaper admitted that there was no anonymous fan: The whole scheme had been created by the sports editor. I suspect that the only surprising thing about that was it hadn't been created by an umpire.

Fiery Tim Hurst, perhaps called that because he was the only umpire to be fired by both the American and National leagues, once claimed that he enjoyed being an umpire because "you can't beat the hours." He believed the proper way to do the job was to "call 'em fast and walk away tough." In the early days the walking-away-tough part was far more important than calling them fast, because players were just as likely to curse the umpire—and punch him—as they were just to curse him. If an umpire and player or manager started swinging at each other today, they would both be fined and suspended, the media would poll the fans to discover which combatant was right, radio sports talk shows would debate the incident for weeks, highlights would be shown on the television news programs and *This Week in Baseball*, David Letterman would invite both participants on his show, a William Morris agent would offer to represent them, book and television-movie rights would be sold, and some smart promoter would try to schedule an off-season bout between the two of them.

During my career I probably received as much attention for my continuing feud with Earl Weaver as I did for talking to the players during play, eating food on the field, and exaggerating my calls. I'm certainly not proud of that, but . . . well, I'm not *that* proud of it. Weaver and I argued over everything from plays in the infield to the correct conjugation of the verb "ejection," but we never came close to hitting each other. Of course, I'm six-four and close to three hundred pounds, and Earl is an entire person smaller, so if Earl had hit me and I had found out about it, I don't know what might have happened.

In the old days, when an umpire fought with a player or manager, he really fought with him. Although the only time a major league game was officially stopped for a prize-fight was in 1941, when the Pirates and Giants paused to allow fans to listen to the Joe Louis-Billy Conn fight from New York, then resumed play, there have been many unofficial fights involving umpires. And, I can assure you, an unofficial punch hurts just as much as an official one. In 1915, for example, Reds' manager Charley Herzog (related to Whitey only by position) got into an argument with home-plate umpire Cy Rigler. Herzog stepped on Rigler's foot with his spikes. Rigler hit Herzog in the face with his mask, cutting his eye, then followed up with a right to the manager's nose. After being separated by police, both Herzog and Rigler filed charges at the local station house, each accusing the other of disturbing the peace. Obviously that was absurd, as anyone knows there is never any peace between a manager and an umpire. A judge fined each of them five dollars, and Herzog was suspended by the National League for five days.

Rigler, a massive machinist by trade, never hesitated to defend his decisions with his voice and his fists. On another occasion he exchanged punches with Dodgers' manager Bill Dahlen, for which both fighters were fined a hundred dollars, enough to buy several computers in those days—if they had had computers in those days.

John McGraw was once fined five hundred dollars, practically a full season's salary for some players, for attacking Bill Byron, "The Singing Umpire" ("It cut the middle of the plate, you missed because you swung too late"), under the stands after a game. There are some singers who deserve to be attacked under the stands, but McGraw was complaining about a play that took place in the game, not Byron's singing. Byron, however, was obviously a brave man. Let us pause here for a moment and speculate on exactly what Jim Rice might have done if I had called him out on strikes, then sang to him, "Oh, golly, oh, gee, I'm afraid that's strike three."

Once, after a disputed call at home plate, Ty Cobb intentionally slid into umpire Billy Evans, knocking him to the ground. Evans challenged Cobb to meet him after the game. In those days "meet" didn't mean a meeting, it meant a beating. When they met under the stands, Evans, aware of Cobb's reputation, asked, "You got a knife?"

"If I did," Cobb replied, "I'd cut your throat with it."

I have to interrupt this story to remind you that this fight was not about loves lost, or money, or family matters—this was about a close play at home plate. Now, back to the story.

"How do you want to fight?" Evans asked.

To Cobb, the Marquis of Queensbury was something that hung over the entrance to a movie theater. "I don't know how to fight," he replied, just before leaping on Evans. Cobb's first punch sent Evans reeling into a post, knocking him out cold. Cobb jumped on him and started choking him, and it took several other players and members of the groundcrew to pry his fingers loose.

And Rodney Dangerfield complains that he doesn't get any respect.

Umpire George Moriarty once got so angry when he broke his hand on the jaw of a White Sox pitcher that he challenged the entire Chicago team to meet him.

In 1917, Red Sox pitcher Babe Ruth walked the lead-off batter of a game and became so incensed at umpire Brick Owens' call that he punched Owens in the jaw. Owens immediately ejected Ruth, and relief pitcher Ernie Shore came in—and pitched a perfect game.

Umpire George Magerkurth once engaged in fisticuffs with the Giants' Billy Jurges over a fair-ball call. First they spat at each other, then started swinging. Magerkurth became the first umpire ever to be suspended for unseemly conduct, which was not really out of character. "The Greek," as he was known, was so big that trouble had no difficulty finding him. Once, in the minor leagues, a fan threw a bottle at him. Magerkurth simply picked it up and threw it right back at the fan. The league president pointed out that umpires are not supposed to throw bottles at fans.

"And fans are not supposed to throw them at me," he replied correctly.

When Emmett Ashford was working in the Dominican Republic, he had the audacity to call two strikes on the St. Louis Cardinals' Julian Javier. "Mr. Javier and I had a difference of opinion over it," Emmett later recalled. "He refused to get back in the batter's box, so I told the pitcher to throw and I called it strike three. And then Javier clipped me with a left to my jaw for strike four, and a right to my head for strike five."

With so much punching going on, it's hardly worth mentioning spitting. But once, when Frenchy Bordagaray was managing in the minor leagues, he spat at an umpire and was suspended for the remainder of the season. When informed of the suspension, Bordagaray supposedly admitted, "I got more than I expectorated."

One complaint I've heard quite often recently is that

umpires have gotten too powerful, that they no longer allow players and managers the freedom to express their feelings. Hey, if players and managers need to express their feelings, let them call Dr. Ruth. The relationship between players and managers, and umpires, has changed. Just before he retired as National League president in 1986, Chub Feeney said that umpires were telling him that the behavior of the players was getting more aggressive, while the players insisted that the umpires were getting too restrictive. "And I think both of them are right," Feeney decided, sounding exactly like a league president.

The players' job is to play; that's why they're called players. If they were supposed to argue, they would have been called lawyers. When a player makes an error, hometown fans eventually overcome their anger to sympathize with him, but if an umpire makes a bad call, no one forgets it. Davey Phillips, one of the best umpires in the game, summed it up correctly when he was selected to work the 1980 World Series in his hometown, St. Louis. "I told my wife before the Series started that I was very excited about it," he remembers, "but I also warned her to keep in mind that if things didn't go well we'd probably have to relocate the family."

Part of the reason for the change is that umpires now know they have a strong union to back them up, but more importantly, they have shinguards to protect them when a player or manager tries to kick them, and a steel mask in case the player swings at them.

The thing every umpire in baseball history has had to decide is where to draw the line. How much abuse to take before ejecting a player? Every umpire is different. Bill Klem drew his line in the dirt somewhere between home and first base and warned whomever he was arguing with that if he stepped over that line, he was out of the game. My line was a fine line: As long as a player or manager was discussing the call I'd made, even if he cursed, that was fine with me—but when he started cursing me or the horse I came in on, he was out of the game.

During Doug Harvey's first major league season he called

Joe Torre out at second base. Torre called him a sonofabitch, and Harvey ejected him. Torre's manager, Birdie Tebbetts, tried to calm down Harvey, explaining that he had to learn to take some minor abuse. "Now, wait a second," Harvey said, laying down the ground rules for the rest of his career. "He ain't gonna call me a sonofabitch, you ain't gonna call me a sonofabitch, and no sonofabitch in this ballpark is gonna call me a sonofabitch."

But in the early 1970s the National League tried to change those rules. "The league told the umpires that they should take more from players before ejecting them," Harvey remembers, "so I decided to find out exactly what that meant.

"What that meant, I was told, was that the league didn't see anything wrong with cursing, that umpires should allow the players to curse. I told them they'd better not be trying to tell me that I have to stand there and let them curse at me, because if they were, I intended to walk into the league office the next day and tell them, 'You lousy #$#@ $%#%$#, I want a raise.'

" 'Oh, if you did that,' I was warned, 'we'd have to run you out of the office.'

" 'Now you get the idea,' I said."

One of the most difficult aspects of the job has always been avoiding arguments and fights. When someone is standing there cursing at you, your natural reaction is to fight back. Umpires are not supposed to do that. From the beginning of baseball, umpires were supposed to have the wisdom of Solomon, the honesty of Abe Lincoln, the vision of Superman, and the ability to take the abuse of an inflatable knockdown doll. But perhaps more than any of those traits, the one thing that an umpire needs most is a good answer. It doesn't necessarily have to be the correct answer, or a funny answer, just one that will end the discussion. As the great Hall of Fame umpire Jocko Conlan used to advise young umpires, "Son, if you got the right answer, you got them screwed."

One of the many things that made Jocko such a great umpire was that he usually had the right answer. He was behind the plate one day when the Phillies' Richie Ashburn complained about a call. "Okay," Jocko told him, "you call the next pitch. I'll wait until you tell me what it is, and that's what I'll call it."

Ashburn was dubious but agreed. The next pitch was just inside. Ashburn paused, then said, "Strike."

"Strike!" Jocko called. Then he called time out and bent over to dust the plate. "Richie," he said quietly, "you just had the only chance in the history of baseball to hit and umpire at the same time. And you blew it. That's the last pitch you'll call. I'm not going to have you louse up my profession."

Dour Bill Klem was not known for his sense of humor, but once, after he'd called a pitch a strike, the batter stepped out of the batter's box and told him, "You missed that one, Bill."

Klem responded, "Well, if I had a bat on my shoulder I wouldn't have."

On a close play at first base, Hall of Famer Billy Evans called the runner out. The runner started screaming at Evans, complaining that he'd called the play before it was completed. "Any umpire can call the play after it happens," Evans replied, "but only the great umpires can call it before it happens. So you're still out."

Evans refined that credo during another game. A batter laid a bunt down the third-base line. Evans waited and waited as the ball rolled slowly down the line in foul territory, and finally he called it foul. But just as he did, the ball hit a pebble, plopped into fair territory, and stopped. "It's six inches fair," the coach pointed out correctly. "Look at it."

There was really no disputing the evidence. The ball had stopped in fair territory. "It certainly looks fair," Evans admitted, "and it would have been a fair ball yesterday and it will be a fair ball tomorrow and it'll be a fair ball for every other game of my career. But right now, unfortunately, it's a foul ball because that's the way I called it."

How can anyone argue with that? Where there's a will, or in my career an Earl, there's a way.

Crusty Bill McGowan also had a disputed play at first base one afternoon. As the player jumped in the air and screamed at him, he listened passively, his approach based on the theory that if a teapot boils long enough eventually all the water inside will evaporate. And finally, when the player demanded that McGowan respond, Bill finally said softly, "If you still think you're not out, look in the paper tomorrow morning."

But even McGowan lost his temper on occasion. One day he fulfilled the fantasy of countless umpires when, after batter Ray Scarborough refused to stop complaining about a call, McGowan wound up and threw his indicator at him. The bad news is that he missed.

Bill Guthrie, another old-time umpire who refused to take any abuse, lived by his well-known philosophy, "It ain't nothin' till I call it." Once he called a strike on a batter who turned around and started screaming at him. Guthrie ripped off his mask and explained the facts of baseball life to the batter, "Listen, fella, when I call 'em, they stay called. They're either dis or dat. And dis," he said firmly, "is dis!" I've always believed that summed it up entirely.

Charlie Berry was a former football player who absolutely demanded respect from the players. Players used to say that they would come to bat and Berry would tell them, "Hey, kid, good to see ya strike one. How's it going strike two."

Beans Reardon was another arbitrator known to run the game with an iron mouth. One afternoon Bill Dickey was catching and Reardon called a pitch a ball. "What was the matter with that pitch?" Dickey demanded.

"Nothin'," Reardon admitted.

"I thought it was right down the middle," Dickey said.

"Was," Reardon agreed.

"Then why wasn't it a strike?"

Beans spoke for every man, or woman, who has ever stood behind home plate when he replied, "Because I called it a ball." Can anyone actually question the irrefutable logic behind that response?

A great answer doesn't necessarily have to make sense. A few years ago an Oriole batter hit a long, extremely high fly ball right down the line. The ball landed foul by inches, but Kenny Singleton, who was on second, complained to third-base umpire Greg Kosc. "Gees, Greg," he said, "why didn't you run out there and get a better look at it?"

"Kenny," Greg replied, "if I start running out there, my eyes will jiggle." Great answer.

Sometimes an umpire doesn't have to say anything to say a lot. Quite often during a game a batter will take a pitch for a strike, then turn around and ask the catcher whether the umpire had made the correct call. The smart catcher will always agree with the umpire—no matter where the pitch was—because even in these days of designated hitters, the catcher comes to bat. Eric Gregg had the plate one day and Gary Carter was catching. Batters kept asking Carter, but Eric didn't hear him reply. Between innings the second-base umpire told Eric that Carter was holding his hand up near his neck to indicate the pitches were too high. So when Carter came to bat, a pitch came in that just might have been a bit low. Eric called it a strike, and Carter stepped out of the box and demanded, "Where was that?"

Eric said nothing. He just looked at Carter and held his hand waist high.

I was never a very quick thinker on the field. When someone argued with me, I always wanted to mail them a reply. Occasionally, though, I was able to come up with an answer that even I enjoyed. I remember one day I was in Chicago working first base in a White Sox-Minnesota Twins game and Bill Veeck had some kind of promotion going on, so there were approximately fifty-five thousand people in Comiskey Park. I'd never seen that old place so packed, or heard it so loud. The White Sox' Carlos May hit a long drive down the right-field line that bounced within an ant's antenna of the foul line. It was close enough to be called either way. I called it fair—and nobody argued. Hey, then it must have been right.

Harmon Killebrew was playing first base for the Twins,

and after the play he said, "That was pretty close, Ron. How much was it fair by?"

I didn't even pause. "By about fifty-five thousand fans."

Unfortunately, at least from the point of view of an umpire, it is not always the umpire who has the last word. In the old days, when a player or manager started arguing, the umpire often would take out a stopwatch and start timing the argument. If the argument went on too long—and "too long" usually was defined by umpires as slightly longer than "that's long enough"—the umpire would eject the player or manager. Once, though, an umpire pulled his watch on Dodger manager Casey Stengel, to which Casey whispered conspiratorially, "You're crazy to show that watch in front of this crowd, you know. The owner might recognize it."

In the 1934 World Series Dizzy Dean disagreed with a call made by home plate umpire George Barr. Dean screamed at him for a bit, then said, "Mr. Barr, will you kindly answer my question." At least Dizzy said he phrased it that way.

Barr told him, "I did answer your question, Mr. Dean. I shook my head."

Dizzy disagreed. "No, you didn't," he said, "because if you did, I would of heard something rattle!"

Emmett Ashford was a black umpire, which, in the early 1950s, was like stepping up to the plate with two strikes against him. Most umpires start with only one strike against them; at least when people didn't like me, I knew it was because I'd earned it. In 1966 Emmett became the major leagues' first black umpire, and often he told us stories about the problems he had faced in his early days. When he had been hired by the Triple-A Pacific Coast League, he was scheduled to work a game in Portland with two other umpires. As he walked onto the field he noticed that Portland's manager seemed particularly unfriendly. So Emmett walked over to him and asked if there just might be some problem. "Ah, it's not you," the manager admitted, "it's those two other guys I'm mad at."

"You mean my partners?" Emmett asked.

"Hell, no," the manager said, smiling. "Branch Rickey and Abraham Lincoln."

When words fail, an umpire must resort to his ultimate defense, ejecting the player or manager from the game. An ejection is an umpire's way of saying: If you were sinking into a bed of quicksand and I had a length of water hose in my hand, I would use it to add water to the quicksand.

In the history of baseball there has been almost every conceivable type of ejection. There is the most common ejection: one player, one time. Usually it's simple. For example, one day when John Lowenstein was playing for Baltimore, Stevie Palermo threw him out of the game. Lowenstein was shocked. "What are you throwing me out of the game for?"

" 'Cause you called me an !#%&(!"

"No way," Lowenstein protested. "I never called you a !#%&(." And after pausing, he added, "I called you a @$*{!"

But from that basic starting point, things have gotten much more complicated. There is the rare no-player ejection. With the permission of manager Casey Stengel, pitcher Bob Miller left the Mets one day before the 1962 season ended to start his long drive home. During the final game of the season someone on the Mets' bench was riding the home-plate umpire. Finally that umpire decided he had had enough. He ripped off his mask, marched to the Mets' bench and said, "That's it Miller, you're out of the game."

Nobody moved. Finally Casey went over to the umpire and explained, "If you really want to do that, you'd better get in your car and start driving, because by now he's probably a thousand miles away."

Slightly more complicated than no-player or one-player ejections are multiple ejections. For instance, take the 1956 Cardinals—all of them. Early in a game against the Giants at the Polo Grounds they started riding plate umpire Stan Landes. Unable to determine exactly who was yelling, Landes decided to clean house—he ordered everyone on the bench, except Manager Freddie Hutchinson, to go to the clubhouse. He got them all, every last one of them—except Hutch.

And there was no way he was not going to get Hutchinson; it was just a question of how long it was going to take him.

Not very long. When Hutchinson ordered the batboy to leave with the team, Landes decided Hutch was trying to make fun of him. The batboy stayed; Hutchinson left.

No player, one player, and the entire team. Now the subject of ejections begins to get really interesting.

In the minor leagues, Ken Kaiser got an entire pressbox. The writers and scorers sitting up there were yelling at him, and Kenny does not like to be yelled at. Kenny does not like to be whispered at. In fact, if you have something negative to say, it's best to talk to Kenny on the telephone. It's best to talk to him on the telephone long distance.

No player, one player, the entire bench, the pressbox—and a fan. In Philadelphia one afternoon, Bill Klem threw a fan out of the ballpark. Chicago manager Frank Chance got into a screaming match with this particularly unruly fan, and Klem went over to the stands to break it up. "That's enough," Klem said. "Let's break it up." He told Chance, "You can't insult the patrons."

"What about him?" Chance demanded.

"Sir," Klem said politely, "you didn't buy that seat to insult the ballplayers."

"Oh, yeah?" the fan responded just as politely. "Just go ump the game, you big fathead." That was probably not the single most intelligent thing he might have said. Klem summoned a police officer and became the first umpire in history to order a fan thrown out of the ballpark.

No player, one player, an entire team, the pressbox, a fan—and a football player. The Miami Dolphins football team was scheduled to play a charity softball game at the conclusion of a regularly scheduled Class-A Florida State League game. When the baseball game went into extra innings, Dolphin linebacker A. J. Duhe walked onto the field and told home-plate umpire Al Migliorato, "Hey, ump, let's just get this damn game over with."

Naturally, Migliorato was a bit surprised to see a football player standing next to him on the field, so he called the Florida Highway Patrol and had Duhe escorted from the ballpark. The president of the Florida State League then requested that the Dolphins management fine Duhe for "abusive language, a threat, and contact," which would have made him the first football player to be fined by an umpire for behavior during a baseball game.

No player, one player, an entire team, the pressbox, a fan, a football player—and himself. In 1955, Jocko Conlan took himself out of the game. After he had called a strike on a pitch to Jackie Robinson that had bounced in the dirt, Jocko left the ball game. "I just couldn't bend over to follow the pitch," he admitted afterward. "And Robinson seemed so honestly shocked over that call I figured I must have missed it. I didn't want any more like that."

And finally there is legendary umpire Al Barlick, who once ejected a fan from a coffee shop. One morning in the coffee shop of a St. Louis hotel, the fan recognized Barlick. Al was never known for his sense of humor. Let me put it this way: Compared to Barlick, William Buckley is a stand-up comedian. For some reason fans think it is clever to kid umpires about calls they've made—which, to an umpire, is like telling bus crash jokes to a mechanic who repairs bus brakes. The fan put his hand on Barlick's shoulder and said, "I was at the ball game Sunday and I saw you blow that one in the first game."

Barlick pushed the man's hand off his shoulder, waved his arm, and shouted, "Get outta here!" The man actually left the coffee shop, and thus Al Barlick made history as the first umpire to throw out a fan outside a ballpark.

Actually, umpires and fans are not natural enemies. For fans, disliking umpires is an acquired trait. Unfortunately, it is apparently an easily acquired trait. The last refuge of an unhappy fan is blaming the umpire. Umpires don't like being yelled at, but they accept it as part of the job—much like cabdrivers accept potholes. It is when fans yell at umpires and try to beat them up or throw things at them that umpires get upset.

Without doubt, as far as umpires are concerned, the most important technological advance in recent history is the invention of the aluminum can. In the old days fans would often express their hostility toward an umpire by throwing a bottle at him. If they were really unhappy, they would throw a full bottle at him. Fortunately, tests have proven that a fan simply cannot throw an aluminum can as far as he or she is able to throw a bottle. And it is very difficult to throw a can with any accuracy.

Throwing a bottle at the umpire was another old tradition, sort of the morons' version of throwing out the first ball. In those days a "high, hard one" did not necessarily refer to a fastball. Newspapers used to describe how angry a ballpark crowd had been by estimating the number of bottles thrown at the umpire. Just as several explorers claimed to have discovered the New World, so several umpires have claimed that their decisions were responsible for the fact that fans are no longer permitted to bring bottles into ball parks. There were sixty thousand cheering fans at Yankee Stadium during the 1937 pennant race, for example, when umpire Joe Rue called a long drive by Yankee George Selkirk foul. Bottles immediately started flying out of the stands at Rue, who stood defiantly on home plate. When the bottle shower ended, the field was littered with bottles. The Harry Stevens concessionaires sent their people onto the field with baskets to collect the empties. Officially, more than four thousand bottles were thrown at Rue, the American League record. "We counted them and we wept," Frank Stevens commented. Unfortunately, his tears were not out of sympathy for Rue. "Four thousand bottles," he continued, "and nearly all of them had been brought into the park from outside, not sold by us."

Jocko Conlan was working a Dodgers-Cubs game at Ebbets Field in 1944. When the third out of an inning was made at third base *before* a runner touched home plate, Conlan ruled the run didn't count. Dodger manager Leo Durocher went berserk, kicking dirt all over Conlan. And then a great barrage of bottles began. Jocko also stood defiantly at home plate as the bottles flew out of the stands. (Do you think maybe that kind of thinking is caused by wearing the mask too tight?) "It's not a very comfortable feeling to be standing at home plate while people you don't even know are throwing bottles at your head," Jocko wrote years later, which makes me wonder if he would have felt any better if he had known the people throwing the bottles. According to Jocko, bottles were forever banned from ball parks after that incident.

Sometimes forever isn't a very long time. Only six years later, Al Barlick forfeited a game in Philadelphia to the New York Giants when Phillies fans objected to his ninth-inning call by tossing ketchup onto the field. Well, it actually hadn't become ketchup yet, it was simply bottles and tomatoes.

In those old days, if anyone had asked an umpire what he liked most about the average fan, that umpire would most likely have replied, "His bad aim."

Unlike umpires and fans, umpires and managers are natural enemies. The only thing a manager is concerned with is his team winning, and it is impossible for him to accept the fact that an umpire really doesn't care whether that team wins or loses. Umpires don't like managers, and some umpires don't like some managers more than they don't like other managers. Throughout baseball history, there have been many great feuds between managers and umpires. Obviously, Earl Weaver and I really didn't get along as well as, say, Roosevelt and Hitler. Earl didn't like me and I didn't like him. I always felt that was his fault—he was born. Our feud eventually got so bad that the American League refused to assign me to Oriole games. To them, that was a punishment. A punishment? Not having to go into Baltimore and listen to Earl whine from the first pitch to the last pitch? If that was a punishment, what were they going to give me for a reward?

But compared to some of the other classic confrontations, our battles were minor skirmishes. Hall of Fame manager John McGraw and Bill Klem despised each other on the field. McGraw apparently wasn't really crazy about any umpire, he didn't even like the color blue, but he really disliked Klem. The two future Hall of Famers first met before a game in 1905, when McGraw presented Klem with a gift from a local high school, a silver ball-and-strike indicator. Their fine relationship survived only three innings. Then Klem ejected McGraw. The next day, as McGraw trotted past Klem, McGraw told him, "I can whip any umpire in baseball."

"No, you can't," Klem responded.

"Who can't I lick?"

"You're looking at him."

Once, I threw Earl out of a game before it had even started for continuing an argument that had begun the day before. Klem and McGraw had the same kind of warm relationship. Because of McGraw and Klem, managers or their representative must now bring the starting lineups to the umpires at home plate before the game. In the old days the umpire had to go over to each dugout to get the lineups. As Klem was doing that one day, McGraw greeted him with a typically friendly remark. "Drunk again, eh, Bill?"

After the usual bantering, Klem said politely, "Mr. Manager, you are a dirty liar." McGraw survived two full innings that day before Klem ejected him.

Managers who don't get along with particular umpires often have a player or coach who tries to soften up that umpire so that their team doesn't suffer. Catcher Rick Dempsey was the go-between, or the "smoocher," as this player was called in the old days, between me and Earl. I liked Rick a lot, but he was not a great smoocher. Several times, after catching a pitch that I'd called a ball, he would indicate to Earl that I'd called it incorrectly, and Earl would start screaming, "There you go again, trying to $#@% me. . . ." And then Rick would complain to me, "Gees, doesn't that guy ever shut up?"

Klem ejected McGraw from just about every National League ballpark; he even ejected him from exhibition games. For a brief period the two men did not speak off the field, until their paths crossed and pitcher Christy Mathewson jokingly asked McGraw if he knew Klem. "Yeah, we know each other," McGraw replied. "And he always gives me the worst of it."

Another question: Which umpire once said about which manager, "He is the king of the complainers, the trouble-makers, the malcontents, the ones who can never, never, never accept a tough decision against them?" Actually, it could have been almost any umpire speaking about almost any manager. In fact, it was Jocko Conlan describing Leo Durocher. Jocko often described Leo as two-faced, the kind of man who, when he patted you on the back, made you suspect he had a knife in his hand. Durocher was a dirt-kicker of the Ralph Houk mold; the difference is that Houk rarely kicked dirt toward the umpire, while Durocher liked to kick it on the umpire. One day Jocko had had enough and after ejecting Durocher followed him toward the dugout. "Turn around!" he screamed at him. When Durocher did, Jocko screamed, "Go ahead and take a punch at me!"

"Why?"

"So I can knock you out right here!" And this, too, is inside conversation between a future Hall of Fame umpire and one of baseball's great characters.

Weaver used to yell and scream and whine and jump up and down like one of those toy baseball cap bobbers that are put in the back window of automobiles, but he never, ever tried to hit me. Because of that I always disagree when someone claims he isn't smart—he was certainly smart enough not to get physical with me.

The relationship between umpires and managers, and umpires and players, and umpires and fans will never change. As I've often explained, every time an umpire makes a decision, half of the people on the field aren't going to like it, and the other half are going to like it but believe the umpire finally gave them a break because he'd called so many against them in the past. But many other things about the job have also changed through the years. The traditional uniform, for example, has evolved from a suit with a formal hat to today's more casual wear. Until quite recently all umpires had to wear a jacket and tie, which they were not permitted to remove during a game, and a long-sleeved shirt. "The men in blue" in the National League actually wore a blue suit, while the American League's men in blue wore maroon blazers with gray slacks.

Without doubt one of the most significant advances in major league umpiring took place in 1967. After a two-day-long meeting, Umpire-in-Chief Cal Hubbard announced that the base umpires would henceforth be allowed to remove their jackets on hot days. The real problem was deciding what constituted "hot." Umpires had long dealt with problems like how dark is too dark and how much rain is too much rain, but what is hot was a totally new concept. It was finally agreed that a majority vote of the three base umpires would determine hot.

It was also decided at that meeting that, while National League umpires wore short-sleeved shirts under their jackets, American League umpires would continue to wear long-sleeved shirts, even when they took their jackets off. This decision was reached because several umpires with hairy arms feared "that the fans might refer to them as apes." I certainly wouldn't have minded that—compared to what they were already calling me, that would have been an improvement.

Eventually, though, we progressed from long-sleeved shirts to short-sleeved shirts to turtleneck sweaters to nylon baseball jackets. One problem we had was that on occasion we wanted to wear sports jackets, but not the ties, and the league insisted that we couldn't wear the jacket without a tie. So what we often did was not wear the jacket at the beginning of the game, then at the end of an inning have the ballboy bring out our jackets but not our ties; that way we could wear the jackets without ties and blame it on the ballboy. Revolutions often begin with very small skirmishes.

The primary function of the equipment worn by the home-plate umpire is protection, although if that were really true, the home-plate umpire would also carry a weapon. Ironically, the greatest change in the protective equipment has been the elimination of the large inflatable chest protector—the "mattress," "balloon," or "bag," as it was known—that was once used by American League umpires, which has been replaced by the National League-style protector— which is worn inside the shirt or jacket and offers much less protection.

Some home-plate umpires, as well as some catchers, have started using a "Stevie," a throat protector that hangs down from the bottom of the mask and prevents foul balls from hitting the umpire or catcher in the throat. This was invented by catcher Steve Yeager—who invented it when he was struck in the neck by a piece of a broken bat as he crouched in the on-deck circle. However, at this time batters waiting on deck do not use the protector.

Perhaps the most recognizable piece of umpire's equipment is the whisk broom used to clean home plate. I think it is worth pointing out that in no other sport are the officials supposed to clean the playing surface. Football referees don't sweep wounded players off the gridiron. Basketball referees don't sweep the court. Soccer officials don't mow the field. Tennis officials don't wash out the players' mouths with soap. Only in baseball is the official responsible for keeping part of the field clean. And they are not paid anything extra for it, either. Umpires actually once used a long-handled kitchen broom to sweep the plate. Contrary to the vicious rumors that umpires adopted the small-handled whisk broom because some kid stole the long handle to play stickball, the whisk broom became an official part of the umpire's equipment in 1904, after some clumsy player tripped over the kitchen broom's handle and broke his ankle. From that point on, umpires have been bending over backward to clean up the mess made by players.

Umpires have successfully determined how dark is too dark, how much rain is too much rain, and what is hot, but one question that long concerned them was how many umpires are enough. In the major leagues, at various times the answer has been one, two, three, four, and six. The only thing proven by the original one-umpire system was that

one was not enough, even when he was being paid the
enormous sum of five dollars per game. That led to the
institution of the two-umpire system—which possibly prevented the institutionalization of the single umpire.

Four umpires were used in a game for the first time in
1909. In the World Series between the Pirates and Tigers
that year Billy Evans was the home-plate umpire and Bill
Klem was working the bases. To accommodate more paying
fans, temporary bleachers were erected next to the permanent outfield stands in Pittsburgh. The ground rules were
amended so that any ball hit into those temporary stands
on a fly or on one bounce was a double, while any ball hit
into the permanent stands on a fly or a bounce was a home
run. With the home team Pirates hitting, a batter hit a
one-bouncer into the seats, but neither Klem nor Evans
could determine if it landed in the permanent or the temporary section. Having no choice, both umpires marched to
the outfield and asked the fans. One fan, sitting in the
temporary seats, held up the ball and said he'd caught it
right there. Evans ruled it a ground-rule double and put the
Pirate batter on second base. Here's my question: What do
you think happened to that fan? Here's my second question: How many pieces can you cut a baseball fan into?
The very next day, however, four umpires were assigned to
work a game for the first time—a memorial, I suspect, to
that honest fan.

Klem lobbied for the use of four umpires in a game
during the regular season, but that was like asking the
criminals to hire more cops. By the 1940s major league
rules required two umpires a game, but most often three
umpires were used. Night baseball, in fact, is primarily
responsible for the introduction of the fourth umpire. Because it was so difficult to see a ball hit deep into the
outfield at twilight, a fourth umpire was needed to make
sure that someone would be in position to determine if a
ball hit near the foul lines was fair or foul.

Six umpires are now used during the World Series. So
finally, when television cameras are able to focus on any

portion of the field and instantly replay the action, more umpires are used than ever before.

Once, it was a matter of honor to umpires that they never left the field or sat down once the game had begun. No matter how many innings the game extended, no matter how many hours it took, no matter how hot or cold it was, an umpire never left the field or sat down. Okay, one person's definition of honor is different from another person's. I don't know why it was so important to uphold this tradition, but it was—and I learned my very first season in the minor leagues that umpires just never sat down on the job. None of us believed the Republic would fall if we sat down, or the stock market would collapse, but there are just some things that weren't done—like voting twice in the Miss Rheingold election. I broke almost every tradition in my career, I spoke to fans, drank coffee during the game, joked with players, laughed at a manager, but I never sat down or left the field—even when some players and managers suggested I should.

If someone had told me when I started working in 1962 that eventually umpires would be wearing short-sleeved shirts without a tie, have long hair, and occasionally leave the field between innings, I would have laughed and told them, "Yeah, sure, that'll be the day that Ronald Reagan from *Death Valley Days* becomes president and umpires get vacations."

Umpire vacations? Umpires now are given two week vacations during the season. How come umpires didn't get vacations when I was working? And we needed them more than they do now, too, because we didn't sit down or leave the field during a game. In all honesty, if I hadn't had to actually work as an umpire, I certainly would have kept the job much longer.

When I was active, instead of vacations we had injuries. The only time we got even a day off was when we were hurt. One day in Anaheim, I remember, I got hit in the knee and went down. Bill Haller came over to me and asked, "What is it?"

"A two-weeker," I said happily. I finished the game and

immediately put ice on it, which was a mistake, because that kept the swelling down and I was back in ten days.

The only other "vacation" I had took place when I fainted during a game from loss of blood due to a bleeding ulcer and had to be rushed to the hospital. When I got to the hospital, still wearing my umpire's uniform, a doctor recognized me and asked, "What are you doing here?"

What was I going to tell him, the stork brought me? Eventually they told me the ulcer had been caused by stress and suggested I do my best to avoid aggravation. "That's great," I said. "From now on when the managers come up to home plate before the game and hand me their starting lineup, I'll hand them my medical report."

Minor injuries were considered bonuses. A National League umpire was stung on the eyelid by a bee, for example, and missed a week. Everybody else immediately went out and bought honey to rub on their faces. Umpires are perhaps the only people jealous of pulled muscles. The great Hank Soar was the individual who taught me an umpire has to take a few days off during the season just to retain his ability to keep things in perspective, as well as his sanity. Hank always took a week off in late August or early September, just before the stretch run really began, to take his canoe out of the water. But until then no one could say he didn't have both oars in the water.

Surprisingly, the thing that has significantly changed all sports in America, television, has had little effect on umpires. Television actually has been very good for umpires, particularly slow-motion instant replay, because it has proven that umpires make the correct decision almost every time. The problem, of course, is that no one except Earl Weaver can be correct all the time, and when a wrong decision is made in a play-off or World Series game, every fan in the nation sees it. But except for the occasional death threat, that hasn't caused any problems.

Occasionally an umpire becomes known as a "television umpire," someone who performs for the camera. Before television, some umpires were called "newspaper umpires," men who performed for the writers. The differ-

ence, of course, is that "newspaper umpires" were at the
mercy of the writers, and you can't wrap fish in yesterday's television program. There is no such thing as a television umpire. Umpires don't perform; they respond to the
action. There is simply no time to wonder how that response looks on TV. At least that is what I always told our
makeup man before the game.

The one thing we had to remember when working a
televised game was not to start an inning before the commercial ended. The difficulty with that was that because
we were on TV, we couldn't watch TV, so we didn't know
when the commercial ended. So the network assigned a
man with a white towel to sit near the camera at third base
to give us signals. A towel on his shoulder meant that the
commercial was still running; when he took it off, we
could resume play. I always had a problem figuring out
what to do while waiting for him to take the towel off his
shoulder. The team in the field would be finished warming
up, the batter ready to step in, fifty thousand fans would be
waiting for me to signal the pitcher to begin, and I had to
wait for a man I didn't even know to take a towel off his
shoulder. It is very difficult in those situations to fake
being busy. Believe me, you can tie a shoelace only so
many times, or inspect the ball, or clean off the plate, or tie
that shoelace again without looking ridiculous. Fortunately,
because the commercial was running, you can look ridiculous only to the people in the stadium. And how smart can
they be? They had paid money to sit in the ballpark, far
away from the field, in the middle of a crowd, when they
could have been watching the game free at home.

Many popular books today include some sort of unbelievable, shocking revelation. And I certainly don't want
this book to be an exception. So here it comes: The most
important thing that television has proven is that there is
no such thing as a half swing. Calm yourself; I understand
that is difficult to believe. But it is true. Think of it this
way: An airplane is either on the ground or in the air, an
umpire is either right or correct, and a batter either swings

or does not swing. A half-swing is like a pasta diet, there isn't any such thing.

It's simple. The hands may be quicker than the eye, but the television camera is quicker than the hands. As far as an umpire is concerned, if a batter starts to swing, he swung. The instant replay is either going to show that the batter actually spun around twice or almost held up—but even if he almost held up, it is going to be close enough to call it a strike.

An invention that did have an impact on the profession was contact lenses. Many people would disagree, but I've always believed it is very important that an umpire be able to see. Over a period of time vision often deteriorates. In the old days there was nothing an umpire could do about correcting that. What was he going to do, wear glasses on the field? Ho, ho, ho, that's a good one. The first umpires to wear glasses onto the field were American Leaguers Ed Rommel and Frank Umont in 1956. And, naturally, the second time Rommel wore them, during a night game at Yankee Stadium, Mickey Mantle hit a ball approximately 450 feet to center field, where it either hit a narrow retaining wall or bounced in and out of the bleachers. Rommel ruled it had hit the wall, and Mantle had to settle for a triple. The Yankees' Casey Stengel protested the game, demanding that Rommel wear his glasses not only during night games but at all times.

Contact lenses solved the problem. Nobody can tell when an umpire is wearing contact lenses because no one can see them, even if they are wearing their own contact lenses.

Umpires have spent more than a century calling them as they see them, when they see them. And they've spent more than a century trying to maintain their integrity while doing a job in which, as Klem once said, "They expect you to be perfect at the beginning and then get better."

I think every young umpire should be aware of the legend of Tim Hurst. One Sunday in the early 1900s an overflow crowd, held back by a rope, ringed the playing field in Cleveland. After a close call at first base went against Cleveland, their manager, Pat Tebeau, threatened Hurst, "You @$*& Irishman. If you make another decision like that, I'll cut the ropes and let the crowd in on you."

Several innings later, a batter hit a little dribbler down the third-base line. As it got near the bag it rolled foul, but Hurst screamed to the batter, "Run, Jim, run! It's fair!" Then he turned to Tebeau, stood up tall and proud, and yelled defiantly, "Cut the ropes, ye spalpeen, cut the ropes!"

8

BASEBALL IS A MONEY GAME

Recently I asked several former major leaguers to name the most significant difference between the game when they played it and the way it is now. Not one of them had to hesitate to think about it. "About a million-three a season," one of them said.

"We had more fun but they make more money," another one stated, then added, " 'though I suppose a lot of them today think making a million dollars a year is a lot of fun."

"Actually, the checks they get today are the same size as the ones we used to get," a third ex-big leaguer explained. "It's just that theirs have more numbers on them."

And finally, a former All-Star pointed out, "I earn more money today playing in Old Timers Games and appearing at autographing sessions than I did in a season when I was an active player."

Joe Garagiola once claimed, "Baseball is a funny game." When he played it certainly was, and for some people it probably still is. But today, more than anything else, baseball is a money game.

An old baseball axiom once stated that home run hitters drive Cadillacs. That is no longer true. Now, home run hitters' chauffeurs drive Mercedes, while singles hitters have to drive their own Mercedes. At one time baseball fans were astonished to learn that Babe Ruth was being paid more per year than President Calvin Coolidge, forcing Ruth to defend himself by explaining, "I had a better year." Many players today earn more money per season than the president, vice-president, and the entire U.S. Supreme Court combined. In fact, Yankee pitcher Ron Guidry turned down a two-year offer of $1.6 million in 1987, saying he was embarrassed by the offer. I believe I speak for many people when I state that I would be willing to be embarrassed for a lot less money.

In the old days contract negotiations were simple. "When I was twenty years old I walked into General Manager Ed Barrow's office for the first time," Phil Rizzuto remembers. "He was sitting there getting a haircut. I sat down and he said, 'Here's your contract.' It was for $5,000. 'Mr. Barrow,' I said, 'I was the Most Valuable Player in the American Association, *Sporting News* Minor League Player of the . . .'

" 'Sign that or get your ass outta here,' he interrupted. In the 1940s that was known as a negotiation."

Rather than a general manager, a player and a barber, a salary negotiation today can easily involve as many as fifteen people, particularly if the club and the player's agent cannot agree on a contract and they submit their dispute to binding arbitration. When the Mets' Ron Darling requested arbitration, for example, he was represented in the arbitration hearing by his agent, who had two assistants with him, and three people from an agency hired to present his case. The Mets were represented at the hearing by two executives, in addition to four people from Tal Smith Associates, who had been hired to present their side to the arbitrator. That's thirteen people, fourteen counting the arbitrator, and it doesn't even include the accountants and attorneys who did the actual mathematics. Obviously, players today have to be paid a lot of money; otherwise they couldn't afford to pay the people who ensure that they are going to be paid enough money to pay them to ensure that they . . .

As Rizzuto's experience proved, before free agency— which theoretically enables players to change teams and thus establish their true market value—players had only two options: Play or don't play. That system also left the owners with two options: Pay or don't pay. The owners tried to combine the two: They paid their players as little as possible to play. Lefty Gomez won only twelve games in 1935, for example, fourteen less than he'd won the previous season, and the Yankees tried to cut his salary from $20,000 to $8,000. Lefty mailed the unsigned contract back to the Yankees, suggesting, "You keep the salary. I'll take the cut."

Dizzy Dean won thirty games in 1934 and got a raise to $18,500. The next year, he won twenty-eight games. "After the season ended I decided I was going to ask for $50,000. Then I got my contract. Branch Rickey cut me down to $17,500 because I'd won two less games than I did the year before."

Joe DiMaggio had a similar problem with the Yankees after hitting safely in fifty-six consecutive games in 1941. "When I came in to talk contract, I was offered a $5,000 pay cut."

St. Louis Cardinals' Hall of Famer Bob Gibson won twenty games in 1965, after winning nineteen in 1964. He told General Manager Bob Howsam he wanted a $15,000 raise. Howsam countered by offering $2,000. Gibson argued that he'd won twenty games the previous year. Howsam responded by telling Gibson, "Gee, Bob, that's only one more than you won last year."

Before arbitration, sportswriters were able to fill countless pages every winter with salary negotiation stories. Each winter the teams and their players would engage in an almost ceremonial charade that included name-calling, arguing, and threatening. As the beginning of spring training got closer, the threats would get louder and louder: Players would claim that they absolutely would not play for the salary the team was offering; the team would respond by explaining it simply could not afford to pay a penny more. The writers would participate in the game, explaining what steps the team would be forced to take if the player held out the entire season. In fact, the writers, the player, and the team knew that there was about as much chance of the player sitting out the entire season as there was of Nikita Khrushchev agreeing to play Maria in the Broadway version of *West Side Story*. But somehow, trusting baseball fans would accept the myth that there was a possibility the player would actually sit out the season! This would happen every year, and every year every player would eventually sign, and the next year it would happen again, and the fans would believe it again. What I want to know is: Where were these fans when I had my sporting goods store? My problem was that my customers bought only things they wanted, and expected to pay a reasonable price.

The annual ceremony would begin when teams mailed out new contracts to the players. Until that contract arrived the player had no idea how much the team was going to offer him to play the following season. "The day your new contract arrived in the mail was always an exciting day," Ed Brinkman remembers. "You knew you were going to turn it down and send it back, but you'd kind of open it up very slowly, wondering how little the team actually thought of you. Then, generally, after opening it, you'd get angry, and send it back with a note explaining why you deserved more."

In 1957, Minnie Minoso returned his contract to the White Sox' Chuck Comiskey with a classic note reading, "I am sending this contract you send me because I guess you was wrong about it. It looks like a contract which belong to me for the year of 1953 or 1954, not for Minoso after fine 1956 year I have.

"I can't think that this contract belong to me, it belong to another player on the club. This salary has expired and is no good for me next season. Contract for me should have more money than one sent by mistake for next season.

"Please send me correct contract. Excuse me. Orestes Minoso."

Sometimes players would get so angry they would tear up the contract and mail the pieces to the general manager. When Camilo Pasqual did that, though, Senators' owner Calvin Griffith taped it together and sent it back to Pasqual.

Actually, some players who had negotiated with Calvin were surprised that he didn't bill Pasqual for the cost of the tape.

Sometimes the salary dispute could be resolved over the telephone. One winter the Milwaukee Braves' Johnny Logan and General Manager John Quinn argued until they were only $500 apart. After weeks of haggling, Quinn called and suggested they flip a coin over the difference. Logan agreed—on the condition that his wife flip the coin. Quinn accepted. After a long pause, Logan returned to the phone to tell him the results. And if you can't figure out who won the toss, I have a sporting goods store and a four-wheeled vehicle only slightly damaged in a minor tornado to sell you.

Usually, though, the player ended up making an appointment and negotiating head-to-head with the general manager. This was very fair. On one side of the large desk sat an experienced businessman who negotiated a minimum of forty contracts a season and had a legal staff available to him. On the other side sat a player who probably hadn't gone to college and negotiated perhaps ten contracts in his entire career. These negotiations were about as fair as a math bee between Darth Vader and Fred Flintstone.

"I was never a very good negotiator," Joe Nuxhall admits. "In 1955 I won seventeen games, six more than anyone else on the team, and asked for a $5,000 raise. They offered me $2,000. Finally the general manager raised it to $3,000, which he said was his final offer, then warned, 'You sign this contract or on your way home, you stop at Fisher Body in Norwood, 'cause I hear they're hiring.' "

On occasion Vada Pinson would go into the GM's office prepared to negotiate a pay cut. "If I didn't have a good season, I was willing to take a cut. One year I remember I went in there and said, 'Okay, I'll take a $2,500 cut.' And they told me, '$5,000.' I don't think that's how things work today."

Perhaps Early Wynn summed up the feelings of most of the players of the 1950s when, after winning twenty-three games in 1954, he received his new contract and announced,

"I think there's probably been a mix-up. I didn't ask for a cut."

Among the toughest of all negotiators were the Yankees' George Weiss and the Senators'/Twins' Calvin Griffith. No matter how good a season a player had, they always found a reason to give him a smaller raise than he wanted. Weiss used to try to convince Yankee players that they should accept less money in salary because they could practically depend on receiving a World Series share, which in those days equaled an entire season's salary for some players. Of course, if the Yankees didn't win, Weiss would attempt to cut salaries that didn't include the raise he failed to give them the year before because they had expected a World Series share, because they'd failed to win the World Series.

In 1949, Eddie Lopat won fifteen games for the World Champion Yankees, and Weiss offered him the same salary he'd received a year earlier, telling him, "You didn't pitch against many contending clubs."

"I had no control over who I pitched against," Lopat responded. "They give me the ball and I go out there and pitch." Lopat received a small raise. The following year he won eighteen games, twelve of them against contenders. "I couldn't wait to get in there to tell him."

Weiss offered a $1,500 raise, explaining, "It doesn't matter who you pitch against. Now you're in a bracket where the money is pretty good and we just can't afford to pay what you want." Years later, Lopat claims, he learned why Weiss was such a tough bargainer—supposedly, he was given a salary budget to work with and got to keep ten percent of anything left in that budget after all the players were signed.

Calvin Griffith didn't need any such incentives—he owned the club. It was his money he was paying, or as he might have said, "giving away." When Jim Kaat won eighteen games for the Twins in 1962, Griffith raised his salary to $19,000. Although Kaat slumped to ten wins in 1963, he figured the Twins might offer him the same salary because the team had finished third and broken attendance records.

But the contract that was sent to him called for the maximum allowable 20 percent cut. "I tried to call Calvin collect," Kaat recalls, "and I knew it was going to be a tough negotiation when he refused to accept the charges. Finally I went up there and met with him.

"His secretary ushered me into his office and he was sitting behind his big desk. He asked her to bring him some coffee but didn't even think about asking me if I wanted some. Then he started shuffling through some papers. It was as if I didn't even exist. All of a sudden he looked at me and asked, 'Are you here to talk about something?'

"I told him I had an appointment to talk about my contract. 'Oh, that's right,' he said, cupping his chin in his hands. 'How much were we paying you last year?' Believe me, he knew to the penny what I was making. Then he turned half around and started looking for a file, and as he did he began complaining aloud, 'Boy, the price of bats and balls is going up again. This game is getting expensive.' What chance did I have against him, really?

"Eventually we started discussing salary. I told him what I wanted and he said he couldn't possibly pay me that much. 'You think you can go out on the street and find another job for $21,000?' he asked.

" 'No,' I agreed, 'but do you think you can go out to the Interstate 36 and find a left-handed pitcher who can win eighteen games?'

"When I reminded him how well the team had done, he said, 'It doesn't make any difference how many people we draw or where we finish, I pay you for what you do on the field.' Eventually I signed for $17,500.

"The next year I won seventeen games, but we finished seventh and drew about one hundred thousand fewer fans. The first contract Calvin sent me was for $19,000. So I'd won twenty-seven games in two seasons and was being offered the same salary I'd earned two years earlier. After holding out for several weeks, his offer got to $26,500. It was less than I wanted, but I finally reached the point where I decided what was more important, the principle or the money. I believe in principles, but I took the money.

"That's the way negotiations were conducted in those days. I think one of the major results of the way we were treated then is that today the principle begins at about $200,000."

Not every negotiation was that difficult. Some Dodger players, for example, trusted General Manager Buzzy Bavasi so completely that they agreed to sign blank contracts. "Usually my negotiations with Buzzy consisted of, 'Can you give me a few thousand more?' " Hall of Famer Duke Snider remembers. "One winter Pee Wee [Reese] and I were the only two players he hadn't signed. Buzzy called and asked me to agree that I would sign a contract in spring training. We didn't even discuss terms. So I did. We got to spring training and Pee Wee and I were about to go onto the field and we were told we couldn't work out unless we were signed, so Buzzy sent his secretary over with two blank contracts and we both signed. We actually didn't know what we were going to be paid until we received our first paycheck."

Oh, sure, I can see players doing that today. Now some of them won't even sign autographs without being paid for it.

Bavasi would often play games with his players. One former Dodger recalls negotiation sessions in which Bavasi wrote figures on three slips of paper, turned them upside down, and told the player to pick one. After the player had made his choice, Bavasi threw the other two in the waste-basket and said gleefully, "I'm glad you picked that one, because it's the lowest of the three." Naturally, the player shared the joke with him. Bavasi then proceeded to give the player the salary he'd originally requested.

Another player once received a contract in the mail from Bavasi that called for an illegal 50 percent pay cut. "I immediately called him," the player remembers, "and he told me they had a pool going in the office trying to guess how quickly I was going to call. 'And if you think you're calling quick,' Buzzy told me happily, 'wait until that big collie [Drysdale] gets his contract!' "

In the spring of 1987 Red Sox pitcher Roger Clemens revived another ancient baseball tradition. Clemens, who had not been in the big leagues long enough to qualify for mandatory arbitration, refused to sign with the Red Sox for their offered $500,000 and actually refused to play a portion of the season. By doing so, Clemens became a "holdout," a player who wouldn't sign for the salary offered by the team. Once, holdouts were an important part of baseball lore, and every spring training opened with photographs of four starting pitchers, arms extended, holding baseballs in their hands and a lone holdout sitting forlornly by himself in the stands. Except for an occasional exception like Clemens, though, the holdout has become as rare as a mile of highway without a McDonald's.

At one time, however, holding out was serious business, and several players sat out an entire season—among them Hall of Famers Edd Roush and Frank "Home Run" Baker—rather than play for what they considered an unfair salary. One of the most significant holdouts in baseball history took place in 1966, when Dodger pitchers Sandy Koufax and Don Drysdale held out together. That was long past the time a player would have signed a blank contract. "In 1965 Koufax had won twenty-six games, I'd won twenty-three, and the team had won the World Series," Drysdale explains, "so I knew that if I didn't get a good salary that year, I was never going to get it. I met with Buzzy Bavasi and we spoke for a few hours about everything except dollars and cents. Finally he asked me what I wanted.

"I named a figure over $100,000. At that time the $100,000 salary was reserved for the superstar hitters; pitchers just weren't paid that much. When I named the figure Buzzy got pale and said, 'Oh, my God.'

" 'What's the matter?' I asked. I thought maybe he was sick.

"He said, 'Are you trying to get me fired? How can you want that when Sandy only wants ...' and he named a much lower figure. I told him I didn't know what anyone else was making, I didn't care what anyone else was making, I just wanted what I considered to be a fair salary.

"Several days later Sandy and I got together for dinner. I didn't intend to ask him about his negotiations because in those days we never discussed salaries. It just wasn't done. But I could see he was a little depressed, and I asked what was bothering him. 'Oh, it's Bavasi,' he said. 'I go in there and try to talk to him and all of a sudden he asked me how could I ask for so much money when you had asked for so much less.'

"That opened my eyes. I told him my story and that perked him up. 'I think I know how to cure this,' I told him. 'We'll just go in together.' " Koufax and Drysdale held out until the end of spring training, before the Dodgers made them baseball's first $100,000 pitchers.

That opened a lot of eyes. Until that time players had successfully been isolated. Another grand tradition of negotiating was that players would never, ever reveal their salary to other players or to the press even if someone stuck chopsticks under their fingernails. Salary figures in those days were only slightly less secret than the Coca-Cola formula. The theory was that keeping those figures confidential prevented jealousy in the clubhouse; the reality was that it prevented players from comparing their salaries. When Jim Fregosi was playing in minor league baseball he remembers the general manager telling him, "Okay, okay, you win, I'm gonna give you $600 a month, but don't tell anybody because then everybody will want that."

When Moe Drabowsky was with the Cubs he had the privilege of playing with Ernie Banks. "It took me a long time to understand him," Moe remembers. "Every day we'd get beat and the next day he'd come out there smiling, telling everyone, 'What a great day for a ball game. Let's play two.' I couldn't understand how he could be so happy all the time. Later, I found out. I was making $6,000 a season and he was making $80,000. No wonder he was so happy. If the situation had been reversed, I would have been as happy as he was."

Although there had been several challenges to baseball's reserve clause, which allowed teams to own the rights to their players in perpetuity and thus keep salaries artificially low, one of the first successful breakthroughs took place in 1975, when an arbitrator declared Oakland's Catfish Hunter a free agent and salaries began escalating. Escalating? Slightly faster than the way a rocket escalates. "Jim Hunter and I had an agreement," Charlie Finley, the A's owner, explained. "He wanted to defer part of his salary, and I agreed to do it. Later on he decided he wanted to take $50,000 of that deferred money, and I told him he couldn't do it, that that wasn't part of our agreement. He had a country lawyer from North Carolina who was pretty smart and they took me to arbitration. I agreed because I didn't think there was a chance in the world I could lose. I'd have been damn foolish to take a chance on losing the best pitcher in baseball for $50,000, but I believed I couldn't lose. Well, I turned out to be a damn fool. I lost. The arbitrator ruled against me and ruled that Hunter's contract was void.

"The next day Catfish called me and said, 'Mr. Finley, I'm sorry about yesterday and I don't want to leave you. There's a farm down here in Hertford that I'd like to have that'll cost $250,000. If you'll buy that farm for me, I'll forget about yesterday and come back and play for you.'

"I then made the darndest mistake I ever made. Well, maybe second to tearing up a ten-year agreement to stay in Oakland and signing a twenty-year contract. Anyway, I felt so bad about losing the decision, I was so hurt, that I said no. I told him I wouldn't do it. I could've gotten him back for $250,000, nothing compared to what that led to, but I had to live with myself."

The Hunter case changed the economics of baseball just as dramatically as the lively ball changed the game on the field. The arbitrator's decision made Catfish Hunter baseball's first true free agent, able to sign with any team he chose. But as baseball's players soon discovered, in some instances the term "free agent" is a contradiction—the one thing no agent is is free.

Baseball's players have never been good negotiators. They don't have to be. Never in baseball history has a pitcher retired a batter with a good argument. Perhaps the negotiat-

ing ability of the average player is best exemplified by
Orioles' coach Jimmy Williams. As a young player he was
invited to attend a Dodger tryout camp in 1948. After
working out for more than a week, he was one of nine
players told to report to the team office, which had been set
up in the rear of a sporting goods store. Before Williams
went into the office, one of the other players advised, "I'm
telling you, whatever they offer you, ask for more money.
You've had a great camp. They really want to sign you."

Finally the great Dodger scout John Carey invited Williams into the office and told him they wanted to send him
to the minor league team in Kingston, New York, and
offered him a contract for $150 a month. Williams remem-
bered the other player's advice and told Carey, "I'd like to
sign with you, but I need more money than that. I'd like to
buy a car, and I'd like to send some money home to help
my parents, and a hundred-fifty a month just isn't enough
to do that."

Carey asked with a sigh, "How much do you want?"

Williams didn't hesitate, "A hundred sixty-five."

Agents are much like adjectives: Their primary function
is to define fully the meaning of the player's ability, although sometimes they also help modify behavior. Of course,
the adjective they are most like is "more."

There is absolutely no question that agents play a necessary role in professional sports today. Athletes know as
much about payouts, annuities, and deferments as I know
about payouts, annuities, and deferments. The real problem is the lack of ability of some agents to do anything
more than convince a client to sign with him. Today,
instead of some high-powered, well-dressed, domineering
owner trying to intimidate a young player into signing a
contract, it is the high-powered, well-dressed, domineering
agents trying to intimidate a young player into signing a
representation contract—so they can negotiate with the
high-powered, well-dressed . . .

Bluntly, some agents are crooks. Certainly not all of
them, not even a majority, but a few. When Mickey Mantle
first joined the Yankees, for example, one of baseball's first

agents convinced him to sign away 50 percent of his income. Recently a young Atlanta Braves' player just promoted from the minor leagues paid his agent $2,500 for negotiating a contract that called for him to receive the legal minimum salary. On the other hand, because of his agent, Dave Winfield is no longer just a right fielder, he's a corporation.

Originally baseball's "agents" simply negotiated off-the-field endorsements and appearances for players. The best-known "booking agent" of the 1950s was Frank Scott, who represented about a hundred of the major leagues' biggest stars and managed to get them fees between $250 and $1,000 for appearing on television shows like *Do You Trust Your Wife?; Masquerade Party,* on which a celebrity panel tried to identify a disguised guest; *Name That Tune; The Honeymooners;* and *Ed Sullivan's Show of Shows.* Scott's clients faced their greatest crisis when baseball expanded to California. "Los Angeles is a $50 town," Scott complained. "That's as much as they'll pay for an appearance by the average player. Maybe they'll offer $100 to somebody like Duke Snider or Gil Hodges, but in New York they pay $500 to $750 for the same thing."

As a basis of comparison, Scott pointed out that Macy's, in New York, willingly paid ballplayers $100 an hour for an appearance—with a two-hour minimum—while the May Company in Los Angeles offered to put a sign in their window urging people to go see Dodger games.

What do you figure the odds would be today that a player would make an appearance in return for a window sign? More or less than the odds that someday I'll be head chef on the *QE2?*

Team owners fully supported Scott's work. "In fact," Scott commented, "most club owners take the attitude that if the player is signed up for the opportunity to earn a little extra income, he has a greater incentive to do a better job on the field. They're not averse to that at all."

With owner support like that, it's hard for me to understand why the players wanted things like more money, pension benefits, or free agency.

Agents first attempted to assist players in salary negotiations in the 1960s, when Earl Wilson of the Red Sox asked Bob Woolf for help. And, of course, the benevolent owners welcomed qualified representatives to the game. "We refused to talk to them," Charlie Finley remembers. "When a player hired an agent he was taking a chance on his job, because we didn't like them at all. I only talked to a few of them before I sold the team. I told them to go fly a kite.

"After Vida Blue had had his first great season, he came into my office with his agent. The agent asked me for $100,000. I was offering $20,000. 'A hundred thousand,' I told him. 'You had to be smoking something before you got here. You got just as much chance of getting that kind of money as I have of jumping out of the window on the twenty-seventh floor. Forget it.'

"The Chicago Baseball Writers' dinner was that night, and at the dinner Vida leaned over my shoulder and whispered, 'Forget the $100,000. I agree, he's nuts. I'll take $75,000.' And that's what he signed for."

When agents first began appearing in negotiations, several general managers refused to speak to them. Supposedly, just as the Green Bay Packers' Vince Lombardi had done the first time a Packer player showed up with an agent, when a Dodger veteran arrived at Buzzy Bavasi's office with an agent, Bavasi excused himself and returned moments later to suggest that the agent negotiate with the San Diego Padres, because he'd just traded him there.

Eventually, however, agents became an accepted and vital part of the negotiating process. In fact, Atlanta Braves' owner Ted Turner was so impressed with the job agent Ed Keating had done in making him pay outfielder Gary Matthews $1.7 million that, after skippering the twelve-meter yacht *Courageous* to the America's Cup, he hired Keating to represent him.

The almost complete elimination of holdouts is primarily due to the existence of the arbitration process. After playing three seasons in the major leagues, if a player and his team cannot agree on a salary, he can elect to have the dispute arbitrated. In that process the club offers what it considers a fair salary and explains why, and the player counters with his demand and his reasons why he deserves it. An arbitrator then picks one of the two figures. The process obviously presents a problem to the ball club, which does not want to destroy a player's confidence. "What we have to do," Mets' vice-president Joe McIlwayne explained, "is try to convince the player that he has done such a good job that we're right to pay him less than he wants."

Probably the easiest arbitration in history involved pitcher Mike Flanagan in 1982. Flanagan demanded $485,000—while the Orioles refused to pay him more than $500,000. That was only the second time a player had actually asked for less than the club offered. Flanagan finally settled for $500,000.

The combination of professional agents, the threat of free agency, and arbitration has made many baseball players millionaires. "When I retired in 1979 after seventeen seasons," Ed Kranepool says, "I was making $110,000. The year after I retired, I read that the man who had been the worst player on our club, a player who would only get in the game when he pinch-hit in one of those twenty-six-inning extravaganzas, signed for $900,000. I couldn't believe it. The only reason he was still on the club was because he didn't play very much. $900,000. 'Wait a minute,' I thought. And that's when I knew the owners had hurt themselves."

"When I started in 1970," Ken Singleton recalls, "there must have been maybe five or six guys making $100,000 a year, and that was my goal. I thought, 'If I can make that much money in this game, I'll be very happy. Well, as it turns out, I made much more than that, and sure enough, I was very happy."

Tommy Hutton remembers having similar thoughts when he signed with the Dodgers. "I said to people, 'Wouldn't it be something if I could make $100,000 a year,' because that was the ultimate, that was what players like Koufax and Drysdale were getting. Now second-year players are getting that, easy."

When Al Hrabosky agreed to a contract worth $5.9 million to be paid over thirty-five years, a reporter asked him if he believed he was worth that much money. "The most obvious answer is, 'No, I'm not.' But if somebody's willing to pay it, then the answer is, 'Yes, I am.' "

It became obvious that the owners, who had underpaid players, were overpaying them. In 1985 catcher Butch Wynegar hit .223 with 32 RBIs and missed a third of the season because of injuries—and signed a three-year contract for $2.2 million. That same year reliever Donnie Moore signed for three years at $1,000,000 a year after appearing in forty-nine games, winning four and losing five, and suffering a shoulder injury and migraine headaches. Pitcher Wayne Garland suffered a sore arm and left baseball in 1981 but continued being paid by the Indians until 1987. Several Royals' players signed lifetime contracts. Reggie Jackson made so much money he bought approximately eighty classic automobiles, probably just to make sure he'll always have something to drive to the bank.

Sometimes the players wanted more than mere money. They wanted love . . . and mere money. When the San Diego Padres' Dave Winfield became a free agent, for example, he signed with the Yankees for a package that will eventually be worth almost $20 million. But he would have stayed in San Diego, according to his agent, the late Al Frohman, if the Padres "had just shown him . . . the tiniest bit of affection—if they had just given him a tie clip or even a congratulatory letter when he won the RBI title. If [General Manager] Ballard Smith had just come to his birthday party, Dave Winfield could still be in San Diego."

Talk about your expensive tie clips. Smith, incidentally, denied that he had forgotten Dave's birthday, claiming, "I was there [at the party]. I even gave Dave a present." Sure, a present, maybe, but I'll bet he didn't give him $20 million. I'll make an offer right here: If Ballard Smith wants to come to my birthday party, he can do so for only $50,000. He can even have a second piece of cake. Okay, three pieces.

I suppose some people reading this might claim I sound just a wee bit jealous. They are absolutely wrong. Wee bit? No way. I'm big-time jealous. Major league jealous. If I had realized that professional athletes were going to be paid this much money, I'd still be on the NFL's disabled list.

Unlike umpires, who simply had to determine how dark is too dark and what is hot, baseball team owners finally had to decide how much money is too much. For many of these people, some of whom had spent their lives believing the phrase "too much money" must be a typographical error, this was a difficult lesson to learn. Unfortunately, it was even more difficult for the players and their agents. Take Bob Horner, for instance; and you can, because nobody else did. The Braves' oft-injured power-hitting third baseman became a free agent at the end of the 1986 season. His agent, Bucky Woy, claimed Horner would have no difficulty signing a new multiyear, multimillion dollar contract, even though he had missed much of the previous two seasons with injuries. "He sells seats," Woy said. "Home-run hitters are the top attraction in baseball. What would he do for a team like Kansas City, that's just begging for a power hitter?" Woy was correct: Several teams did want Horner—it's just that they all happened to be in Japan. Horner signed to play with the Yakult Swallows. That's one long road trip to Atlanta.

By 1986, the gold rush had become a gold stand around and wait. Star players were still receiving large contracts from their teams, but role players were no longer being offered huge salaries. Most teams had ceased bidding for players who had become free agents. The players countered by suing the owners, claiming that they had to bid for free agents even if they didn't want them, even if they couldn't afford them, otherwise free agents really weren't free. Well, I knew that.

The salary boom may well have been the greatest thing that ever happened to players and Mercedes dealers, but many people suspect it has had a negative effect on the quality of the game. "I don't think there is any question that long-term large contracts have hurt motivation," believes Hawk Harrelson, who has been a player, general manager, and broadcaster. "There's a definite pattern, pitchers especially—once they've signed a long-term contract, their performance level goes down. It was true in my own case. When I went from $50,000 a year to $100,000, I didn't work as hard that year. Instead of running fifteen wind sprints when everyone else was running twelve, like I used to, I was running nine. For years I was doing that extra running to reach a certain point, and when I got there I stopped doing what had gotten me there.

"The philosophy of the game has changed. Now it's protection. Fifteen, twenty years ago, everybody played for the good of the club. Today it's more play for yourself. If I was playing today, I really believe I'd be doing the same thing these kids are doing. If you're talking about making a million and a half dollars a year, I may not be cursing at the pitcher, because if I do, he's liable to hit me, and I won't get a new contract."

"I think some players probably weren't as hungry after they signed long-term contracts," said Milt May, whose fourteen-year big league career spanned the salary explosion. "I think there may have been some individual cases where a player thought, 'My leg's a little sore, or I'm not feeling so well because I've got a cold, so I can stay out today because it isn't going to affect my contract, I'm locked in for five years.' "

"It's hard to play the team game today," Montreal manager Buck Rodgers agrees, "because we have an arbitration system based on statistics. It used to be that if you had a runner on second or third the batter would be trying to hit a ground ball to the right side to advance the runner. But players don't want to give themselves up like that anymore because that doesn't go down on the stats."

Rather than not trying hard enough, or not being willing to sacrifice themselves, Al Hrabosky believes some performances suffered because the players were trying too hard. "They got the contract for whatever they did in the past. Suddenly they start thinking they have to start justifying the big numbers. I did it to a degree. I went out there feeling like I had to convince everyone I was worth what I was being paid. That can put tremendous pressure on a player. Suddenly he starts trying to do more than he did to earn the contract."

To summarize, rather than continuing to do what he had done, which had enabled him to get what he got, he tried to do more than he had, to prove he was worth getting what he got, but instead often ended up doing less than he had done to earn what he had gotten. Personally, I like the part about not being hungry anymore.

One means teams are using to counter the effects of long-term contracts are bonus or incentive clauses. These clauses are the general manager's way of saying "have a good season but not a great season." Bonus or incentive clauses cover everything from total at-bats and relief appearances to remaining injury-free and keeping weight below a certain level. For example, André Dawson earned $150,000 for not suffering another knee injury in 1987, and the Giants' Jeffrey Leonard earned an extra $50,000 for being named Most Valuable Player in the National League Championship Series, while Roger Clemens failed to earn his $50,000 bonus when he was not named to the American League All-Star team.

Since umpires' salaries are determined by length of major league service and are not subject to individual negotiations, umpires receive no incentive bonuses. Even if they could, what would they be for? Ejections? No umpire I know ever needed an incentive to eject a manager. The only bonuses available to an umpire are paid for being selected and working in the All-Star Game, play-offs, or World Series, although I suspect that if I had really pushed, certain managers would have offered me a bonus for *not* showing up at the ballpark.

Until recently, incentive bonuses, which are now an important part of many contracts, were illegal—although before they were illegal, they had been an important part of many contracts. Supposedly baseball's first incentive bonus was agreed to in 1888, when Baltimore pitcher Matt Kilroy received an extra $10 for every victory. It was not just individual players who received bonuses, either. Around the turn of the century it was not unusual for a

team to send a "present" to another team as an induce-
ment to play harder against an opponent. Usually these
"presents" were silk shirts, suits, or hats, but on occasion
teams sent money—the theory being, I suppose, that with
money the other team could afford to buy their own silk
shirts, suits, and hats. With only four games left in the
1916 season, for example, Brooklyn gave Boston $10,000
to bear down against the Phillies. That investment paid
off: The Braves beat the Phillies, and the Dodgers won the
pennant.

The problem with incentives is that they can pit teammates against each other. A classic example of this problem took place in 1931, when St. Louis Browns' pitchers
Sam Gray and George Blaeholder each had a contract clause
calling for a cash bonus for winning more than twelve
games. Toward the end of the season both pitchers had
eleven victories. Gray started the game. With the score
tied, Manager Bill Killefer brought in Blaeholder to relieve.
At least he tried to bring in Blaeholder. Gray refused to give
him the ball. Blaeholder demanded the ball. The two pitchers started arguing, then finally began wrestling over the
ball on the pitcher's mound. (Both finished the season with
eleven victories.)

Weight clauses probably are easier to earn, but if a player
is supposed to receive a bonus for staying under 200 pounds,
and instead Lucianos up to 270, who's going to tell him he
isn't getting the money?

Although teams were at one time prohibited from
awarding incentive bonuses to their own players as well
as to other teams, one owner tried to get around that
rule in the 1970s. Now, who could that have been? Which
owner would really try to circumvent the rules? Name
one. Name twenty-six. In 1977, in an attempt to inspire
his Oakland A's, Charlie Finley offered $200 to anyone
who could advance from first to second on a fly-out, $1,000
to any batter going four-for-four, and $2,000 if he was
five-for-five. Pitchers received $1,000 for a shutout, al-
though Mike Norris was promised $2,000 for a shutout

"because," Finley explained, "I know I don't have to worry about that."

After listening to Finley present his price list, third baseman Wayne Gross perhaps got a bit carried away, proposing, "I'd kill a second baseman for $200."

In the old days, when major league players were more concerned about their team's manager than their money manager, and relief pitchers out in the bull pen discussed pitching instead of deferred payments, many major leaguers actually had to get a job in the off-season. Let me repeat that: Many major leaguers actually had to get a job in the off-season. Just like real people. In fact, finding a job was often a problem, because employers knew that the players were going to be leaving the factory/plant/showroom/bar/restaurant/bank/office in February to report to spring training.

The range of occupations was as varied as those of . . . real people. Mickey Mantle literally came out of the coal mines to the major leagues. During one off-season Bill Skowron worked as a plumber's helper, another year he put up neon signs in bowling alleys, and he was in the trophy business. Pitcher Milt Pappas was a bowling instructor, remembering, "I even got my diploma in bowling instruction." Richie Hebner was a gravedigger in the family-owned business. The famed Mets' catcher Clarence "Choo Choo" Coleman painted white lines for the Florida State Highway Department. Jerry Casale worked in a candy factory, earning $2 an hour "and all I could eat. Another winter I delivered used cars that were going to be exported to the docks; that was okay except that to prepare the cars for the trip they tied down the springs and took out the windshield. Believe me, if the owners want players to appreciate spring training, they should get them jobs driving through New York City in the winter in a car with no springs and no windshield." Pitcher Don Rudolph had one of the most interesting jobs, working as a catcher for his wife, who was a professional striptease artist.

Bob Gibson toured with the Harlem Globetrotters. "It took me a while to understand their program," he explains.

"In college I had been a pretty good shooter. During the first game I played with the Trotters I came down the floor and realized there was nobody guarding me. Jump shot, two points. The next time I came down the floor there was still nobody guarding me. Another jump shot, two more points. The coach immediately took me out of the game and started screaming at me, 'What are you doing? What are you doing?'

" 'Hey,' I told him, 'there was nobody guarding me.'

" 'Throw it in to Meadowlark,' he said.

" 'But there was nobody . . .'

" 'Throw it in to Meadowlark,' he repeated. Every time I tried to say something, he interrupted and told me, 'Throw it in to Meadowlark.' So I went back into the game and when I got the ball I threw it in to Meadowlark, then I made a quick cut off a screen to the basket. I was completely free underneath, and turned to look for a return pass, instead I saw everybody else on the team running around in a circle.

"By the time I finished with the Globetrotters I'd learned that our playbook consisted of one play: Throw it in to Meadowlark."

In 1987 the Royals' Bo Jackson decided to play professional football in the off-season. Not because he needed the money, he explained, but because he needed a hobby. A hobby? Play pro football as a hobby? Whatever happened to stamp collecting? How about making model airplanes? If he needs to do something physical, how about smashing model airplanes? But pro football as a hobby? I played pro football, or I would've played pro football if I hadn't been smart enough to be hurt for four seasons, and believe me, if Bo Jackson really needed a hobby, he should've taken up something safe, like cliff-diving, or underwater bomb disposal.

Jackson is the first baseball player in recent years to play another pro sport in the winter, although many stars from other sports, including football Hall of Famers Jim Thorpe and George Halas and basketball Hall of Famer Dave DeBusschere, had brief major league careers. Pitcher Gene Conley played several seasons with the Boston Celtics.

Catcher Vic Janowicz attempted to play pro football with the Washington Redskins.

I worked as a substitute teacher in the winter. That job served an important purpose for me, besides preventing starvation. After spending six months trying to manage rooms full of whining kids, I was fully prepared to handle a few whining managers. Several umpires, including Doug Harvey and Baby Davey Phillips, worked as college basketball officials, and Davey eventually became the supervisor of officials of the Metro Conference. Larry "six-three-one even" Napp was a boxing referee. We called him "six-three-one even" because he judged every fight he worked six rounds for one fighter, three rounds for the other, one round even. It didn't matter if the fight lasted only four rounds, his card still read six-three-one even. Marty Springstead had the best job of all: He handed out money. He worked for a bank and used to say it was the first time in his life that people liked him.

Kenny Kaiser was a professional wrestler known as "The Hatchet." He briefly worked as André the Giant's partner, although he admits, "André did the wrestling, I did the watching. I like André a lot, his head is bigger than most people. I remember the first time we went out to dinner together. He ate a salad that was about the size of a swimming pool, two twenty-ounce steaks and eleven baked potatoes, and he drank a quarter keg of beer. At that time he only spoke French, and at the end of the meal he said something I didn't understand to an interpreter. 'What'd he say?' I asked.

" 'He wanted to tell you he'll pick up the check,' the interpreter said.

" 'No kidding,' I said. The check? Big deal. If he had really wanted to, he could have picked up the building."

In addition to holding real jobs in the off-season, players often supplemented their incomes by endorsing products and making personal appearances. Most players usually received something like a meal and $25 for appearing at a dinner. In Boston, one former Red Sox player remembers, if they were really lucky, they would also receive a pair of

Bostonian shoes. That player soured on dinners after talking with Ted Williams, who was on his way to make a brief appearance for which he was going to be paid $1,000. "How can I get one of those jobs?" the player asked.

"Start by hitting .388," Williams suggested.

Countless players have endorsed everything from cigarettes to automobiles. Mickey Mantle, for example, claimed, "I want my Maypo" long before Joe DiMaggio became spokesma . . . spokesperson for a New York bank and gained true national fame as "Mr. Coffee." I have been asked to endorse everything from umpires' shoes to the great Car X Muffler Shops in the Midwest. When I was first approached to become a spokesma . . . spokesperson for Car X, I figured an automobile manufacturer had hired someone popular to identify with their brand, while I was going to be the standard-bearer for Car X, as if they were saying, "If you buy car X, you'll end up looking like this poor man." As I found out, Car X was actually an extremely wonderful chain of muffler and brake repair shops, each of them run by brilliant and understanding professionals. They wanted me as their spokesma . . . person, it was explained, because when people saw me they thought about muffling sound.

Old-timers often would capitalize on their fame in the winter by touring the vaudeville circuit. Hall of Famer Waite Hoyt, for example, was a singer who often appeared on the same bill as Eddie Cantor and Burns and Allen. In the 1950s, stars often would appear in the audience of Ed Sullivan's Sunday night variety show to receive the ultimate in recognition: Ed would ask them to stand up. Some stars would put together an act in the off-season, appear in places like Las Vegas, and receive an outrageous fee. The quality of these performances can best be described as not quite up to the talent level of Miss America contestants. After the 1969 Miracle Mets had won the World Championship, for example, seven of them formed a singing group and appeared in Las Vegas—at $5,000 per person per week. The winter after winning eighteen consecutive games, Pirates reliever Elroy Face toured with an act consisting of strumming a guitar and yodeling.

Certainly players today would never yodel for money; instead, many current and former players appear at autographing sessions at which they are paid by the signature. I have no intention of criticizing people who do this, and not just because someday I hope to be asked to appear at one of these shows. Collectors have turned the hobby of trading and selling baseball cards, mementos, and autographs into a multimillion-dollar business. Many of the people who buy autographs at these shows are not young people adding to their own collection but rather people who intend to sell them at a profit. Given that, I don't see anything wrong with athletes being paid to appear at these shows. If I have any complaint at all, it is that the current market value of my autograph is just about equal to that of one glass of water. Let me put it this way: If thieves broke into someone's autograph collection, they would take what they wanted and in its place leave two of my signatures.

Hey—how about autograph-collecting as a hobby for Bo Jackson?

The most important thing about making a personal appearance, I've learned, is that you have to have at least one good anecdote to tell. If the story is good enough, you can tell it over and over. One of the best things that ever happened to me, for example, was calling a foul ball hit by the Angels' Tommy Harper a home run in Baltimore in 1975. I've probably told this story a thousand times on television, at banquets, in my living room, in my first book, to the dogs. Admittedly, at the time it happened I did not think it was one of the best things that ever happened to me. Coincidentally, the Orioles had their largest regular-season crowd in history in Memorial Stadium that day, and after I'd made the call against the home team it appeared that most of them were charging at me. I was surrounded by so many orange-and-black-uniformed Orioles that I thought I was in the middle of a Halloween parade.

I'd lost sight of the ball before making the call and never saw where it went into the stands. I called it fair because the fans were quiet, and I figured they would have been cheering if the ball was foul. I had to call something, and I knew I couldn't call a time-out. And because I wasn't sure, I decided I really had to sell my call. So I leaped into the air, I spun around twice, I . . . stop me if you've heard this story.

Oh, perhaps I have told it too often. In fact, lately every time I open my mouth, my mother says, "You'd better not be telling that story again."

A good story can be very valuable. For example, Joe Ginsberg had a mediocre career but one great story. "I've told this story in many places," he explains. "When my friend Joe Garagiola was doing the *Today Show* he had me on and I told it on national television. The story takes place in 1957. I was catching for the Orioles, and in those days we used a big round glove that required catching everything with two hands. At Yankee Stadium one day, Yogi Berra lined a single to center field and Mickey Mantle tried to score from second base. The throw beat him, but as I tagged him out the ball started to roll out of the glove. I barely managed to hold on to it.

"After the game our manager, Paul Richards, said, 'You almost dropped that ball.'

" 'I know,' I told him. 'It's not easy holding on to it sometimes.'

"Richards had an idea. 'With a runner on second base, when a line drive is hit to center field, where does the pitcher go?' he asked, then answered his own question: 'He goes behind home plate in case there's an overthrow. So what's to prevent the pitcher from giving his glove to the catcher as he runs by him? The catcher can put it on his hand and use it like an infielder. That way he can hold on to high throws and scoop out low throws.'

"It seemed like a good idea. So in spring training the following year Gus Triandos, our other catcher, and I started working on it. It seemed to be working very well—on a base hit to the outfield with a runner on second, the pitcher ran to the plate, handed his glove to the catcher, the catcher quickly put it on, boom. He could hold the throw and make the tag.

"A month or two into the season we were in Cleveland.

A veteran pitcher named Bill Wight was on the mound for us. With an Indian runner on second, sure enough, Roger Maris hit a line drive to center field for a base hit. This is it, I figured, this is what we'd been practicing for. Wight came running to the plate and flipped his glove to me and I started to put it on . . . and started to put it on . . . and that was the first time I realized Wight was left-handed. I couldn't get the glove on. The runner rounded third and headed to the plate, the center fielder made a good throw, and I couldn't get the glove on my hand. After the play Richards said . . . I can't tell anyone what Richards said.

"Garagiola had me on his show and I told the story and he gave me a check for $200. I was only making $6,000 a year, so that was a lot of money. Two months later, though, I got another check from NBC for $200. I called Joe and told him they'd made a mistake, they had double-paid me. 'You idiot,' he said, 'that's a residual. Every time they play that tape you'll get $200.'

" 'Let me get this right,' I said. 'You mean, every time they show that thing I'm gonna get a check for two hundred bucks?'

" 'That's right.'

" 'Gees,' I said, 'that's great. How 'bout showing it once a day?' "

Former players also can earn additional money by appearing at "fantasy camps." These are instructional camps for adults, at which former stars work with people to improve their baseball game so they can return to their homes and be better dentists, stockbrokers, and accountants. In addition to baseball camps, at which the campers wear facsimile uniforms of their favorite team, some baseball players are scheduling fantasy fishing camps, at which people can fantasize, I suppose, that they caught a big fish. I didn't know you had to pay for that privilege. I have never been invited to one of these camps, even though I am relatively well known, easily recognizable, and like people, which leads me to the inescapable conclusion that me not being at these camps is apparently a lot of people's fantasy.

As I've previously stated, there are certain things that

make no sense to me. For example, as a professional eater, I've learned that the slowest thing in the world is a fast. And I know that when dealing with lawyers, the one thing you can depend on is that a brief isn't going to be. And when I first came up to the major leagues, the one thing the hotel rooms in which we stayed didn't have was room. How small were they? I'm glad you asked. They were so small the bunk beds had to be on separate floors. They were so small that the Gideons left only abridged Bibles in the room. They were so small they didn't have mirrors because there was no room for a reflection. I mean, they were small.

And at the same time, I learned the biggest thing in the world was a major league baseball player's ego. And I used to love to watch teams trying to fit two huge egos into one small room. It was always interesting to see two men, both of them used to getting their own way, both of them accustomed to having people do what they want, try to get along. They had about as much chance as Mother Teresa and Idi Amin.

In the old days every player—with the exception of superstars like Ted Williams and Willie Mays—had a roommate. But most contracts signed today have a clause guaranteeing that the player will have his own room on the road. I think that is incredibly ironic; now that hotel rooms have finally gotten large enough for two people to share comfortably, everybody stays alone.

Roommates are another old baseball tradition that has gone the way of the clean-shaven face. Major leaguers, like the animals on Noah's Ark, were always paired off two by two—although I suspect the animals kept the Ark cleaner than many players kept their hotel rooms. Players were always carefully paired by the team's traveling secretary and general manager who, for example, would attempt to put a calm veteran player with a rookie, or a player who stayed in at night with someone who liked to run around, so the good citizen could set the example. That didn't always work. Babe Ruth's roommates, for example, always boasted that they "roomed with Babe Ruth's luggage!" And when Joe Pepitone first joined the New York Yankees, Manager Ralph Houk tried to calm him down by pairing him with quiet, reserved, strong first baseman, Bill Skowron. "That lasted one day," Skowron remembers. "I told him if he was going to stay out all night, call me. He didn't call. But about four o'clock in the morning I heard a knock at the door. I was fast asleep and as I opened the door, I heard this dog barking at me, so I slammed the door fast—slammed it right on Mickey Mantle's head, in fact. When I heard the scream I opened the door again. There was Mantle, on all fours, on the floor. He was with Whitey Ford and they were looking for Pepitone. Imagine what would have happened if I had slammed the door on Mickey's fingers instead of his head."

(By now the reader should be able to fill in his own line here.)

There really was no way of determining which players would get along with each other. Some players had strange habits that made it difficult for them to room with anybody. One ballplayer from the Dominican Republic, for example, insisted on closing the windows and running the hot water all night because he was accustomed to sleeping in a humid climate. Pitcher Dean Chance spent much of the time he was in his hotel room on the telephone speaking to people in various parts of the world. One former roommate of his remembers coming in to discover Chance talking to someone in Tel Aviv. There were players who were sticklers for neatness and demanded that their roommates hang up every piece of clothing. And, at least in the old days, there were players who drank too much. Buck Rodgers remembers one of his roommates coming in very late and very inebriated and mistaking the closet for the bathroom. "He opened the door and threw up. Then he apologized for missing the toilet. Fortunately, I hadn't unpacked my bags yet so I had no problem. Unfortunately, he had."

Perhaps the oddest of all baseball couples was 6-2, 245-pound slugger Ted Kluszewski and 5-5, 140-pound non-slugger Albie Pearson when both were with the Angels.

"The Big Klu" used to warn Pearson that if he didn't be-
have himself he was going to lock him in a suitcase. Supposedly Klu would open the top drawer in the bureau and
put in a blanket and pillow, then pick up Pearson and put
him in there while he took both beds. Maybe it's true,
maybe not. I always believe people as strong as Kluszewski.

The two most important items in any room apparently
were the television and the mirror—although unlike women,
most arguments between players involved the TV. "Tim
Foli was a great roommate," Ken Singleton remembers, "as
long as you wanted to watch whatever he wanted to watch.
I'd be in the middle of a program, he'd walk into the room
and start turning the dial. 'I was watching that,' I'd say.

" 'Yeah, but it was no good,' he'd tell me as he turned
on something else."

In Cleveland, pitchers Gary Bell and Jack Kralick once
actually started fighting over what to watch. Sometimes
the fights didn't involve anything as complex as deciding
between programs; sometimes they were just a matter of
on or off. "I roomed with Robin Roberts for a while," Milt
Pappas remembers. "One night, I remember, we watched
the late news and then I turned on Johnny Carson. Robin
got up, walked over to the TV, and turned it off. 'That's it,'
he said.

" 'What are you talking about?' I complained. 'This is
New York. I want to watch TV.'

" 'I don't,' he said as he climbed back into bed.

" 'You don't have to,' I told him, getting up and turning
it back on. 'I want to watch TV.'

"As soon as I laid down, he got up. 'Why don't you go
down to the lobby and watch?' he suggested as he turned it
off again.

"And as soon as he laid down, I got up and turned it
back on. 'I don't have to,' I snapped. 'This is my room, too.'
Both of us were pretty strong-willed.

"This went on for about ten minutes. Finally Robin got
up again, walked over to the television set, ripped the plug
out of the wall, then took the rubber part of the socket and

snapped it off. 'Now,' he said with finality, 'no one's gonna watch TV.'

"I was so mad at him I couldn't sleep, but I wouldn't give him the satisfaction of leaving the room. So I laid awake for hours, staring at the blank television set."

The most difficult pairing of all, according to most position players, was rooming anyone with a pitcher. "I don't know why they roomed anyone with a pitcher," outfielder-first baseman Art Shamsky says. "If he was pitching the next day he didn't want you getting phone calls after a certain hour, he didn't want the television set keeping him awake, he didn't want the air conditioning on because he was worried about his arm.

"I roomed with pitcher Sammy Ellis in Cincinnati. The first year we were together I'd wake up in the middle of the night and see him standing in front of the full-length mirror, in uniform, pretending to be snapping off curveballs. The thing that really surprised me is that he was pitching from a stretch. 'What's the problem,' I said to him once, 'the mirror get somebody on base?' But he won twenty-two games that year.

"The following season he lost nineteen games. I saw a complete turnaround. One night that year I woke up and there he was, standing in front of the mirror again. This time, though, he had a golf club in his hand and was practicing his golf swing. I figured he must have known something."

Evidently a lot of batters practice in front of the mirror at night. The Orioles' Jim Gentile used to stand there naked swinging a bat, telling himself, "I think I can adjust, I think I can do something." Lou Piniella's roommates with both the Royals and the Yankees talk about how they would awaken during the night to find Piniella swinging his bat in front of the mirror. It wouldn't have surprised me to hear that he also practiced complaining about the umpire's call.

It's not just the pitchers and batters who use the mirror. In umpire school Ken Burkhart would stand in front of a mirror practicing "safe" and "out" calls for hours. Three o'clock in the morning, he'd be screaming "safe!" and "out!" I've heard of people counting sheep, but outs?

Because major leaguers have so much free time when they're on the road, inevitably they are going to attempt to play practical jokes on their roommates and teammates. In 1944, for example, Giants' outfielder Danny Gardella opened his hotel room window and left a suicide note for his roommate, Nat Reyes. Gardella then hung by his hands outside the window until the distraught Reyes got back to the room and found the note, then ran to the window and looked out.

One of the classic practical jokes was played on Mets' roommates Ed Kranepool and Ron Swoboda by Ken Boswell and Shamsky, who had the room next door. "The team was in Atlanta one Saturday and Ronnie and I had stayed in the room all day to watch *The Game of the Week*," Kranepool remembers. "We'd ordered room service, and when it arrived, I managed to convince him to pay for it. But when he looked for his wallet, he claimed he couldn't find it. I thought that was his way of avoiding paying the check, but when I looked for my wallet I couldn't find mine, either. When we couldn't find our watches, we realized we'd been robbed. The scary part about it was that the robbery had obviously taken place while we were asleep in the room.

"From Atlanta we went to San Francisco. Both Swoboda and I were upset and a little edgy. In the middle of the night, after we'd fallen asleep, Shamsky and Boswell managed to get the door between our rooms open and started screaming, 'Get him! Grab him! Hit him!' Ronnie obviously woke up just before I did and leaped over my bed toward the sound of the voices. I woke up just in time to see this figure leaping over the bed, and I grabbed him and started swinging. Ronnie started swinging back, and the fight began. We really went after each other, each of us convinced we'd caught the thief. Fortunately, neither one of us was a particularly good fighter, Ronnie never hit anything too squarely, and I only had a few foul tips.

"Suddenly the lights got turned on. It took a few seconds for my eyes to adjust, and a few more seconds for me to realize that Swoboda and I were the only people in the room.

"That's when we heard Shamsky and Boswell laughing and screaming. We then tried to beat down their door, and I would have to say it was lucky for all of us that we didn't succeed."

George Maloney, an excellent umpire, played what I consider the worst trick I've ever heard of on his roommate. It had to be the worst because I was the roommate. It happened in Anaheim very early in my career. Perhaps I shouldn't admit this, but the one thing that irritates me more than anything in the world is a continuous, rhythmic sound. The sound of a dripping water faucet, for instance, drives me crazier than a manager's whine. What Maloney did was hide an electronic metronome behind the air conditioner. I walked into the room and heard this faint ticking sound. Tick. Tick. Maloney was reading. Tick. "You hear something, George?" I asked. Tick.

He shook his head. Tick. Tick. "What?" Tick.

"It's like . . ." Tick. ". . . a ticking sound."

"No, I don't hear anything." Tick. Tick.

I looked under the bed. Tick. I searched the closet. Tick. Tick. Finally I tracked it down to one of the walls. Tick. "What's wrong with you, Ronnie?" George asked. Tick. Tick.

Tick. "That sound is driving me nuts." Tick.

"Maybe you should see a doctor."

I finally figured out what it was. Tick. Tick. I decided it had to be the heat rising in the ducts. Tick. I started banging on the walls, trying to get it to stop. Tick. I called the manager. Tick. He said the heat was not on.

Maloney went downstairs to get something to eat. Tick. The ticking went on, the incessant tick, tick, tick, tick. The ticking went on until the battery in the metronome wore out two days later. There are several people who believed some of the things I did on the field were crazy. If so, it was not my fault. It was George Maloney's fault, and it started in that hotel room in Anaheim.

But when roommates did get along, they often became

lifetime friends. Art Shamsky's first roommate in Macon, Georgia, in Class D, was nineteen-year-old Pete Rose. "He was this real gung-ho, rambunctious, gregarious type," Shamsky remembers, "but if you had seen him play baseball then you would have said there's no way he's going to make Class A, much less the big leagues.

"At that time there were only sixteen major league clubs, and it was much more difficult to make it and, honestly, I didn't think I was going to make it, either. In those days the main thing roommates talked about was baseball. Then girls, but baseball was first and probably a close second, too. When we weren't talking about baseball we were busy getting in trouble. One night we missed curfew and tried to sneak up the fire escape to our rooms. The night watchman caught us and pulled his gun. One of the greatest careers in baseball history almost ended that night. And mine too. We got in so much trouble that the farm director tried to get us to calm down by reminding us he knew our parents. Then he told us we were never gonna make the major leagues, that we were going in the wrong direction. This was in Class D. There was nothing below us.

"Tony Perez was with us then, too. He didn't speak any English. His real name is Atanasio Rigal Perez. We called him Tony because we couldn't understand him when he told us his name. The team used to drive to road games in station wagons. We had three of them, and eight players rode in each one: three guys in front; two in the next seat; and three in the jump seat, facing backward. Pete and I always took the jump seat so we could see where we'd been. About 4:00 A.M. one morning we were driving down a highway in Georgia at about sixty miles an hour. Most of the other people in the wagon were asleep, even the driver was half asleep, and it was very quiet. We were tired and we weren't playing very well and I was very frustrated. 'Pete,' I said, 'what do you think's gonna happen to us? What are we doing down here?'

" 'I dunno,' he said, 'but I'm going crazy myself.' With that he put down the rear window and crawled out of the car. I didn't say anything, it was terribly hot, and I figured he wanted some fresh air and was going to ride on top for a few miles. Pete was capable of doing that sort of thing. Instead he crawled across the top of the station wagon to the front and suddenly SLAPPED his hand down on the windshield.

"I would say that woke the driver up quite rapidly. Woke up everybody else in the car, too, when the driver slammed on the brakes and the car started swerving across the road. One of the greatest careers in baseball history almost ended that night, too. Mine too.

"From being roommates we became best friends. When Pete got married in 1963 he even wanted my wife and me to stay with him in the honeymoon suite. 'Pete,' I told him, 'it's your honeymoon. You can't have us—'

" 'It's okay,' he insisted. 'She doesn't care.'

" 'No,' I told him. 'You gotta do the right thing,' I explained.

" 'C'mon,' he said, 'we'll talk a little baseball. . . .'

"But that was Pete. That was Pete."

Tick. Tick.

Although no one would begrudge players the right to earn as much money as possible—no one but an umpire, perhaps—the astronomical salaries have changed the game in many ways. But I don't believe I ever fully appreciated how large the salaries have really become until I read that when the Yankees exercised pitcher Neil Allen's option clause for the 1988 season, his salary was *reduced* by $1 million. Think of it this way: His salary was cut more in one season than most players who have ever played the game earned in their entire career. Or think of it another way: even after being cut, he was earning slightly more than $250,000, more than most players in history earned during their career. As Lefty Gomez once said in a similar situation, "You keep the salary. I'll take the cut."

9

T.V., OR NOT T.V.

Contrary to popular belief, money does grow on trees. In fact, without trees to be made into paper, there would be no such thing as paper money. But as far as major league baseball is concerned, the money needed to continue paying large salaries and operating costs grows on television.

Baseball and television go together like love and marriage or heaven and hell; sometimes their relationship is like a love affair with a beautiful woman; at other times it's like being married to the devil. Obviously, major league baseball can be played without anyone watching, as the Indians and Mariners prove every September. But if fans didn't watch the games on television, sponsors wouldn't pay to show their commercials, and without those commercials there would be no revenues to the television station, and without revenues to the television station there would be no rights payments to the teams, and without rights payments the teams would have to do without certain luxuries—like salaries, new baseballs, uniforms, and players. Therefore, television is only about as necessary to baseball as blood is to a vampire.

Baseball survived and prospered for decades without television. Baseball fans—or "cranks," as they were once known—got information about the games from newspapers, or gathered in front of the telegraph office, where the scores of important out-of-town games were electrically posted in the window. The only advantages of this system were that there were no commercials on the telegraph, and instead of a play-by-play announcer and a "color man" there was a guy who knew Morse code. There were no former ballplayers doing Morse code, probably because baseball was still so new there were no former ballplayers. In some places a rudimentary play-by-play was reenacted on a theater stage, with boys moving around the bases as details were received on the wire.

The invention of radio caused drastic changes. Instead of having to stand in front of the telegraph office to watch scores posted, fans could stand in front of the radio store and listen to the game on a loudspeaker. The first broadcast of a baseball game over wireless telegraphy, as radio was originally called, emanated from Pittsburgh's Forbes Field on August 5, 1921. The Pirates beat the Phillies, 8–5. Two months later the first World Series was broadcast from New York's Polo Grounds on a massive three-station hookup. Radio sets in those days cost as much as $70 or $80 and, even at $2 a week, that was a lot of money.

The owners of the major league teams greeted radio broadcasting with only slightly more enthusiasm than France greeted Kaiser Wilhelm's army. These far-thinking businessmen believed that free broadcasts of their games would hurt ballpark attendance, their primary source of revenue. In New York, for example, the Yankees, Giants, and Dodgers agreed not to broadcast any regular-season games because of fears it would keep fans at home. The concept of "exclusive rights" had not yet been discovered, so any local station that desired to could "aircast" home team games. In 1924, WMAQ in Chicago became the first station to broadcast every home game of the local teams, and several other stations quickly joined them. Since rights were free, a lot of stations were willing to make offers for them. Radio station WWJ in Detroit, for example, even refused to accept sponsors for their baseball aircasts, claiming, "We're doing a public service." I suspect that NBC and ABC and many local television stations feel much the same way today; it's just that the price of doing a public service at a profit has risen.

As far as the owners were concerned, however, the real history of baseball broadcasting began in 1934, when the Ford Motor Company agreed to pay $100,000 a year for four years to sponsor aircasts of the World Series. Whoo, were those owners sharp businessmen: radio broadcasting was developed, and only thirteen years later they realized they could charge money for the right to broadcast games. It was as if the owners had suddenly discovered that they controlled the heating rights from the sun, and it marked the beginning of baseball's economic explosion.

Because the only earth satellite in those days was the moon, the range of live aircasts was severely limited by things like hills, making live broadcasts of away games prohibitively expensive, so "re-creations" were invented. These were broadcasts in which an announcer in a studio would pretend he was actually at the game, using sound effects to create a ballpark atmosphere and telegraphed information to give a pitch-by-pitch report of the action. Among the "re-creators" of the time were Jack Graney, the very first ex-major leaguer to become a broadcaster, and Ronald Reagan, the very first ex-re-creator to become president of the United States. These studio announcers would imitate the crack of the ball hitting the bat by banging sticks together and the echo of the public-address system by broadcasting from a tiled bathroom. When the Western Union tape bringing them details of the game slowed down or stopped completely, these announcers would have to invent action to fill the time until the ticker resumed, so if a batter fouled off more than four or five consecutive pitches it usually was the fault of a slow ticker rather than a live fastball.

Once, long before the major leagues moved to California, announcer Dean Maddox was re-creating a Pacific Coast League game featuring the Oakland Oaks. For some reason Maddox got confused and broadcast the top half of the fifth immediately following the top of the fourth, skipping a half inning. Suddenly he realized his mistake, and knew he had to explain honestly to his listeners what had happened. "Ladies and gentlemen," he admitted, "for the first time in baseball history the same team has batted twice without interruption."

Baseball tuned into the television age on August 26, 1939, when a doubleheader between the Dodgers and Reds was televised on an experimental basis in New York. The ratings of the game, if there had been ratings, probably would have been around fifty, primarily because there were only about fifty television sets then in existence. Reports on the quality of the telecast were mixed, the players were easy to see, but it was impossible to see the ball. That was potentially a serious problem: It would be difficult to attract an audience for televised baseball games if the viewer couldn't see the baseball.

Within a year, though, the Dodgers were broadcasting a game a week to their local viewers.

One of the most historic events in sports history took place in 1946, when the Yankees sold the rights to broadcast their games to New York's five hundred television set owners—mostly bars that used them to draw customers—to DuMont for $75,000. As always, the owners and general managers immediately realized the enormous potential of television. "I was scared of television at first," onetime National League president Warren Giles admitted. "I thought we were giving away something for nothing that might be too good. I was worried it would hurt attendance."

Senators' owner Clark Griffith had no such fears. "Television doesn't show you enough," he said. "You can't follow the play. If it ever becomes good, I'll throw it out."

"What some people forget is that television got off the ground because of sports," NBC director Harry Coyle, who started with DuMont in 1947, remembers. "Today, maybe, sports need television to survive, but it was just the opposite when it first started. When we put on the World Series in 1947, heavyweight fights, the Army-Navy football game, the sales of television sets just spurted."

Dodgers' owner Walter O'Malley once recalled, "In the

early days, baseball was the greatest circulation or listener-builder TV had. They needed us. The station that televised our games told me they wouldn't be able to keep us on when more sets were sold and networks were set up."

"We didn't know anything about televising baseball," Coyle admits. "In fact, we didn't know anything about television. We had to invent things as we went along. Our equipment was so primitive at that point that once, when we were doing some event, a tube blew in one of our transmitters. We used the same tubes that were used in radios. So we just took out the tube, went to a local radio store for a new tube, and put it back in. We were off the air for about ninety minutes.

"We used two portable cameras to cover a game at Yankee Stadium, and they were located in cages hanging behind first base and third base. In those days, 'portable' meant anything that had two handles on it. It might have weighed four hundred pounds, but if it had handles on it, it was portable.

"There was no such thing as technique. The most common suggestion we got from people was why didn't we show the whole field with one camera and just leave it there? That's not a stupid suggestion, except that the players would be about the size of mice and you wouldn't be able to see the ball."

Most improvements in coverage resulted from technical advances and trial and error. Often there were more errors than anything else. For example, a camera could go only as far as the cable that connected it to the power source could be stretched.

"Each year," Coyle remembers, "we would go a little further, until finally we decided to experiment with a camera out in the right field stands at Yankee Stadium. It seemed to be working all right, but what we were really waiting for was a home run to right field. We figured we would see the ball coming toward the camera, the right fielder moving back; it should have been a great shot. Sure enough, somebody hit a long drive to right field, directly at the camera. But when I looked at my monitor, instead of seeing the ball and the fielder, all I saw was grass. Grass? I couldn't understand it.

"Eventually I learned that our cameraman was a great baseball fan. He'd brought his glove with him to the ball park, and when the ball was hit toward him he got so excited he forgot all about his camera. He picked up his glove and tried to catch the ball. The weight of the lens had pulled the camera straight down."

Baseball broadcasting today bears as much resemblance to the pioneer days as convertibles do to covered wagons. Rather than directing the action from the back of a station wagon, sitting on the equipment to stay warm, as Harry Coyle did in his DuMont days, broadcasts are directed from multimillion-dollar mobile studios in large trucks or vans. Instead of one or two monitors, the van includes as many as thirty-six screens, videotape equipment, instant-replay facilities, slow-motion discs, a vidifont machine to provide graphics, and an Arvin Echo to freeze the action, as well as heaters to keep the crew warm and air conditioners to keep them cool. These days when someone refers to cable, they mean the array of new stations rather than the metal cord that connected cameras to their power source. In fact, truly portable minicameras, weighing about fifteen pounds, are battery-powered and can be carried by a single cameraman. Lenses vary in size from eighty inches, which were once barred from center field because they allowed players in the dugouts to read catchers' signs, to the tiny microminicam, which can be attached to an umpire's mask. Instead of two cameras, networks use as many as sixteen cameras to cover important games, and small crews of technicians have been replaced by small armies of technicians. "When NBC comes in to Minnesota to cover a game," Twins' publicity director Tom Mee explains, "they bring about eighteen people and hire local camera crews. ABC flies in about seventy people from New York. I never saw anything like it. They had one guy whose only job was to tell the broadcasters whether the official scorer had ruled hit or error on a certain play—after we'd already announced it loudly in the booth. They flew him in from New York, so he must have been very good at it."

Technique has changed just as much. Rather than putting cameras in position and simply following the action, broadcasting strategy is more complex than a pro football team's game plan. For the 1986 World Series, for example, each of NBC's fourteen cameramen was told exactly what to follow when there were no base runners and a right-handed hitter at bat, no runners and a left-handed hitter at bat, a "normal" runner on first, a "fast" runner on first, a runner on second, on third, two runners on base, and the bases loaded. When the bases were loaded and a left-handed hitter was at bat, for instance, Cam 9, designated as a "field snooper," was assigned to a "C.U. of Batter—Stay with him for reaction on home run and wherever he goes," while the job of Cam 13 in high right field in the same situation was to "SHAG—but do a golf shot—between pitches show entire infield and batter."

Do I know what any of that means? Let me put it this way: When NBC hired me as a broadcaster, I heard a director tell someone to "show hero." I didn't know what that meant, so I asked what a "hero" was. Someone explained that it was simply a graphic.

"Oh," I said. "What's a graphic?" So, no, I have no idea what any of that means. My understanding of the technical side of television is limited to the knowledge that you're never supposed to plug the TV into the same socket as the toaster.

Even with sixteen cameras, twenty-eight engineers, twelve production men, a three-man broadcasting crew, a statistician, other support personnel, a carefully planned strategy, and a pregame rehearsal, "You still have to be lucky," Coyle concedes. One of the most unforgettable images in baseball history is that of the Red Sox' Carleton Fisk using body English to push his game-winning home run fair in the twelfth inning of the famed sixth game in the 1975 World Series. "We decided to be innovative so we put a small camera inside the scoreboard in Fenway Park," Coyle explains. "The cameraman was instructed to stay on the batter, but if the ball came directly at him, follow the ball. As Fisk came up to bat the cameraman called me and said, 'Harry, there's a rat out here, sitting about five feet away from me.'

" 'Is it a big rat?' I asked. Obviously it didn't make any difference. It just seemed like the right thing to ask.

" 'It's a big rat, Harry,' he said.

" 'What's he doing?' Meanwhile, the game is going on.

" 'He's not doing anything, Harry,' he said. 'He's just looking at me. Harry, the big rat is looking at me.'

" 'Well,' I suggested, 'try to pay attention to the game.'

"I know this cameraman had one eye in the viewframe and one eye on the rat. I suppose he really had one and a half eyes on the rat and half an eye on the game. When Fisk hit the ball there was no way the cameraman was going to take his eye off the rat to follow it. So he stayed with Fisk, who was bouncing down the base line waving at the ball, finally leaping happily into the air when it went over the fence.

"We knew it was a good shot when we made it. But it was only after we replayed it that we realized how good it was."

Ironically, the easiest game Coyle broadcast in his career was Don Larsen's perfect game in the 1956 World Series. As he points out, "Nothing happened. There were no base runners."

By now most players and managers have become accustomed to performing on television and recognize its importance. "I had had something like a hundred pinch-hits before I played in the 1979 World Series," the Orioles' Terry Crowley recalled. "But when I pinch-hit a double on national TV, suddenly everybody opened the record books and recognized my ability. That double was probably the most important hit of my career—not because of the situation, but because so many people saw it."

Some players and managers, in fact, have learned to make the camera their best friend. "Few managers have ever been better on TV than Tommy Lasorda," NBC's executive producer Mike Weisman, my former boss, said. "When

we televised a Dodger game we used to make bets in the
truck on how quickly Tommy would be out to visit his
pitcher. If it was nationally televised, we were pretty sure
he'd be out by the second inning. If it was just a local
telecast, he probably wouldn't be out until the sixth. If it
was just on cable, he wouldn't be out at all.

"Anyone who knows Tommy knows that in private,
when he is with men, he uses extremely colorful language.
Every other word is a curse word. Just after he had become
the Dodgers' third-base coach under Manager Walter Alston,
we thought about putting a mike on him during the game,
but we were worried about his language. 'I will not curse,'
he told us. 'Trust me, you'll be safe, I'll remind myself, I'll
write on my wrists.' Obviously he wanted to do it, so we
put a wireless mike on him and held our breath. In the very
first inning Dodger catcher Joe Ferguson hit one into the
gap and came into third base huffing and puffing. Sure
enough, Tommy remembered the microphone was on and
was very careful. 'Way to go, Joe!' he yelled. 'That's the
way to go, Joe, baby.'

"To which Ferguson replied, 'Gees, Tommy, did you
see that #@$%&&%$ ball sail?' "

Few players have ever performed better for the television cameras than Reggie Jackson, both as a batter and
when being interviewed. Once, Weisman did a pregame
interview with him that Mike intended to use as an insert
when Reggie came to bat during the game. Reggie's answer
to Weisman's question ran thirty seconds, too long to use
between pitches. Weisman explained that to Reggie and
asked if he'd do a shorter version. "No," Reggie said, "that's
my answer. I don't want to change it, so I'll tell you what.
The second time I get up, roll that thing. Trust me—just
roll it."

When Reggie came to bat for the second time Weisman
took him at his word and rolled the tape. Ten seconds into
it, Reggie stepped into the batter's box. "Uh-oh," the director said, "I'm gonna miss the pitch if I don't lose the tape.
I'm ready to lose it right—" But just before he cut off
Jackson's answer, Reggie called time, went over to the

on-deck circle, and rubbed the handle of his bat with pine
tar. And just as the tape finished rolling, he looked up at
the production booth and smiled, then stepped back into
the box.

Like all love affairs, Reggie and the television camera
have had their difficulties. During his final big league season in '87, for instance, he struggled at bat. Once, after
grounding out, he came back to the dugout frustrated and
angry. In the old days, a player would have kicked the
water cooler. In this case Reggie threw the Gatorade cooler
against a wall. When he realized his tirade was being shown
on television, he stormed toward the camera and slapped it
in the lens, spinning it around. It's often a brutal thing to
see when love goes out the window.

Another player who had an affair with the camera was
Milt Pappas, who might well have been the greatest pitcher
in television history. Television, not baseball. "I was 11–0
on national television," he says proudly. As far as most of
America's television audience was concerned, Pappas never
lost a game, although the same thing might be said about
Cy Young.

Many people believe that umpires don't like working
televised games because more people can see them make a
mistake. That's just not true. Most umpires get just as
excited as the players when the game they are working is
being shown on national television. I mean, do I seem shy?
I took to television like a lion takes to catnip. I never ever
performed especially for the camera, I still ate when I was
hungry and spoke to players when I was lonely; but I knew
that that red light on the camera did not mean stop.

Admittedly the first few times I worked nationally televised games I was nervous, but it became obvious to me
that the more cameras televising the game, the better I was
going to look. I knew that no matter what kind of play I
was involved in, the director was going to have twenty
different angles of it, and from at least one of those angles it
was going to look like I'd made the right call.

Baseball players may not realize how large a debt they
owe to television; if it weren't for television, I'd probably

still be a major league umpire. Because I was such a notice-
able umpire I was often interviewed on television. Because
I proved during those interviews that I could be humorous
for approximately one minute, NBC hired me to comment
on games that lasted three hours. As NBC and I both learned,
after one minute I was in trouble. I immediately encoun-
tered the same problem Al Hrabosky ran into after he had
retired and made the transition to the broadcasting booth.
"The first game I broadcast was wonderful," 'the Mad
Hungarian' remembers. "I spent two hours telling all the
great stories I knew, talking about my career and the things
that I'd learned. As I walked out of the booth that day
people were congratulating me, and I suddenly had a terri-
fying thought: 'I've now told all my good stories, what do
I say for the next twenty years?' "

The real problem with broadcasting, I discovered, is that
people are listening to you. That awareness made me try to
change. Rather than continuing to do the same things that
had gotten me the job, I tried to become my image of what
a broadcaster should be. And I would have to say honestly
that I did a good job, except for the speaking part. I dressed
correctly and I showed up on time.

Broadcasting is very easy as long as you're sitting in
your living room. It becomes difficult only when you're up
in the booth and suddenly you remember the most important thing about the job: Don't make a moron of yourself.

The job of the baseball broadcaster is to tell the viewer
what he or she has just seen. Some people are better able to
do it than others; apparently everybody was better able to
do it than I was. That very first televised game, from
Brooklyn in 1939, was broadcast by Red Barber, who is to
the history of baseball broadcasting what silk is to fabrics.
Broadcasting "from the catbird seat," as he called it, Barber's colorful descriptions of the action down on the "pea
patch" set a standard for announcers. When the business
begins with someone like Barber, it makes it very difficult
to improve.

As the baseball broadcasting business developed, two
distinct types of announcers have emerged: former players

and professionals. There is actually a very important difference: Former players can become professionals—as people like Joe Garagiola, Bob Uecker, Tim McCarver, and Tony Kubek have proven—but professionals can never become former players. Professionals can never really know what it *feels* like to be on the field, although many former players never really know how to describe what it feels like to be on the field.

Players joke that a .240 batting average is nature's way of telling them to become a broadcaster. Beginning with Jack Graney in 1932, there has been a constant trickle of ballplayers becoming broadcasters; only recently has that trickle turned into Niagara Falls. The list of former players and managers who became baseball announcers is even longer than the list of managers fired by George Steinbrenner. Among the many are Frankie Frisch, Tris Speaker, Harry Heilmann, Phil Rizzuto, Pee Wee Reese, Charlie Grimm, Paul Richards, Bill Rigney, Dizzy Dean, Dizzy Trout, Buddy Blattner, George Kell, Fred Haney, Lou Boudreau, Jerry Coleman, Bill White, Brooks Robinson, Ralph Kiner, Duke Snider, Al Kaline, Herb Score, Early Wynn, Jim Palmer, Jim Kaat, Fran Healy, Joe Garagiola, Tommy Hutton, Tony Kubek, Tim McCarver, Mickey Mantle, Joe Nuxhall, Mike Shannon, Bob Uecker, Bob Montgomery, Bobby Murcer, Duane Kuiper, John Lowenstein, Rex Barney, Ken Brett, Joe Torre, Steve Busby, Ray Fosse, Del Crandall, Harmon Killebrew, Don Drysdale, Al Hrabosky, Johnny Bench, and Bob Gibson. Well, I'm wrong: It isn't as long as the list of fired Yankee managers.

Originally, the elements that a ballplayer was expected to bring to the broadcasting booth were inside knowledge and personality. It was considered a bonus if he could actually describe the ball game. The first real star to rise above the field was Hall of Famer and former vaudevillian Waite Hoyt.

After retiring Hoyt became the voice of the Cincinnati Reds. As an athlete-turned-broadcaster, he was proud of the fact that his tenses always matched—even if it was the wrong tense. Hoyt often described action as it took place on the field in the past tense.

But even that was thoroughly acceptable compared to some of the other former players who followed him to the microphone, especially Dizzy Dean, who spoke in no known tense. Few players were less likely to become broadcasters than Diz. His understanding of the English language was probably best described by his brother Paul. After Dizzy had been hit in the head during a game and carried off the field, a reporter asked Paul if Dizzy had regained consciousness. "He wasn't unconscious," Paul said, "he was talkin' all the time."

The reporter asked what he was saying.

"Nothin'," Paul replied, "he was just talkin'."

But what Dizzy Dean lacked in erudition he supplied in personality. Dean began broadcasting for the St. Louis Browns and Cardinals in 1941. "I got into the business because I couldn't pitch no more," he once explained, "and the brewery which sponsored the Cardinal and Brown radio broadcasts sent a man to see me and he blowed up this broadcasting business something terrific.

"I slud along fine until 1950. But my career in St. Louis ended one day when I said the Browns were nothing but a lot of Humpty Dumpties. That's when I came to New York."

Diz immediately ran into a problem in New York. Having almost gotten through second grade in school—"I didn't do so good in first, either"—he had difficulty when the Yankees told him he would have to read their Ballantine Beer commercials exactly as they had been written. "Cain't I just tell people to drink the beer?" he pleaded. Somehow he managed to struggle through the commercials, although after finishing that chore he was known to ask his listeners, "I done that one pretty good, didn't I?"

As a broadcaster Dean became known for his creative use of the language, relying on folksy expressions like "They was really scrummin' that ball over today, wasn't they?" and "Folks, I wish you could be here. This is the nuts," to describe the action. Upon hearing complaints that perhaps these phrases were difficult to understand, he claimed, "When I tell people that the score is nothin'-to-nothin' and nobody's winning, why, folks knows exactly what the score is."

Dean was as much of a character in the broadcast booth as he had been on the field, leading some people to suggest that much of his folksiness was an act. Ole Diz vehemently objected to that, explaining, "It's the best I know."

It's quite possible that Dizzy Trout got more than his nickname from Dean. Like the most Dizzy, Trout became a broadcaster when his career ended, then spent decades in Detroit fighting a never-ending war with grammar. Once, for example, after a batter had fouled off several pitches, he said in frustration, "That guy ain't in a class with this Luke Appling, what used to play shortstop for the Chicago White Sox. There was the foulingest batter I ever see. In one game he keeps foulin' off every strike pitch I throws up there an' finally I get so sore I throws the glove at him. The umpire throws me outta the game and I go up to the plate to have a few words with the umpire and this here Appling says to me, 'Why, if I'd saw you throwed that glove I'da fouled that off, too.' And I guess he would've, too. Nobody ever hit so many fouls as him."

Although his use of the language left much to be desired—tenses, plurals, and pronouns, for starters—he usually found wonderful words to say exactly what he meant. "They call him 'Ole Cucumber an' Onions,' " he said of infielder Billy Goodman, "on account of he loves 'em both. They'll keep him from catching cold and sure keep him from makin' friends." And when a scrap of paper floated gently across the outfield one windy afternoon, he described it perfectly: "That piece of paper looks like Dutch Leonard's knuckleball did five or six years ago."

Phil Rizzuto spent thirteen seasons as the Yankees' shortstop and has spent more than three decades in their broadcast booth, which is probably the only thing that enables him to keep his job while boasting that he leaves the stadium before the game is over to beat the traffic—although, he claims, "I always listen to the end of the game on my way home." Once, in the seventh inning of a spring training game, he left the booth to get some coffee for broadcasting partner Frank Messer. And sure enough, the next day he walked into the booth with a cup of hot coffee. An announcer talking about leaving the game before it's over is like a mailman picking up the mail he is supposed to deliver and mailing it to the people on his route.

Rizzuto's style in the broadcasting booth is sometimes as much stand-up comedy as it is broadcasting. While doing play-by-play one night in Chicago, for example, he took a short break, and partner Fran Healy divulged to listeners that "the Scooter" had gone to the men's room. When Rizzuto heard about that, he told Healy not to say that on the air and suggested that instead Healy tell listeners that Rizzuto was visiting White Sox General Manager Bill Veeck. Several times that night Healy informed listeners that Rizzuto was visiting Veeck, forcing Rizzuto finally to explain, "When you drink a lot of coffee on a cold night you have to visit Bill Veeck often."

On the air Rizzuto seems to be as much a host as a broadcaster, turning Yankee games into episodes of "The New York Home Companion." Often he barely manages to fit in details of the game in progress between reading lists of people celebrating birthdays and anniversaries, sending good wishes to people recovering in hospitals, recommending restaurants, and talking about his family and friends, especially his wife, Cora. Yankee fans willingly accept the fact that he doesn't always have his facts correct—he once had the wrong Indian pitcher shutting out the Yankees for seven innings—as long as he continues to entertain them. Only a hometown hero like Rizzuto could be excused for telling listeners that he disliked round hotel rooms because "I'd have trouble cornering Cora there."

Unlike professionals who spend years perfecting their style working college and minor league games, a former major leaguer's training to become an announcer often consists of good range on ground balls, a great fastball, or, in my case, a mastery of five basic hand signals. Among many others, the Cardinals' Mike Shannon, the Yankees' Bobby

Murcer, and the umpires' Ron Luciano, for example, didn't even know how to keep score when they became broadcasters—which made it difficult to tell listeners how the player had done his previous times at bat. Rizzuto invented his own scoring terminology, including the symbol "w.w.," which was interpreted to mean, "wasn't watching."

It certainly isn't the athlete's fault he hasn't had the training. After spending much of his life perfecting playing skills, he finally reaches a point of success at which he qualifies to do something he has never done before in his life. In fact, the one thing not at all necessary for success on the baseball diamond, talking, is just about the only thing required of the announcer. I could talk, I'd proved that. I just didn't know when to talk or what to say; unfortunately, I also proved that. And when I was hired, the entire extent of my professional training consisted of someone saying, "Stand over there."

"My training for baseball basically consisted of doing three years of college basketball," said Joe Nuxhall, who had become a Cincinnati favorite during his two decades with the Reds. "In 1967 a local brewery asked me to consider broadcasting Reds' games, but I wasn't sure my career was over. I went to spring training as a pitcher, one of the only two experienced left-handers on the club. But when our other left-hander got shot by his wife, and the general manager began talking about trading me to Detroit or Philadelphia, I knew it was time to become a broadcaster."

The practice of hiring former players who have little or no broadcasting experience is often criticized, particularly by the professional broadcasters who are in competition with them for the jobs, and really in particular by Howard Cosell, who derisively refers to them as the "jockocracy." Naturally, former players disagree with that. "I think television needs people who have actually been on the field," former Red Sox catcher and current Red Sox broadcaster Bob Montgomery explained. "On radio, the announcer can say anything, he can say the ball took a bad hop when it didn't. Who'll know? In fact, on radio the announcer doesn't even have to be up with the play. But the television viewer can see what's happening, so what's needed is not so much someone to tell them what's happening but to explain why it's happening. As a catcher I was involved with everything that took place on the field, and I think that experience enables me to interpret the game for the viewer."

Of course, experience is not always a good thing. "Obviously my primary qualification as a broadcaster was my pitching career," the Cardinals' Bob Gibson admits. "ABC offered me a job and I took it. The first interview I ever conducted was with pitcher John Candelaria in Pittsburgh after he had pitched a no-hitter. I asked him that traditional question, 'Did you know you were pitching a no-hitter?' But even before I finished the question I realized, from my own experience, that it was a ridiculous thing to ask. So before he could answer, I answered for him, 'Well, of course you did.' Then he started talking about his ex-wife and I asked him if his family was there. I got so flustered I threw it back upstairs before I was supposed to."

One of the things that numerous former players have proven is that you can take the player out of uniform but you can't take away his loyalty. The primary reason many players get jobs as announcers is because they were popular players in that city. Often they live near the city, they usually know most of the people working for the organization, they're listed in the team's pressbook, and the team pays their salary. Yet the professionals consider them unprofessional if they show the slightest loyalty. I never understood what was so bad about rooting for your employer. Probably the only advantage I had as an umpire-turned-broadcaster is that during my career I rooted against everybody. To expect a player who has been with one organization his entire life to suddenly become neutral is like asking a zebra to wear paisleys.

Former players like Dean and Rizzuto rooted openly for their former teams. Dean would communicate with the Cardinals' dugout with a set of hand signals and used to say things like, "I'm broadcasting to you about the greatest team in baseball, and they will run them Yankees right out of the ballpark." Once, when an opponent failed to touch a base on a play, Rizzuto unsuccessfully tried to phone the Yankee dugout to tell them so they could appeal before the next pitch. "I'm so much a Yankee I can't help it," he admitted. "I know there's supposed to be a fairness thing, but those things don't hit me at the time."

Obviously, some professional announcers also express loyalty to their employer. The Pirates' famed Bob Prince, for example, always ended his broadcast of games won by the Pirates by reminding listeners, "We had 'em all the way."

And in 1964, legendary announcer Harry Caray screamed to St. Louis fans, "I can't believe it! Roger Craig hit the left-center-field wall! The Cardinals are going to win the pennant!" In fact Caray was right, the Cardinals did win the pennant—but this particular declaration was made during the fourth game of the season.

Announcing would be much easier if the game wasn't being broadcast. Unfortunately, as I learned, people not only listened, they also expected me to know what I was talking about. Broadcasting for me was a continuing dilemma: My mother always told me to keep my mouth shut if I didn't know what I was saying, while producer George Finkel wanted me to talk. In fact, the only time I really got in trouble on the air was when I spoke. One day in Toronto I made the terrible mistake of trying to describe the temperament of the Blue Jays' redheaded third baseman Roy Howell. "He's not really redheaded," I started, and that's really where I should have finished. What I wanted to say was that although he had red hair, he didn't have the kind of temper associated with redheads. But I continued, telling my broadcast partner Merle Harmon, "You know what redheads are like, very volatile. I knew a girl in Baltimore once and she had a red beard. Now, she was volatile. There's a lot of crazy people in Baltimore. Baltimore, you know, is full of crabs, and I love them."

That seemed all right to me, but not to George Finkel, who warned me to be careful what I said, because people might misinterpret what I meant. So I made sure everyone would understand my meaning. "I miss those crabs," I concluded. "They are soooooo good to eat. That's what I meant."

When we had Kansas City on *The Game of the Week* I tried to compliment their manager, Jim Frey, whom I liked. "If it's true that people learn from their mistakes," I complimented, "then someday Jim Frey is going to be one of the greatest managers in baseball history."

That was supposed to be a compliment. As I discovered, it's not so easy to think when your mouth's full of words. Too often, my words often got in the way of my thoughts. As every person who has broadcast a game has learned, that is an occupational hazard. So when I quote the mistakes made by other broadcasters, my intention is not to criticize or embarrass them. As anyone who ever heard me working a game will attest, the only thing that prevented me from making more mistakes than anyone else was the fact that NBC failed to renew my contract. They didn't just fail to renew it, they tore it up in little pieces, put the little pieces through a shredder, and gave the scraps to Oliver North for safekeeping. Making mistakes is part of the business of broadcasting—NBC hired me, didn't they?

During a New York Giants' game, for example, Frankie Frisch told his radio listeners, "It's a beautiful day for a night game."

Phil Rizzuto once began a broadcast by greeting viewers, "Hello, everyone, I'm Bill White," while former White Sox manager Jack Onslow started his radio show by telling listeners, "Hello, Jack Onslow, this is everybody speaking." Philadelphia's legendary By Saam, who has always never been a former ball player, opened his very first major league radiocast by saying happily, "Good afternoon, Byrum Saam, this is everybody speaking." Nervous?

New York Mets' fans collect samples of the wit of Ralph Kiner, the Hall of Fame slugger who has been broadcasting for the team since their first game in 1962. Kiner, for example, once told Met fans, "Darryl Strawberry has been voted into the Hall of Fame for the fourth consecutive year, the first National Leaguer to have done that." During a holiday broadcast, the popular Kiner told listeners, "On

this Father's Day, we again wish you all a happy birthday."
It was Kiner who once claimed a pop-up hit by Keith
Hernandez *inside* the Astrodome "got caught in the wind"
and suggested viewers stay tuned after the game to see the
movie *Kartroom*.

Kiner's difficulties with names is well known in New
York. For example, the Cubs' Ryne Sandberg has been Ryne
Sandbag, or simply Ryneberg. On Kiner's postgame show,
Kiner's Korner, currently the longest-running show on tele-
vision, Gary Carter became Gary Cooper. Kiner later
explained that he made that mistake because he was think-
ing of the movie *The Natural*, which reminded him of the
movie *Pride of the Yankees*, which starred Gary Cooper.
And even Ralph Kiner once identified himself as Ralph
Korner.

During a Met game against the Pirates, Kiner informed
fans, "Rounding third base is Mel Ott," which came as an
extreme surprise for all those aware that Ott had died
decades earlier. Actually, that one is easy to understand.
The base runner was catcher Milt May, whom Kiner was
simply mistaking for catcher Ed Ott, whom he mistakenly
identified as Mel Ott.

Once he referred to his broadcasting partner Tim McCarver as Tim MacArthur. "Ralph," McCarver gently corrected,
"my name is McCarver."

"What I'd say?" Kiner asked.

"MacArthur."

"Well," Kiner decided, "that was pretty close."

During the off-season, when a broadcaster for the San
Diego Chargers football team got sick, Kiner graciously
agreed to substitute. "Can you do football?" a Charger
official asked.

Kiner replied that he knew a lot about football, then
opened his broadcast with the greeting, "Hello, baseball
fans!"

Few announcers are credited with making more mistakes than the Padres' Jerry Coleman. "Credited" is the key
word. The former Yankee second baseman has become the
Casey Stengel of broadcasters; writers often credit him

with humorous mistakes made by other broadcasters or sometimes just make up funny lines and attribute them to him. Once, for example, Coleman's broadcasting partner, former Padre infielder Dave Campbell, suggested, "The Padres better make sun while the hay shines." Campbell immediately realized his error and said, "I can't believe I said that."

"Don't worry about it," consoled Coleman. "I'll get credit for it anyhow."

High on everyone's list of favorite "Colemanisms" is his classic description of a long fly ball, "Winfield is going back, back . . . he hits his head against the wall. He picks it up and throws it into second. . . ." And maybe he did say it, but Byrum Saam had said precisely the same thing about outfielder Bob Johnson more than two decades earlier. Certainly Coleman makes mistakes, the best of us do—and so, as I proved, do the rest of us. But among the many humorous remarks *credited* to Jerry Coleman are:

"Johnny Grubb slides into second with a stand-up double."

"I challenge anyone, even with a radar machine, to hit that slider."

"Senior Citizens' day is Sunday. If you want to become a senior citizen, just call the Padres' office."

"In a bunt situation, the batter always looks at the third-base coach to see if he wants him to do what he wants him to do."

"Sanguillen is so unpredictable to pitch to because he's so unpredictable."

"From the way Denny's shaking his head, he's either got an injured shoulder or a gnat in his eye."

"Nettles leaped up to make one of those diving catches only he can make."

"When the time calls for it, Dick Williams will put the bat in his teeth."

"That noise in my earphones knocked my nose off and I had to pick it up and find it."

"That home run ties it up, 1–0."

"Ozzie Smith just made another play that I've never

seen anyone else make before, and I've seen him make it more than anyone else ever has."

"If Rose's streak had still been intact, with that single to left fans would have been throwing babies out of the upper deck."

"Kennedy has that one quality you look for in a catcher: size, strength, and stamina."

"Again we have a high sky, and that can be a problem if it's in the wrong place."

"Only Winfield's six-foot-six arm allowed him to reach that ball."

"Enyart is a typical left-hander. When he throws the ball, nothing happens."

"This game is like a yo-yo. When one side goes up, the other side goes down."

Once, while interviewing Hector Torres, he asked, "How can you communicate with Enzo Hernandez when he speaks Spanish and you speak Mexican?" After Torres explained that Spanish and Mexican were the same language, Coleman concluded, "I didn't know that. . . . You learn something new in this game every day."

Coleman was so popular in San Diego that in 1980 he was brought down from the booth to the field to manage the team. After a disastrous season he happily returned to the broadcast booth, explaining, "You rarely stay awake at night second-guessing a broadcast."

Professional broadcasters are just as prone to speakos, the broadcaster's version of a writer's typos—typographical errors—as any player-come-lately. Jerry Coleman supposedly said, "The score at the end of nine innings . . . wait a minute, that's the end of the game," but the Red Sox' Ken Coleman, certainly among the top professionals, once ended a game an inning early. "We were ahead of the Indians 2–1 in the eighth," he recalls, "and Cleveland had runners on second and third. Bob Stanley came in to pitch for us and Mike Hargrove singled to left. 'Here comes the tying run,' I said, 'and here comes the winning run.' As far as I was concerned, the game was over. But I noticed Bob Stanley was still on the pitcher's mound. It was then I discovered that they played nine innings. I admitted to my listeners, 'Ladies and gentlemen, I'm sitting here in the broadcast booth in Cleveland, Ohio, red-faced because I've just found out that they are now playing nine innings instead of the eight . . ."

The great Harry Caray was broadcasting a game in Chicago in 1984. That year the Cubs had a very pretty ballgirl whose uniform consisted of a Cub jersey and extremely brief shorts. One cold day, however, she appeared on the field wearing sweat pants, causing Caray to tell his listeners, "And the Cubs' ballgirl has just come onto the field. This is the first time I've seen her without her pants."

When Philadelphia's By Saam broadcast his very first game from Montreal in 1969, he informed his listeners, "Most people up here speak French. However, they *are* nice people." Saam matched that *non sequitur* one year in spring training, telling fans, "Down here in St. Pete there's artificial turf on the infield and natural grass in the outfield. Nevertheless, the Cardinals have runners on first and second." During his career Saam gained the affection of countless fans, including an elderly New Jersey woman who wrote asking him, "Would you please talk a little louder? My radio batteries are getting very weak."

Mistakes are the exceptions, of course; otherwise they wouldn't be called mistakes. The amazing thing to me is that broadcasters work as many games as they do without making many more of them. Being a professional broadcaster means being prepared; being aware of the game situation, knowing your facts, listening to what the people you're working with are saying, being able to take advantage of a situation, and being even more prepared. At least those are the mistakes they told me I made. I've found that the best broadcasters have complete confidence in their ability. Vince Scully was doing play-by-play when Detroit's Jack Morris pitched a no-hitter in Chicago. When Morris retired Ron Kittle to complete his no-hitter, when I would have been busy yelling and screaming and telling viewers what they had just seen, Scully had enough confidence to be absolutely silent. It was the loudest silence I've ever heard. The crowd and the scene told the story far more than even the poetic words of Scully could have. And finally, when the roar of the crowd subsided, he found the perfect words to describe the moment, saying softly, "And then there were none."

Scully has the gift of making twenty million listeners each feel he is speaking directly to them. One Saturday afternoon, NBC's Bob Costas was doing the primary game in Milwaukee, while Vin was doing the backup game in Cincinnati. When Costas switched to Scully for an update of the Reds' game, Vin suggested to viewers, "Welcome, all of you who have been watching the Milwaukee-Baltimore game. Why don't you all pull up a chair and watch what's happening?" All across America you could hear chairs being pulled up to the set.

However, when the network returned to Costas, he complained, humorously, "I never realized that all you people watching this game had been standing up."

Although every game is different, most of the things that happen in those games are not unusual, so announcers are prepared for them. Or at least I was supposed to be. The ability of the announcer to adapt to unusual situations is what marks a great professional. For example, when a Yankee broadcast was interrupted by the tragic news that the Pope had died, Phil Rizzuto was so moved that he admitted that that would even put a damper on the Yankee victory.

Perhaps the announcer who best adapted to the unexpected worked for a small cable station in Detroit. "I was sitting home watching the Mets-Dodgers game we were doing," Mike Weisman remembers, "and it was a blowout. But at the same time, Walt Terrell was pitching a no-hitter in Detroit. I wondered if that game was being telecast, so I called producer John Filippelli and asked him to find out. Flip found that a very small Detroit cable station was doing the game. This station probably reached a few thousand homes. We located their office in Detroit and quickly made arrangements to pick up their feed, which included their local broadcaster. I really didn't think about the announcer.

"We made the switch. The Tiger game came up and all

of a sudden I hear this booming voice I didn't recognize saying, 'Welcome to the NBC Television Network!' It was the local announcer. Then he started ad-libbing. I think it was about then I realized that I had just handed over the entire NBC Television Network to someone I knew nothing about. I had no idea what he was capable of. We couldn't break away, because Terrell still had his no-hitter going. All I could do was watch and hope. This broadcaster was having a wonderful time. He did the play-by-play, he ad-libbed promos of our upcoming schedule, he did everything he had heard our network announcers do.

"I don't think anyone ever rooted for a game to be over, no-hitter, no no-hitter, more than I did that day. Without doubt, the best words I heard him say the entire time were, 'Now back to Vince Scully.' "

Actually, there exists a third type of broadcaster, the celebrity. Announcing is much like turning over the letters on *Wheel of Fortune*—everybody thinks they can do it. Occasionally a celebrity who is a baseball fan visits the pressbox and ends up doing some play-by-play. This is not to be confused with the celebrity who ends up announcing that his special program, "A real diversion for me, something I've always wanted to do," will soon be shown on the same channel. In spring training one year, for example, San Francisco mayor George Moscone did a few innings of a Giant-Cub game. Moscone's major problem was highly unusual for a politician: there were times during which he had nothing to say. Giants' announcer Lon Simmons prodded him, suggesting, "You might sing something between pitches. Or mention a lot of names. You could practice a speech."

When a Giant batter hit a long foul ball, Moscone said, 'Oooohhhhh." Simmons gave him some important technical advice, explaining, " 'Oooohhhhh' just won't do it, George."

New York film critic Jeffrey Lyons predicts his epitaph will read: Cause of death: Boston Red Sox. Lyons claims he grew up believing the name of his favorite team was actually the "Long-suffering Red Sox." During a visit to Fenway

Park in the summer of '87, Lyons was being interviewed on radio by Ken Coleman and Joe Castiglione when Coleman said suddenly, "Okay, Jeff, the next three batters are yours."

"I wanted to say, 'Thank you very much, Ken Coleman and Joe Castiglione, and hello, everybody. It's a beautiful night for baseball in Fenway Park, the wind is blowing slightly out to right-center, and Boston leads it 5–0 in the top of the fifth before 31,119 delighted fans. Bruce Hurst has been very sharp tonight, getting nine of the last twelve batters he's faced on just fifty-one pitches, most of them fastballs and curves down and away. It's his best outing since May 19, when he struck out fourteen Yankees. . . .' I wanted to say that. Instead I said, 'The pitch . . . in there for a strike, one and one.' When Coleman put me on I felt as if I'd been given the controls to a 747, or presented with the baton in the middle of a concert and asked to lead the Boston Pops. What I really felt was all alone."

When the Cubs' Harry Caray missed a portion of the season after suffering a stroke, several celebrities sat in for him, among them actor-comedian Bill Murray. Murray took advantage of his opportunity to express some of the real emotions felt by Cubs fans. When Montreal Expo's pitcher Floyd Youmans was thrown out of the game for arguing over a call, for example, Murray said, "You hate to see that sort of thing happen, especially when we're hitting him so well." After Cubs outfielder Chico Walker had taken a mighty swing—and missed—Murray told listeners, "He was trying to tie this game up with one swing of the bat, which isn't easy when your team is winning 7–0." At the end of the game, Murray explained he was particularly pleased with the work of pitcher Rick Sutcliffe, "Because, frankly, he owes me money."

During his stint as a celebrity broadcaster, Murray also had a guest in the booth: his mother. Cub broadcaster Steve Stone took advantage of the opportunity to ask her, "Was Bill really raised by wolves?"

Players can be rated by skills, but it's much more difficult to rate a broadcaster. A player might be fast, or great defensively, or throw a good curveball, but what can you say about a broadcaster? He's got great adjectives? He never splits an infinitive? All a broadcaster is armed with when the game begins and he throws out his first noun is his vocabulary. For a broadcaster, words are the offense and the defense, which might be one of the reasons I had a problem. The only words an umpire must know are "safe," "out," "ball," and "strike." He probably can fake "fair," and "foul," and "Weaver, you're out of the game."

One of the few things I was good at were clichés. Basically, clichés are phrases that have no meaning but are repeated so often that they sound like they have meaning. I often found myself using clichés when I was broadcasting, without thinking about what they meant. "He came to play," for example. Well, of course he came to play. Why else would he come all the way to the ballpark and put on his uniform? He came to watch? He came for dinner? Once, after George Brett had made a great play, I described him as "a real professional." What's a fake professional?

I remember hearing "a real professional," Yankee broadcaster Hank Greenwald, announce a Yankee deal in which they gave up "a player to be named later." Made sense to me, until Greenwald added, "Actually, the player was named at birth; he's simply going to be identified later." Greenwald started in San Francisco, and when the Giants obtained José Uribe, who had changed his name in the minor leagues from José Gonzales to José Uribe, Greenwald explained, "He really is the player who was named later."

On another occasion I heard former player Tommy Hutton tell his listeners on Yankee radio, "The rain is really coming down hard now." Then he paused and added, "Although I guess the real story would be if the rain was going up." That's my kind of announcing.

Baseball has a language all its own, and like every language, and like every other aspect of baseball, it is constantly evolving. Roger Maris's "tonks" became Reggie Jackson's "jacks" and are now Mark McGwire's "dingers," for example. As far as umpires go—and some players will tell you it isn't far enough—one generation's "Blind Tom" became another generation's "Mr. Guess," or "robber," and now is simply !#%&(!. Part of the job of the broadcaster is keeping up with the latest fashion in terminology.

A lot of wonderful baseball terminology has almost completely disappeared from the vernacular. The object of the game was to win the league pennant, or the "gonfaloon," as it was once known. Fans were once called "pluggers" and "grandstand managers" as well as "cranks," but to some players they'll always be "wolves." When was the last time a "pheenom," or "morning glory," a rookie having a great spring, was referred to as an "April Cobb"? Of course, too often that "April Cobb" became a "June bug" and had to be sent back to the minor leagues. Remember "bargain bills," more commonly known as doubleheaders? The major leagues—or "bigs," as they are currently known—used to be "the big tent," and that was before they played indoors. The first-base coach, now known as "the first-base coach," once was "the barker," while the third-base coach, now known as "the third-base coach," used to be a "yodeler," "traffic cop," or "flagman." Coaches in general were "wig-waggers." The umpire working third base was the "ukulele umpire." The number four hitter in the lineup, the "clean-up" hitter, used to be "Big Bertha," although I don't know that anyone would really want to call Kent Hrbek "Bertha." Certainly one thing that has disappeared is "coffee and cake," or "fish cakes," which was an extremely low salary. "Collisions" was a derisive term used to describe college-educated ballplayers, who were considered too smart to know what they were doing on a baseball diamond. A line drive to the outfield—a "frozen rope"—was once a "daisy scorcher," probably because it took the tops off daisies growing in the infield, when there were daisies growing in the infield, when there was grass growing in the infield. A "leather player," or good fielder, was totally dependent on his "eagle's claw," his glove, which he used until it became a "pancake" and wore out.

After a long trip on a "gully jumper," a train, the one thing that "house Dick's" players who used to hang around hotel lobbies always had to be wary of were "ear benders," or fans who wouldn't leave them alone. Of course, if they "saw the barrels," or passed a barrel wagon on the way to the "orchard," the ballpark, they knew they were going to have good luck.

A lot of slang terms were named after people: Infielder's were always hoping for a "Bill Hasmer" or an "Arlie Latham," an easy ground ball, especially one that came to them on a "big Bill," a big hop, which they often got when playing on a "pool table," a smooth infield. When playing on a "contractor's backyard," or an "ash heap," a bad infield, however, batters would often get a "base on stones," a hit, when a ball hit a rock and took a bad bounce. A pitcher with a tricky delivery was a "Houdini," an umpire a "Jesse James." A "clubhouse lawyer"—a player who had an opinion about everything—was known as a "Daniel Webster." In the days of short hair, a star who needed a haircut was a "Rubinoff." A player who kept to himself and rarely picked up the check when with his teammates was a "Dick Smith." Women were not forgotten, either: An "Annie Oakley" was a base on balls but later became a ticket to the game. A black bat is still occasionally referred to as a "black Betsy," and a player more concerned about his own statistics than winning or losing was a "percentage Patsy." Of course, a player who made excuses was, is and always will be an "alibi Ike."

Many terms derived from professions: a "barber," which later became a pitcher who threw close to a batter's head, used to be a player who talked too much. The "barber's cat," though, was someone who often played practical jokes. The manager was, naturally, the "teacher," while his assistant was his "shadow" or "bobo." Today's "fireman" is a relief pitcher, while yesterday's "fireman" was a player who showered and dressed quickly after the game. A "goaltender" was a batter with an "eagle-eye" who swung at only good pitches. The groundskeeper, who "scratches the diamond" or drags the infield between innings, is still a "manicurist," although he used to be a "groundhog"; an outfielder is still a "gardener"; and a player who grew up on a farm remains a "plow jockey." Surprisingly, a "burglar" was not an umpire, but rather a fast-thinking player able to take advantage of a situation.

Pitchers, like Frenchmen, had their own language. A bad arm was a "putty arm." Left-handed pitchers are now "portsiders," but they used to be "cockeyed" and have always been "crooked-armed." A pitcher who threw mostly change-ups was a "cunnythumb." Every once in a while a pitcher would have to shave a batter with a "gillette," a pitch thrown at his head, particularly if he'd had a few "blows," or hits, or had "unbuttoned his shirt," taken a big swing, and quite often he'd do it on the "pay ball," or the pitch thrown with two strikes, no balls on the batter. A "pitcher with arteries" was a veteran who used his head as well as his heart, sometimes to overcome the lack of a good "dipsy doo," or curveball.

Today's players worry about falling below the "Mendoza line," the .200 batting mark. They dislike facing a pitcher with "high cheese," a great fast ball, or a "yellow hammer," "Uncle Charlie," or "yakker," a good curveball. And finally, according to the U.S. Department of Labor, they can no longer get their "lumber," or bat, from the batboy; instead, they get it from the nonsexist "bat-handler."

Admittedly, I did not know most of these terms when I began my announcing career. In fact, I didn't know them when I ended my announcing career. But during that brief span I did learn certain key phrases: When something happened I couldn't explain, which was a problem for someone working as a "color man," whose only job is to explain events, I would say, "You ever see anything like that before, Merle?" When something exciting happened I would say, loudly, "Look at that!," which television viewers could do easily. And finally, when I got in serious difficulty and I couldn't figure out how to save myself, I'd resort to the seven most important words in television: "We'll be right back after this message."

10
THE ELECTRONIC GLOVE AND OTHER SHOCKING DEVELOPMENTS

Almost since its invention, baseball has been so popular that people have never stopped trying to change it. And today almost everything about the game has improved: ballparks, gloves, uniforms, playing conditions, certainly salaries, conditioning equipment, training techniques, medical expertise, almost everything, in fact—except perhaps the quality of the players. The one thing that certainly has never changed is the belief held by many former major leaguers that the players of their era were better than they are currently, whenever currently is.

"I figure the teams and players before World War II were 65 percent better than the teams and players today," Bobo Newsom said in 1954. "How many players on today's teams could have made those teams? Take the Yankees, for example. Rizzuto, that's it. With or without tape measures, you aren't going to say Mantle in the same breath with Combs and DiMaggio, are you? If most teams have two players who could have made their teams of the twenties and thirties, they're lucky."

"When I came up to the Dodgers in 1956," Don Drysdale remembers, "the average age of the players was twenty-six, twenty-seven. They had served their apprenticeship in the minors. Today the accent is on youth; it's not the kids' fault, it's just the way the game is played. Consequently a lot of players in the major leagues today should really be playing Double-A ball in the minor leagues."

"Expansion has reduced the caliber of the major leagues as we know it," Ted Williams explained in 1962. "I don't want to take anything away from Maris and Mantle, but they're batting against guys they never would have seen in previous years."

"It's all diluted now," Tony Kubek, who played with Maris and Mantle, believes. "There are simply more teams than there used to be, and there's not enough talent. Look at the kids who are rushed up to the majors now and all the old-timers hanging on."

"I believe the quality of baseball has declined," Art Shamsky agreed. "When we [the Mets] won the pennant in 1969, every team had several really good pitchers. Look at the National League in 1986. There wasn't a team that had more than two good pitchers. I'm not putting today's players down, I just think the talent is spread too thin."

"I'm not taking anything away from the players nowadays," said Milt May, who came up to the big leagues in 1970, "because they're making the best of the situation, but I think there's some guys hitting .280 or .300 who really aren't quality hitters. I was fortunate enough to play with a lot of great hitters in the seventies."

"The biggest difference is that we have 26 teams today," Mike Shannon believes, "and we have fewer minor league teams than we did when we had sixteen teams. The players just don't get the coaching they once did."

"The caliber of the players today is excellent," Hawk Harrelson claims. "They're stronger, faster, and off the field they're smarter. But certainly the teams aren't better. We're talking dilution. There are 240 more players in the big leagues now than there were when we had sixteen teams. If you took the top eight players from the 10 expansion teams and distributed them among the 16 original teams, you'd see better baseball by far than you see now."

Basically, baseball has always been not as good as it used to be.

I would guess that almost every former major leaguer

believes that the players of his era were better than those who played before him or after him. That belief is one of the great traditions of the game. Without doubt, ten years from now today's players will be better than they are today.

How good are today's major leaguers compared with major leaguers of the 1960s? Were players in the 1950s better than those of the 1960s? The answer is definitive: Don't ask me. One of the very few things about baseball that hasn't changed is the argument over how much baseball has changed. No one can really answer that question about the ability of the players. In the 1950s, for example, someone asked Ty Cobb what he thought he would hit if he were playing then. "Only about .320," he supposedly replied, "but don't forget I'm almost seventy years old." I suspect that great players in any era would have been great players in every era.

It's much easier to answer that question about other aspects of the game. One of the few constants of the game has been that people have constantly been trying to improve the conditions under which those players, who may or may not be better than their predecessors, play. Take uniforms, for instance, which have rarely been uniform. Uniforms for baseball were first worn by the New York Knickerbockers in 1851 and consisted of long navy blue trousers, a webbed belt, a white long-sleeved shirt, and a straw hat. The hat was replaced a few years later by a flat-topped mohair cap. Knee-length quilted pants patterned after a style worn by cricket players, called knickerbockers, were introduced by the Cincinnati Red Stockings—not to be confused with the New York Knickerbockers, who wore long pants—in 1867, and were quickly adopted by all the other teams.

By 1876, when the National League of Professional Baseball Clubs was founded, teams were wearing an all-wool, eight-ounce athletic flannel uniform consisting of a shirt with a laced, buttoned, or shield front with a high "sun collar" replete with bow tie, and cuffed pants with a braided side seam and silk pocket. The White Stockings of the 1880s even wore silk white stockings. Remember, this is a uniform to be worn while playing in the dirt. Either those players had cleaner dirt or didn't mind mussing their silks. Bow ties or four-in-hands were worn with uniforms until 1911, when John McGraw's Giants eliminated both ties and collars.

The modern uniform evolved gradually from that point. Sleeve lengths were shortened and were even temporarily eliminated by the 1956 Cincinnati Reds when they got in the way of their muscles. The length of the pants has moved up and down as often as the length of women's skirts. The knee-length knickers that replaced long pants were worn knee-length (that's why they were called knee-length), but "King" Carl Hubbell decided the elastic band impeded blood circulation in his legs, and he changed baseball fashions by wearing his short pants long. Others followed like ... ballplayers. The shortest pants, Bermuda shorts, were first worn in a game by the Pacific Coast League Hollywood Stars on April 1, 1950. General Manager Fred Haney explained, "We think these suits will give us more speed. I predict these new duds will become standard equipment in baseball for hot weather within a year or so. These outfits weigh only a third as much as the old monkey suits." Naturally, these uniforms were immediately accepted by everyone in baseball. The first time they were worn, in fact, the manager of the opposing team thought they were so lovely that when he came out to home plate to give the starting lineup to the umpires, he was wearing a bonnet and carrying a bouquet of flowers, which he presented to Haney.

Although several other minor league teams experimented with shorts, they disappeared until 1976, when Bill Veeck's Chicago White Sox wore them. By this time, of course, ballplayers had become sophisticated enough to accept the practical uniforms. Pitcher Dave Hamilton announced that teammate Clay Carroll "looks like a Pilgrim going out to shoot a wild turkey," while Kansas City first baseman and noted fashion critic John Mayberry warned he would kiss any White Sox batter reaching base.

That, basically, is the brief history of shorts in baseball.

For more than half a century uniforms were made from all-wool flannel weighing eight ounces a yard and the socks were 100 percent wool. The best thing that could be said about those uniforms was that they kept players warm on cold days. Unfortunately, they kept them warmer on hot days. After pitching nine innings one hot day in 1948, a Cincinnati pitcher weighed his uniform and sweat shirt and discovered they had gained twenty-two pounds.

"In those days we only had one uniform when we went on the road," Duke Snider remembers. "So if we were playing a doubleheader, at the end of the first game we'd just wring them out, change sweat shirts, put the uniforms back on, and go at 'em again."

At least in the big leagues, uniforms were cleaned and pressed after every game. In the minor leagues they were cleaned after every road trip. "After the first few days there was this aroma there that you never forget," Braves' coach Ralph Rowe says. "We couldn't wash our uniforms because they never would have dried. So after about four days on the road you could just take it off and it would stand up by itself in the corner. After a game we'd climb onto that old bus and I'll tell you what: it didn't take more than one breath and you knew those uniforms hadn't been cleaned in a while."

"It's no surprise that teams didn't run too much in those days," Jim Fregosi says. "When a player started sweating, those s.o.b.'s got heavy. Steal a base? You couldn't pull the uniform that far."

"You actually could hear those old flannels," Jim Kaat claims. "They were so blousy that when I was on the mound on a windy day I could hear the infielders' flannels flapping around. And players knew how to use them to gain an advantage. Players like Minnie Minoso would let their shirts bulge out over the plate so a close pitch would just catch an edge and ftttt, hit by a pitch."

Woolen uniforms generally came in one size: too big. The uniforms were so loose, in fact, that several fielders lost batted balls inside their shirts. A line drive once hit pitcher Dutch Leonard in the stomach and dropped down his pants leg. A ground ball once rolled up infielder Eddie Joost's arm and disappeared in his sleeve, finally ending up lodged in the small of his back. Another grounder ended up inside infielder Billy Klaus's shirt. For official scoring purposes, players who lost balls in their uniform were not charged with an error; the most they could be charged with was bad tailoring.

Question: Suppose a player catching a ball in his uniform had stepped on a base before a forced runner got there. Would the runner have been out? Answer: No. The ball has to be caught and held in the hand or glove for an out to be recorded.

Some players—"stylemasters," as they were known—had their woolen uniforms tailored, but most players did their own "home tailoring"—they washed them in hot water until they shrunk to the proper size.

Until synthetic fabrics became available, any reduction in the weight of the flannel affected its durability. The teams had a choice between making their players more comfortable or having to spend considerably more money replacing torn uniforms. Guess which choice they made?

Teams actually began experimenting with synthetic fabrics in 1946, but it wasn't until 1959 that a uniform made of a nylon-wool blend weighing half as much as flannel was accepted. Minor league teams continued to wear the heavier flannels, though, because their rocky infields were tougher on uniforms than major league fields. So, in fact, it was absolutely true for a time that minor leaguers sweated more than major leaguers.

Lightweight, form-fitting, wash-and-dry, cool and colorful elastic doubleknits began appearing in the late 1960s. "The first team I saw wearing them was Cincinnati," Ken Singleton remembers. "They had Bench, Morgan, Rose, and those form-fitting uniforms looked great on those guys. Of course, on those guys any uniform would have looked great."

Form-fitting doubleknits were perfect for television as long as the player had a nice form. There were some forms over which a tent would not have looked good. Those doubleknits made Terry Forster's belly look like a painted mountain, for example.

Actually, because Singleton was allergic to wool he became one of the first Expos to wear the doubleknits. While other players were still wearing their somewhat dull white flannels, Singleton was dressed in bright white doubleknits. "When he was standing with the rest of the team," someone once commented, "he looked like a light bulb turned on."

"It's sort of a trade-off," Kaat believes. "You still got your stylemasters in the game today, and they wear those babies tapered to their bodies. On hot days instead of getting ventilation, like we got from the blousy flannels, the doubleknits stick right to their bodies."

Those uniforms are worn so tightly that if a player somehow managed to catch a batted baseball inside one of them, it would take a team of surgeons hours to remove it.

For decades, major league uniform colors were as bright and colorful as concrete. Absolutely every team wore an eggshell white uniform at home and a prison gray uniform on the road. Yankee home uniforms were considered daring because they included a blue pinstripe. In 1961, Charlie Finley brought color to the big leagues, dressing his Kansas City Athletics in kelly green and Fort Knox gold uniforms. "None of my players complained," he points out, "but admittedly, they knew I was signing their checks. At first I thought there might be some problems with other teams. One night Hank Bauer, an ex-Marine, wore them against his former team, the Yankees. When he stepped into the batter's box Yogi Berra told Bauer he looked very sweet and asked him for a date. That's not a good thing to say to an ex-Marine."

Outfielder Gino Cimoli made certain there would be no such problems, telling a reporter who looked at him in his new uniform and started to smile, "Say one word and I'll sock you."

Actually, brightly colored uniforms first appeared—I mean *really* appeared—long before the turn of the century. As early as the 1880s, teams were wearing brightly-colored uniforms, some teams even donning red, white, and blue uniforms. An 1882 rule required players at each position to wear a shirt and cap of a designated color. Catchers wore scarlet, for example, second basemen orange and black, shortstops maroon, and substitutes green, among others. Ironically, that was the year that prim, acerbic Englishman Oscar Wilde saw his first baseball game. "He admired the game very much," a newspaper columnist reported with remarkable tact, "but the uniforms were not quite to his aesthetic taste."

The home whites and road grays that became traditional were adopted in 1911. And with some rare exceptions—superstitious John McGraw once dressed his Giants in special black uniforms for the World Series, and the White Sox of the late 1920s wore dark blue road uniforms—uniforms came in any color, as long as it was gray or white, until Finley bought the A's. The brightest of all uniforms was the rainbow-colored uniform worn by the Houston Astros. It was said that the Astros' management couldn't decide which color the team should wear, so they wore them all.

The baseball uniform of the future, according to Japan's Mizuno Corporation, is a one-piece jumpsuit made of all-weather polyurethane that will keep players cool in the heat and warm in the cold. Uniforms with padding in different areas will be worn by players at various positions. A catcher's uniform would have additional padding in those areas vulnerable to foul tips, for example, and an infielder would have padding in the shin areas to protect him from being spiked.

Whatever color the uniform was, baseball spikes were always black. Laces, however, did come in various colors and allowed players to show their independence. Finley changed that, too, by introducing white shoes "made from the rare albino kangaroo" in 1967. Several other teams eventually introduced footwear to match their uniforms, but old habits died hard. In a 1973 game Eddie Leon of the White Sox claimed he was hit on the foot with a pitch.

Umpire Larry Barnett examined the ball and, finding a telltale smudge of black shoe polish on the ball, agreed that Leon had been hit and awarded him first base.

It was probably a good thing that nobody pointed out to Barnett that by then the White Sox were wearing red shoes.

The only thing that tops the colorful uniforms today are batting helmets. Going to bat in a major league game without a protective helmet would be like entering a bull ring wearing a Red Sox cap, but until the 1950s players were just too hardheaded to wear them. Wearing a batting helmet was seen as an admission of fear, and players were afraid to admit that they were afraid. They would rather be afraid. Players generally said they wouldn't be caught dead in one of those sissy devices, which in fact was absolutely true.

The first protective helmet, patented in 1875, was basically an iron hat with iron earmuffs. When that proved too cumbersome, lead was substituted. In those days, lead was the lightweight metal. Lead also proved too unwieldy, but this is not where the expression "get the lead out" derived from. Attempts were made to produce helmets out of wood and paper, but they also failed. A paper helmet? That was probably designed by someone who had already been hit in the head.

In 1907, Hall of Famer Roger Bresnahan became the first player to wear a protective helmet in a game, using a rudimentary device he designed after being beaned. In 1939, an inventor named Victor Brunzell patented a felt-covered protective helmet made of a resilient substance. Brunzell's helmet featured a swept-back visor that offered additional protection for the batter's temple. This was the same Victor Brunzell who invented a device for hooking a motorcycle sidecar onto an automobile, which would enable a garage attendant to deliver a car to a customer's home and still have his own means of transportation back to the garage with him. Brunzell's baseball helmet was briefly manufactured by Spalding but became another casualty of World War II.

Branch Rickey invented, patented, and manufactured a

plastic helmet with an air foam lining in 1952, and almost immediately the entire Pittsburgh Pirate team started wearing it at bat and while running the bases. The fact that Rickey was the general manager of the Pirates was probably just an unusual coincidence. But any doubts Pirate players had about the value of the helmet was erased when base runner Paul Pettit was hit in the helmet by a shortstop trying to complete a double play. "I doubt Pettit was more than ten feet away from the shortstop," Manager Fred Haney reported. "The ball struck him smack above the eyes and caromed all the way into the stands in back of first. That's how hard it was thrown. But my guy merely blinked. He was unhurt. Without the helmet he'd have been killed." Rickey's helmet sold for ten dollars.

Players called them "bowlers," "space helmets," and "miner's caps," but mostly they called them ridiculous. Baseball officials refused to make them mandatory. Yankee clubhouse attendant Pete Sheehy claimed that one reason Joe DiMaggio retired was because of the helmets. Supposedly DiMaggio picked one up and said, "Wear this thing? You got to be kidding me." and figured the game was changing so much it was time for him to get out. In 1954 Phil Rizzuto was the only Yankee to wear a helmet at bat. He was hit in the head several times, while players who didn't wear them were not hit at all. Even most of the players who wore them at bat took them off on the bases, claiming it slowed them down. Jimmy Piersall wore one when hitting, but he took it off when on base because, he claimed, it was so tight it constricted his thinking process.

Rather than the outer helmet, some players began using the plastic liner from a football helmet that fit inside their caps. These "skullies," as they were known, were popular because they weren't visible, and they helped players keep the one hat per season they were issued by their team in good shape. Cass Michaels of the White Sox was wearing a "safety crown" when A's pitcher Marion Fricano fractured his skull with a fastball. He credited the skully with saving his life but also blamed the skully for his skull fracture.

Veterans complained they needed the "anti–beanball cap" like they needed a good hit in the head. It took several near-fatalities to wake up the players. Don Zimmer and Minnie Minoso were both hit in the head while batting without a helmet—and both suffered fractured skulls. Zimmer almost died. In 1955, Jackie Robinson's Fiberglas and polyester resin cap was dented by a fastball that otherwise would have drilled a crater in his head. And twenty-year-old rookie Brooks Robinson believed his life was saved by a helmet in 1957 when pitcher Ned Garver's fastball broke off a four-inch piece of plastic.

Gradually, the helmet stuck. Newspaper stories of the early 1950s named those few players willing to risk ridicule by wearing them. Newspaper stories of the late 1950s named those few players willing to risk a fractured skull by not wearing them. In 1959, for example, Willie Mays became the only Giant to refuse owner Horace Stoneham's order to wear one, claiming the helmet bothered him. However, he soon decided that the helmet bothered him less than having Don Drysdale's fastball imbedded in his temple, and he began wearing one.

Old-timers like Frankie Frisch poked fun at the helmets, referring to them as "garbage cans" and claiming players of their generation would never have worn them. Of course, many of these same players also claimed they preferred the fun of their era to the larger salaries younger players were receiving.

The "hardhat," which originally resembled a plastic cap, evolved into the device used today, which has earflaps that protect both sides of the batter's head. Some players—Dave Winfield, for example—refuse to wear the earflaps, sticking to a "straight up" helmet. Thurman Munson felt the same way until Dick Drago hit him in the head—that made him feel differently.

The helmet continues to change. Originally, major league helmets had to be painted several times a year to cover dirt and scratches. Now there is a special cloth to remove scratches, and a polish that makes them shine, putting players in the unusual position of having to wax their hats.

And, according to the Mizuno Corporation, the helmet of the future will have a clear Plexiglas front shield to protect the batter's face and contain a microwave receiver with a built-in speech synthesizer, enabling the batter to receive spoken commands from the manager.

Possibly the single greatest endorsement the batting helmet ever received came from pitcher Don Drysdale, who was often accused of throwing at batters. While still pitching for the Dodgers, Drysdale took a job with the Daytona Helmet Company, a manufacturer of baseball helmets, and immediately began passing out free samples to National Leaguers.

Doubleknit uniforms and Fiberglas helmets are far from the only recent innovations in baseball equipment. As long as people have been playing the wonderful game of baseball, other people have been trying to sell them devices to help them play it better.

One of the problems players have always faced, for example, has been playing in extreme heat or cold. In 1961, the Macon Peaches of the Southern Association tried to solve part of that problem by supplying plug-in jackets to players. These electrically heated jackets, developed by the Army Air Force during World War II for aviators to wear in unheated aircraft, had to be plugged into outlets in the dugout. The thing about this that surprises me is that they were used in Macon, Georgia. Georgia, not Alaska. I saw *In the Heat of the Night.* That's Georgia. How cold does it get in Georgia in the summer?

Keeping cool has always been difficult. In the old days some players would put soaked cabbage leaves under their hats in the field. Before dugouts were air-conditioned, players would dip their hats and handkerchiefs into a bucket of ammonia, then rub the ammonia on their faces. "Maybe it wouldn't cool you off," Yankee clubhouse attendant Nick Priori explained, "but it sure would wake you up." In 1958, Cincinnati experimented with air-conditioned caps. The "Vapo-Cool," as it was named, was made of the open mesh similar to that used in caps today, but rather than the old-fashioned sweat band, which cracked, caked, and held sweat very well, the hat had a strip of aluminum foil folded over a thin layer of insulite sponge. The player dipped the hat in water to soak the sponge, and as the water evaporated it cooled the aluminum, which made the player comfortable. This probably was the first time a sportswriter could accurately use the old cliché "Tempers were heated, but cooler heads prevailed." Evidently the Reds abandoned the experiment early in the season.

There have been many other attempts besides the helmet to provide protection for players. A batter's chest protector was patented in 1961. This was a padded vest that hung over one shoulder and covered the heart, stomach, kidneys, and other vital organs, sort of like a fencer's jacket. It was reversible, so it could be used by both left-handed and right-handed batters as well as switch-hitters. Although I suspect it might have changed the time it took a batter to get from home to first base from about four and a half seconds to maybe a minute-twenty, it also would have provided great protection for a runner who slid on his stomach —if a runner would try to steal wearing that contraption.

Two pieces of protective equipment that have disappeared are sliding pads, which players wore under their pants, and sliding gloves which stretched from the hand to the elbow. Both devices were intended to prevent "strawberries," or scrapes and bruises caused by sliding on rocky infields. Sliding pads consisted of two long pads that covered the player's thighs and were tied around the waist and to each leg like a holster. Because pads were uncomfortable to run in, or, I suppose, to walk in, sit in, bat in, field in, pitch in, or even talk in, rather than wearing them, players often taped sponges or kneepads to their thighs for protection.

To me, the most important invention since the McMuffin is the McNugget. But other people have spent a considerable amount of time and money perfecting devices to help players hit better, throw better, pitch better, and catch better. Playing baseball well requires perfecting a number of skills, and whatever skill a player wants to perfect, someone has invented something to help him.

In the old days players believed there was a ratio between the weight of the bat and the distance the ball traveled when hit. Modern players know that bat speed— how fast a player swings the bat—is at least as important as the size of the bat he is swinging. The first "velocity bat," a device that measures bat speed, was manufactured in 1956. A three-inch-long gauge was imbedded in the barrel of an ordinary bat and registered the speed of the swinging bat in miles per hour. "A player can be measured when he's hitting the ball well," a velocity bat salesman explained to Yankee manager Casey Stengel that year. "Then, when the player goes into a slump, he can be clocked again to find out if he is swinging slower. If he is, then you know he is doing something different."

"You know he's doing something different by looking at his batting average," Stengel replied logically.

Moose Skowron's swing was measured at 110 miles per hour, while Ted Kluszewski registered at 116 and Duke Snider at 115.

Suppose a player discovered that he was suffering from tired swings. What could he do? There were no bat speed pills. In the old days, when waiting on deck, players simply swung two or more ordinary bats at the same time. When they discarded the extra bats, the bat they were using felt lighter and they were able to swing it faster. Obviously swinging several ordinary bats at the same time was con- sidered too complicated, because an entire industry seems to have developed around making bats more difficult to swing. For example, there are weighted bats, regular-size bats made of wood and plastic that simply weigh more than regular-size bats made of wood. Then there is the Top Hand bat, which looks like an ordinary aluminum bat but has a sliding weight inside and, when swung correctly, simulates the feel of hitting a ball solidly. There is the "doughnut," a weighted piece of metal shaped like a dough- nut that fits over the barrel of a player's regular bat and is easily discarded when he goes up to the plate. And then there is a 1973 import from Venezuela, the Power Swing, which most resembles the tail of a rocket. It consists of four plastic fins attached to a plastic tube that fits over the end of the bat; the device created tremendous wind resistance when swung. The harder the bat is swung, the manufacturer explained, the more resistance is created, making it more difficult to swing. The only problem with that theory is that the easiest swing of all would be no swing, which would make it very difficult to hit the ball.

Probably the most expensive of all the devices was the "swimming pool." This is a swimming pool, complete with water. When a player stands in the pool and swings a bat, the water creates resistance. When the player gets out of the pool and swings a bat that is not waterlogged, his bat speed improves immediately. Perhaps the greatest benefit of the "swimming pool" is that it enables a player to deduct the cost of the "swimming pool" from his taxes as a business expense.

Of course, being able to swing a bat rapidly is important only if the batter hits the ball. Otherwise a fast swing just enables a batter to get back to the bench more quickly. Fortunately, many companies have been willing to sell equipment to players to help them become better hitters. When Stengel was shown the velocity bat, for example, he said, "I think it's a fine thing. Now I'd like to see someone invent a bat that helps 'em hit a curve." Well, they didn't invent that bat, but they did invent that ball. The "Major League Breaking Ball" has a flat surface on one side, enabling anyone to throw curves, sliders, sinkers, and screwballs. Thus batters can get all the practice they need against breaking pitches without facing a pitcher who can throw breaking pitches. This ball is one of the few products guaranteed to break even when brand new; in fact, if it doesn't break, it's broken. An aerodynamic principle ensures that the ball always curves in the direction opposite the flat side. I can't even spell "aerodynamic" without a copy editor, and I can't explain what it means without a scientist. All I know is that it's cheaper than a Bert Blyleven and does the same job.

Brothers Joe and Frank Torre developed the "Iso-Swing Batting Coach" in their basement in the 1960s. The "coach" consisted of two large rubber jaws that moved up and down, and the object was to swing a bat between them. The jaws could be adjusted to enable batters to practice hitting in various situations, and the resistance of the jaws could be regulated to approximate the speed of a major league fastball. "Once the device gets into general use," Frank Torre was quoted as saying, "anyone with the desire to practice can become a .300 hitter." Here's my question: If Pee Wee Herman bought an "Iso-Swing Batting Coach," practiced diligently, and *did not* become a .300 hitter, could he sue for false advertising?

There are bats to help solve every problem. Uppercutting or chopping down at the ball? Twisting your wrists? Try a "Prac-Bat," an odd-looking bat with a hole measuring seven by three and a half inches in its barrel. If the batter swings properly at a pitch, the ball will go through the hole; if the batter hits the ball, he is swinging incorrectly. So when you miss the ball you're actually swinging well enough to hit it. The object is to learn how to miss the ball. For decades people have been jeering fielders by suggesting they had a hole in their glove, the "Prac-Bat" finally enables them to tell batters the same thing.

Former major leaguer turned college baseball coach Danny Litwhiler invented the bunting bat, an ordinary bat with its barrel sliced in half lengthwise, which forces players to bunt down at the ball with the flat side of the bat if they want to lay the ball on the ground. What I would have liked to have seen was somebody trying to hit a "Major League Breaking Ball" with a Danny Litwhiler bunting bat.

There are even more bats. The patented "ambidextrous bat" had two finger grooves cut into the bat handle, forcing players to grip it correctly, which supposedly resulted in a faster swing and a reduction in bat-twisting. Everybody knows how distressing bat twisting can be. The "ambidextrous bat" was just about as successful commercially as the famed square hula hoop.

The Bud Harrelson bat choke, which was actually devised by Billy Martin, was a piece of rubber with a hole in it that fit snugly over the handle of the bat and enabled batters to choke up but feel as if they were holding the bat at bottom knob. Harrelson's lifetime batting average was .236; Martin's was .257. Seems to me that the thing to do is find out what Wade Boggs is using.

Probably the invention that has done the most to help hitters is the pitching machine. It works on a basic principle: It throws the ball, and the batter tries to hit it. The first pitching machine was patented in 1871, and apparently it was little more than a hand-operated slingshot stuck in the ground. Motor-powered machines began appearing in big league training camps in the late 1940s, and they were basically motor-driven slingshots. "The problem with them," Oriole coach Jimmy Williams remembers, "was that the batter had no idea when the machine was going to release the ball. Pffft. It was on you. You couldn't hit it because you couldn't time it. The one thing that machine proved was how valuable it is to a pitcher to hide the ball before throwing it. The manufacturer finally put a half-moon dial on front, and when there was no moon showing, the ball was released.

That was replaced by "Iron Mike," a machine that looked like a small metal scaffold with one continually rotating arm that released a pitch at the apex of every rotation. Every team liked Iron Mike: He drank only a small amount of oil, he never held out for more lubricant, he didn't have an agent, he pitched whenever the manager asked him to, he finished what he started, he was rarely injured, and he was not a bad influence on young machines. Best of all, he could pitch all day. Once the Orioles' Eddie Everready, Iron Mike's relative by manufacturer, springed his arm—which was quickly unscrewed and removed and replaced with a brand-new one.

Unfortunately, Iron Mike threw only straight balls, and like all pitchers, he was eventually replaced by something with a better variety of pitches. The "Curvemaster" consists of two spinning bald, rubber tires. By adjusting the speed and direction of these wheels, a spin is put on the ball, causing it to curve in the desired direction. If both wheels are turning at the same speed, for example, the ball has no spin and acts as a knuckler; if one tire is going forward while the other one is spinning backward, the ball curves. In other words, on a good day two tires from an abandoned '57 Chevy might have outpitched Tom Seaver.

Patent 3,009,451, filed in 1961, was for the only known baseball pitching robot. This pitching machine supposedly had a steel frame covered with papier-mâché or plastic sculpted to look like a human being. It moved its arms, head, torso, and one leg. Now, I don't want to cast any aspersions, but wasn't it shortly after that patent was filed that Nolan Ryan signed his first professional contract? And nobody in baseball history has thrown a ball as hard for as long, without ever suffering a serious arm injury, as Ryan. Perhaps it's just a coincidence, but maybe there's a reason why no one has ever seen an X ray of Ryan's arm.

Numerous devices have been developed to help pitchers counter the numerous devices developed to help hitters. An army lt. colonel patented a baseball with markings on its cover showing where to place the thumb, forefinger, and second finger to throw a fastball and breaking pitches. Also printed on the cover were arrows that showed in which direction the ball should be spun for each of those pitches. There were also three colored bands circling the cover, one color representing each type of pitch. When that pitch was thrown correctly the colors blended into a designated shade, providing evidence to the pitcher that he had thrown a good pitch. After getting his patent, the inventor said he hoped someone would manufacture the ball so he could buy one for his son. The inventor also filed for a patent for a device that was to be hung on a wall and, when a ball was thrown against it, the ball would bounce back. Um, one question: What was the wall for, to hold up another wall? I mean, why not simply throw the ball against the wall? Because, I guess, then there would be no market for the device.

An invention of Danny Litwhiler's designed to help pitchers is an unbreakable mirror six feet high, three feet wide, and three inches thick. Pitchers are able to observe their windup or pick-off move in the mirror and actually throw a baseball against it without damaging it. The only problem with the mirror, of course, is that a player sees himself in reverse; thus a left-hander seems to be throwing right-handed, while a right-hander seems to be throwing lefty.

A less practical idea that was never fully developed was a rearview mirror worn on the brim of the cap that enabled the pitcher to watch a runner on second while looking toward home plate. The inventor claimed that the experimental device performed exceptionally well in a test game; he successfully picked his brother-in-law off second three times and a cousin once. "I had my mother-in-law nailed, too," he told a San Francisco reporter, "but my next-door neighbor dropped the ball."

In 1975 baseball began using the "radar gun" to measure how fast pitchers were throwing. The lightweight, portable "gun" was adapted from "speed guns" used by highway policemen to time motorists and replaced the "electric eye," which measured velocity by length of time it took a thrown ball to pass through an electric beam. "They started using the gun at the end of my career," Bob Gibson remembers, "and they timed me at ninety-three, ninety-four miles per hour, but I was forty years old. That speed didn't surprise me; I had always figured I was throwing at about ninety-five, ninety-six. The thing that did surprise me was that low pitches were always clocked as fast as or faster than high pitches, and I know that no pitch can be as fast as a rising fastball."

Pirate pitching coach Ray Miller disagrees with Gibson about low pitches, pointing out, "If that's true, how come the radar guns clock a low-slung sports car the same as a ten-foot semi?"

Questions have continually been raised about the accuracy of radar guns. "I was pitching on *The Monday Night Game of the Week* in Philadelphia in 1978," Jim Kaat claims, "and somebody came in and told me ABC had clocked me on the gun at ninety-one. 'Are you kidding?' I said. 'I couldn't drive ninety-one.' " And NBC broadcasters were sued for libel by a radar gun manufacturer when they told viewers during a World Series telecast, "Some speed guns have clocked trees going forty-five miles per hour."

Radar guns are frequently used by scouts to time a prospect's fastball, and some scouts refuse to recommend that a player be drafted or signed unless he registers more than eighty-five miles per hour. "The problem with that," Whitey Herzog explained, "is that speed doesn't make that much difference as far as the success of a pitcher is concerned. Catfish never threw that hard, but his fastball had movement, he had location, it didn't make any difference how hard he could throw. Now people complain if a pitcher 'only' goes eighty-four. Who gives a damn? Does he have control? Does he have a breaking ball? The gun stunk up scouting. All they go by now is how hard they throw."

It's not so much how fast a pitcher throws as where he throws it, when he throws it, and who he throws it to. As I learned during my years behind home plate, some of the best fastballs never reach the catcher. Besides, how would you time a knuckleball? With a cardiograph?

Batters have pitching machines to practice against, and now pitchers have "Mizuno's Pitching Training Center." This computerized system utilizes a screen on which a batter, catcher, and umpire appear. The computer tells the pitcher where to throw the ball, and after he has thrown it, reports his speed and accuracy. In the old days young pitchers used several less sophisticated devices to help improve their control. These included "a pyramid of wooden milk bottles sitting on a table at a carnival," and "an old tire hung from a rope in front of the barn."

Besides the wall hung in front of the wall to bounce balls off, there have been several other inventions intended to help fielders. For example, bug glasses intended to keep gnats and mosquitos out of fielders' eyes were ordinary eyeglasses in which the glass had been replaced by tiny mesh screens. Mizuno has developed a six-fingered fielder's glove that can be worn on either hand. They have also produced a glove with a sunshade webbing that fielders can use like sunglasses to see fly balls on sunny days. And finally, they have invented the electronic glove. The electronic glove contains transistorized signaling devices that enable a pitcher and a catcher to communicate without using finger signals. By pressing buttons on his glove, the catcher can signal the pitcher to throw one of four different pitches to one of four different locations. A device in the pitcher's glove enables him to agree, or to tell the catcher what pitch he wants to throw. With this device Japanese manufacturers have succeeded in making the pitcher's head shake obsolete. Perhaps the greatest advantage of the electronic pitcher's and catcher's gloves is that they will allow a manager to say someday, with a straight face, that his battery ran out of batteries.

Outfielders can look forward to the installation of an electronic warning track. This is not a new concept. As far back as 1960, teams were considering installing loudspeakers on the outfield fence to prevent collisions by having a dugout coach shouting who should make a catch. In this modern version, radarlike sensors imbedded in the outfield wall start beeping when a player comes within twenty feet and grows louder as he approaches the wall. At its loudest, the wall successfully reproduces the lovely sound of a garbage truck backing up.

Without doubt, the greatest change in fielding has been the change in the field. For better or worse, depending on whom you speak to, the development and acceptance of artificial surfaces has changed the way fielders play the game. "You always get a true hop on the artificial turf," Royal's infielder Greg Pryor said. "On the artificial turf the ball comes to you and says, 'Catch me.' On grass it says, 'Look out, sucker.' "

The original artificial surface, known as Chemgrass, was installed in the Astrodome in 1966, when it was discovered that real grass would not grow indoors. At least not inside those doors. The cost of covering the field was $575,000. Astro owner Judge Roy Hofheinz thought Monsanto, inventor of the turf, was paying *him* for the publicity they would gain. Surprise! The statistic that most dazzled fans was the fact that it required a record-setting three miles of zippers to keep the Astrodome's "carpet" in place.

There has always been mixed feelings among players about artificial turf. Some players dislike it, while others truly hate it. A baseball travels much faster on the turf than on grass, supposedly picking up speed when it hits the plastic surface. This enables fielders to play much deeper because the ball will get to them much more quickly—and also forces them to play much deeper for their own safety, because the ball gets to them much more quickly. The only thing that doesn't move quickly on the grass is a diving outfielder. Fred Lynn once tried to make a diving catch on it—and stopped short as soon as he hit the ground. "I just hit the turf and stuck there. And when a ball bounces thirty feet over your head, that's not the way baseball was meant to be played."

When subjected to continuous sunshine, the turf gets unbearably hot. "I remember one time before a night game when it was 140 degrees at five o'clock on our turf," the Royals' George Brett says. "You couldn't stand still out there. We always have a bucket of ice in the dugout so that when we come in off the field, we can step in it and cool off."

Ironically, artificial turf came in just as flannel uniforms were being replaced by lightweight doubleknits. It took the major leagues a hundred years to figure out how to make players more comfortable—and they did it just in time to make them uncomfortable.

The electronic age has also come to umpires. The dream of every player, an infallible ball-strike indicator, was patented in 1985. The "Baseball-Strike Indicator and Trajectory Analyzer" uses an array of cameras and a computer to produce a three-dimensional "picture" showing the path of the pitch through the strike zone. I've actually seen several other devices that supposedly did the same thing. One of them was an electronic eye that had one small problem: It signaled a strike every time a bat crossed the plate. As soon as the inventors solved that problem, Thurman Munson discovered he could trip the beam by tipping his glove over the plate. The inventors finally ended up putting a miniature signaling device inside every baseball that worked very well—except the balls cost several hundred dollars each.

Umpires really entered the age of electricity around the turn of the century. Before public-address systems were installed in ballparks, criers with megaphones would circle the field and announce the starting batteries to the fans. In an attempt to modernize, the New York Giants installed microphones at home plate in the Polo Grounds. The umpire was supposed to stand on the plate, which closed the circuit and activated the microphone, and announce the batteries. One day umpire Cy Rigler stood on the plate, just as he had been told, and started reading. Nobody could hear him. He started again, and again no one heard him. Finally he lost his temper and screamed, "What the @#%$#%#$ $#*&%$ is wrong with this @#&*&% thing?" Nothing, as it turned out, as all fifteen thousand fans in attendance heard that quite clearly. The next day the microphone was removed, quickly ending umpires' sojourn into the newfangled world of electricity.

Mizuno's vision of "baseball in the future" includes electronic foul lines which signal whether a ball lands fair or foul. Personally, I don't believe electronic devices will ever replace the umpire, fallible as he might be. I just can't imagine an angry fan screaming from the stands, "Reprogram the umpire!"

The players' eternal quest for improvement has taken place off the field, too. At one time a complete conditioning routine consisted of throwing a medicine ball around for a few minutes. Today players work out year-'round. Many of them have bought Nautilus equipment for their homes. Most teams have installed fully equipped weight rooms in their ballparks and hired trainers to work with players on their individual problems. Don Mattingly has gone just a little farther: He's installed a batting cage in his house. I suppose it makes sense; hitting is what he does best. Using the same theory, I installed a bigger table in my kitchen.

Through the years many different methods have been used to try to improve performance, some of them probably a bit less than scientific. In spring training in 1940, for example, the Dodgers experimented with Japanese bar exercises. Two players would face each other, standing about five feet apart, holding the ends of two long, thin rods in their hands. The players were supposed to try to push the other player backward. This exercise was an early form of isometrics, the application of pressure against pressure. The Dodgers used the rods for almost two full days before abandoning them.

In the 1960s the Phillies experimented with a "shoulder wheel" that supposedly strengthened a pitcher's throwing arm. The shoulder wheel was an upright wooden disc four feet in diameter with a handle attached. The pitcher stood next to the wheel, grabbed the handle, and turned the wheel, round and round and round and round, theoretically loosening and building up his shoulder muscles. If someone had been smart enough to attach the wheel to a grain thresher this device might have been very profitable as well as helpful.

Many players once considered bowling an excellent exercise for the baseball season. "I know I'm throwing harder since I began bowling in the off-season," Twin pitcher Lee Stange said.

Phillie pitcher Art Mahaffey agreed, claiming, "Months of hurling that sixteen-pound bowling ball, then switching to a light baseball, made the transition much easier for me."

Three-hundred-game-winner Early Wynn, working as the Indians' pitching coach, wasn't sure about the benefits of bowling as exercise. "It depends on the player," he said. "Bowling could develop some muscles that are important for a young pitcher, but veterans are usually developed enough. I don't think it could hurt a throwing arm. Although I don't encourage bowling during the season, I certainly don't plan to impose a rigid no-bowling policy on the staff this season."

Gil Hodges, then managing the Washington Senators, believed bowling was an excellent conditioner. "If some of my players decide to go out and bowl after a game, I'll be happy to join them if I can *spare* the time." Oh, that Gil was some kidder. In the off-season, incidentally, Hodges owned a bowling alley.

The Cardinals got all the benefits of bowling, without actually having to bowl, when their trainer invented "the metal ball." The metal ball consisted of . . . a metal ball weighing between three and five pounds, to be used for various exercises. The ball sold for about six dollars, but that included "the metal ball" instruction booklet. Some players claimed "the metal ball" had great psychological benefits, too, because when they put it down and picked up a baseball, which weighed about 5¼ ounces, the baseball felt much lighter. Hey, any bowler could have told them that.

Some teams are willing to try anything. In 1962 the Reds brought shooting instructor Lucky McDaniel to spring training in an attempt to improve their players' hand-eye coordination. McDaniel had previously worked with Olympic boxing champion Pete Rademacher. McDaniel's method consisted of putting a piece of cotton inside a washer and throwing it in the air, then teaching players how to hit the washer with a BB gun. "I don't know if it did us any good," Reds' general manager Gabe Paul commented, "but by the end of spring training everybody was impressed with how much their marksmanship had improved."

Rademacher was eventually destroyed by heavyweight champion Floyd Patterson, proving that sometimes it's easier to hit a flying washer than a punching heavyweight.

San Francisco shortstop José Uribe devised his own method of improving hand-eye coordination: trying to hit thrown peanuts. "My brother stood about twenty feet away from me and threw me two hundred peanuts a day all winter," Uribe explained, "and I tried to hit them. Then he threw me corn for change-ups and curves. I only hit about thirty out of two hundred."

In recent years the martial arts have replaced bowling as one of the more popular conditioning methods. Years ago martial arts, which have nothing to do with Marshal Dillion, was actually martial art: judo. But gradually other forms of oriental hand and leg fighting have become popular in the United States, and major leaguers study them in an effort to increase their strength and flexibility. Steve Sax and Pedro Guerrero practice karate, or empty-hand fighting emphasizing kicking and punching. Terry Whitfield preferred aikido, which involves dodging an opponent and turning the force of his momentum against him. Gary Lavelle, Steve Carleton, Mike Krukow, Bob Boone, and Atlee Hammaker all practice kung fu, a Chinese art of self-defense. Among the many advantages martial arts have over bowling is that if a player ever gets attacked by a bowling ball, he can break it in half.

Years ago players saw little difference between psychologists and witch doctors; head shrinking was head shrinking. Today, in addition to physical conditioning, many players practice various forms of psychological conditioning. Psychocybernetics, for example, is a basic form of imagery. The theory behind it is that if you visualize yourself doing something successfully often enough, your body will be physically prepared to act out that visualization. One of the earliest experiments with this took place in 1950, when Indians' coach Muddy Ruel had his players stand at the plate as he wound up and threw them phantom pitches. As he pretended to release the nonexistent ball, he yelled out what kind of pitch he would have thrown if he had been throwing a pitch, and he required the batters to adjust to that particular pitch. Although this particular exercise probably seemed strange to the players, they knew that Ruel had graduated from law school, which explained a lot.

In spring training decades later the Reds were doing a remarkably similar exercise. Johnny Bench was at bat and nobody was pitching. The pitch didn't come in, but Bench took a big swing, and he stood on his tiptoes to watch the nonexistent ball sail over the fence for a home run, then broke into his home run trot.

In the old days, if a player had asked for psychological assistance, his team would most probably have told him he was crazy. No more. In 1972 the Astros became the first team to hire a "head coach," putting a psychologist on retainer. That same year the Royals brought two visualization experts to spring training to work with their players. During the 1970s numerous players began practicing Transcendental Meditation, a form of relaxation. In 1983 the White Sox hired a team hypnotist who told their players, "You can hit any pitcher who ever lived. You are going to hit the ball harder. You can see that baseball. It will be large, brilliantly white, with flaming red seams." And they did win their division championship.

In the past few years hundreds of major league players have privately visited sports psychologists. The goal is always the same: to learn how to approach the game with a positive attitude, to learn how to deal with the pressures of major league baseball, to be able to relax on the field, and to improve concentration and coordination. "The key word is 'centering,' " one of the Royals' experts explained to a reporter. "The word is probably indefinable, but you might term 'centering' a recognition of a degree of organization that takes place when you apply the sensory system to a task." He might term it that. Dizzy Dean most certainly would have termed it something entirely different—and been no easier to understand while termin' it, either.

For a game that is often criticized as being too slow, baseball has moved rather quickly. Within a relatively brief period, franchises moved to the West Coast and the leagues expanded from sixteen teams to twenty-six teams. The number of black and Hispanic players in the big leagues increased significantly, and those players have begun to dominate the game. The players' union became strong and staged several strikes. The minor leagues were reduced in size, and college baseball became more important than ever. A player draft replaced the old system in which any team could sign any unsigned player at any time. The draft practically eliminated the job of the legendary scout, who lived out of the trunk of his car in his eternal search for "the next Bob Feller," replacing him with a "scouting combine." State-of-the-art ballparks have been constructed. Women have just begun to make inroads in the game, and one woman is even working as an umpire in AAA baseball.

I got a job as a baseball broadcaster. I got fired from my job as a baseball broadcaster. Everything about the game has changed, but somehow the game seems very much the same.

The dreams never change. Young boys of all ages still dream *the* dream: playing in the big leagues. Ironically, those people whose dreams came true, who made it, still dream about playing there again. For some, though, the dream has become a nightmare. "Every once in a while I dream I'm at bat again," Johnny Pesky said. "I dream I hit the ball and I can't run. My legs are set in concrete and I can't get to first base."

"It's a simple dream," Joe Nuxhall said. "I dream about being on the mound and pitching one more time."

"I dream I'm at bat and I hit one in the gap," Ed Brinkman explains. "I get out of the batter's box fine and all of a sudden I'm moving in slow motion. I can't make it to first. The defensive players move faster and I can't move, but I always wake up before I find out if I made it to first or not."

"I dream that there's a ball coming right at my head," Joe Ginsberg said, "and I have to get out of the way. Sometimes I actually fall out of bed trying to avoid the pitch."

Jerry Casale dreams, "I'm outside the park and they won't let me in. Or I'm ready to pitch and they won't give me the ball. It's like an unfinished symphony."

"I dream I'm standing on the pitcher's mound, in my uniform, but the game never starts," Bob Gibson said. "I wait and I wait to throw the first pitch, but for some reason the game never starts."

But for many people who didn't make the big leagues, the original dream never died. "I often get letters from people asking for a tryout," Mets' vice-president Joe McIlwayne said, "but the most unusual request I ever received came from a sixty-two-year-old man. He wrote asking for a chance, explaining that he works out in the gym every day and is in much better physical shape than men thirty years younger than he is. He was a pitcher, he wrote, and he threw a drop, sinker, slider, and knuckleball. 'Just think how much publicity a sixty-two-year-old pitcher would get. What kind of crowds that would draw for you.' "

I liked the thought that a sixty-two-year-old man still dreamed about playing in the major leagues when he grew up, but I realized it was an impossible dream. If the Mets signed him, even if he spent only three years in the minor leagues, he'd still be sixty-five in his rookie season.